Essentials
of Engineering
Economics

Essentials of Engineering Economics

Erick Kasner

Manager of Process Engineering and Development
Industrial Chemicals Division
NL Industries Incorporated
Hightstown, New Jersey

Gregg Division

McGraw-Hill Book Company

New York	Mexico
St. Louis	Montreal
Dallas	New Delhi
San Francisco	Panama
Auckland	Paris
Bogotá	São Paulo
Düsseldorf	Singapore
Johannesburg	Sydney
London	Tokyo
Madrid	Toronto

Library of Congress Cataloging in Publication Data

Kasner, Erick.
  Essentials of engineering economics.

  Bibliography: p.
  Includes index.
  1. Engineering economy.   I. Title.
TA177.4.K37   658.1′5   78-13052
ISBN 0-07-033323-8

1 2 3 4 5 6 7 8 9 0   DODO   7 8 6 5 4 3 2 1 0 9

The editors for this book were Gerald O. Stoner, Susan L. Schwartz, and Frances D. Bond; the designer was Tracy A. Glasner; the art supervisor was George T. Resch; and the production supervisor was Laurence Charnow. It was set in Times Roman by Waldman Graphics, Inc. Printed and bound by R. R. Donnelley and Sons Company.

To My Wife Susan, Who Gave Me
The Necessary Encouragement To Go On
Writing When The Chips Were Down

Contents

Preface

Essentials of Engineering Economics is designed for students of technology, pre-engineering, and engineering at two-year and four-year colleges and institutes. Its purpose is to introduce students of technology—chemical, civil, electrical, energy, environmental, mechanical, or any other—to essential economic principles. It sets forth what is needed to determine whether technically feasible engineering projects are also attractive business ventures. Excellence in technology and engineering must include economic analysis and evaluation of cost and benefits (profits).

Economics is particularly important in a technical environment, regardless of the level, for it provides the tool for analyzing available resources, energy, and labor and the value of the new venture to society. More and more firms are looking for technologists and engineers capable of supervising a project from its conception through its economic analysis and on to completion.

Too many schools have permitted their technical students to enter the business world without a sound technical economics background. Accordingly, a great deal of time in the first year at work is spent in exposing the individuals to applied engineering economics. Most employers would prefer that this teaching be done in the academic world.

Essentials of Engineering Economics is an introductory text intended for one-semester and two-quarter courses. The text also lends itself, through choice of topics, to use in shorter courses with the emphasis on application. Practicing technologists will find it valuable for on-the-job training.

The mathematics background required for successful use of this book is minimal. A knowledge of high school algebra is adequate.

All chapters have examples and problems varying in numbers, depending on the number of concepts requiring reinforcement. Almost all the examples and problems have been drawn from practical experience and, therefore, should be especially useful. Names of firms, products, and projects have been disguised wherever necessary to protect confidentiality.

This book is unique in its simplicity, practical application, and compactness. Chapter 1 introduces the essential principles of economic analysis. The next two chapters deal with static analysis. Different kinds of costs are examined along with methods of evaluating them. Their application to break-even analysis is presented, including the effect of variables such as sales revenue, fixed and variable costs, and output.

The next two chapters—4 and 5—deal with dynamic analysis by examining different methods of investment evaluation and decision making. The reasons behind various criteria utilized for evaluating investment alternatives are explained. The concepts of investment due to necessity and of payback time are examined in depth, as are return on investment, discounted cash flow analysis, benefit to cost analysis, incremental analysis, and sunken costs. Chapter 5 also covers the time value of money, including the use of interest formulas and tables.

Chapters 6 and 7 deal with tax considerations, depreciation, estimation of useful life, and tax rates. The final two chapters deal with economic planning and decision making. Chapter 8 examines project planning and control in a manner never previously considered in an engineering economics book. The chapter focuses on techniques such as the bar chart, network analysis, and the critical path method. Chapter 9 deals with a vital part of an economic analysis: report writing. This crucial subject is neglected in other engineering economics books also.

I want to thank NL Industries, Incorporated, for its encouragement and cooperation and for its help in the attempt to show the "real" world. Special thanks go to Dianne Bendel for handling the typing and necessary correspondence the first time around, and to Pat Zorn and Lorraine Brooks for typing the revised manuscripts.

Erick Kasner

Symbols and Abbreviations

The following symbols and abbreviations are used in the various mathematical expressions presented in this book. Because of a shortage of letters, some have had to be used for more than one meaning.

a	number of years asset in actual use, intercept in cost equation
ATCF	after tax cash flow
b	variable cost per unit of output
BE	break-even point
BES	break-even point in sales dollars
BEV	break-even output or volume
C	cost
CP	critical path
C_f	fixed cost = a
C_t	total cost
C_v	variable cost
d	depreciation rate, %
DCF	discounted cash flow
dI	annual depreciation, dollars per year
e	Naperian constant 2.71828 . . .
f	fixed percentage factor in declining-balance depreciation method
G	gross profit, gross income
i	interest rate, %; DCF rate of return
i_{eff}	effective interest rate, %
$\bar{i}$	average interest rate
I	fixed investment capital
I_A	initial outlay for project A
I_B	initial outlay for project B
I_w	working capital
I_{wA}	working capital for project A
m	interest periods per year
n	number of years, useful life
n_{BE}	Break-even point in years
N	number of pairs of items in a sample
p	selling price, price per unit
PW	principal, present worth
P	net profit, net income
r	correlation coefficient
PT	payout, payback time
PT_M	maximum acceptable payback time

R	revenue or sales
R	uniform periodic payment
ROI	return on investment, %
ROI_m	minimum acceptable return rate, %
S	Principal plus interest due, future worth
Syx	standard error of the estimate
t	income tax rate, %
tdI	tax credit for depreciation
t_{eff}	effective, or average, tax rate, %
V	Original value of asset at year zero including installation cost
V_b	Book value of an asset
V_s	salvage value of asset at the end of useful life
X	cost capacity factor
x	volume of output sales
y	sales revenue, cost
y_e	y estimate
Σ	Summation

Introduction
to
Economic Analysis

1

An engineer or technologist is a creator. What an engineer designs and creates—machines, plants, automobiles, computers, products, environments, etc.—is a function of his or her area of specialization.

The design, regardless of the magnitude, must be workable; that is, it must pass the "will-it-work" test. This test, however, is incomplete. Practicality and economic feasibility are equally important tests. The former asks, "Is it technically useful to society?", while the latter asks, "Is it capable of being used successfully from the monetary standpoint?" Practicality and economic feasibility are what *Engineering Economics* is all about. In essence, engineering economics is the search for and recognition of alternatives which are then compared and evaluated in order to come up with the most practical design and creation. The primary objective of this book is to introduce the student to engineering economics, that is, to provide the principles, concepts, techniques, and methods by which alternatives within a project[1] can be compared and evaluated for the best monetary return. If economic criteria are not considered properly when profit is the ultimate objective, the result is bad engineering. Many technologically brilliant projects have been destroyed as a result of unsound economic analysis. In large measure, what distinguishes

---

[1] A *project* is the temporary bringing together of human and nonhuman resources in order to achieve a specified engineering objective.

engineering from science is that engineering requires a broad understanding of the technological environment and the ability to organize all available resources, human and nonhuman, to achieve economically and socially desirable objectives.

To illustrate, one of the problems of Consolidated Edison of New York is that the costly electricity-generating facilities must be sufficient to meet peak demand, and then, during off-peak hours, a portion of these high-cost facilities is idle. Suggestions have been made to store some of the unutilized electric energy as chemical energy using batteries. Although the technology is sound, the economy is not, because of the size of the batteries required. An alternative method proposed by engineers at Consolidated Edison is to utilize the off-peak energy to pump water to an elevated reservoir and then reverse the process at peak load times. Thus, off-peak electric energy is converted to potential energy, then during peak load times the potential energy is converted back to electric. This alternative is much more practical as well as economically feasible.

1.1   Objectives of Economic Analysis

The primary objective of our economic analysis is to identify and evaluate the probable economic outcome of a proposed project so that available funds assigned to it may be used to optimum advantage.

The analysis is always made from the viewpoint of the owner of the project and usually involves a comparison of alternatives on a monetary basis. It should be recognized that an action always involves at least two possible courses: doing it or not doing it. If the analysis is to yield results, the criteria by which alternatives are evaluated should have the following objectives:

1.   Profit maximization
2.   Cost minimization
3.   Maximization of social benefit
4.   Minimization of risk of loss
5.   Maximization of safety, quality, and public image

The above list is by no means complete. This book will deal primarily with the first three; however, when applicable, the others will not be neglected.

1.2   Procedure for Economic Analysis

An economic analysis revolves around three processes: *preparation, analysis,* and *evaluation.* The process of *preparation* can be broken down into three steps: understanding the project, defining the objective, and collecting data. Similarly, *analysis* involves: analysis of data, interpretation of results, and formulation of alternative solutions. Finally, there are two steps to *evaluation:* evaluation of the alternatives and identification of the best alternative(s).

Analysis and evaluation can be handled by computer. In fact, nearly all medium- and large-size firms in the United States have this type of capability, yielding quick feedback for decision-making. Decision-making can be considered to be the fourth process involved in economic analysis. The eight steps that make up preparation, analysis, and evaluation will now be briefly discussed.

Understanding the project: One cannot and should not attempt to perform an economic analysis without clearly understanding the project. This is often a substantial difference between what one thinks the project is and what the project really is.

Defining the objectives: Failure to clarify the objectives of a project will often create dissatisfaction. The objectives must be clearly stated and compatible with each other. Some examples are:

1. Meet or exceed a specified minimum rate of return on an investment.
2. Return the investment (break-even) within a specified time period.
3. Obtain a specific share of a market.

The firm's objectives and criteria must be specified and defined quantitatively. That is, for example, if return of the investment within a specified time period is sought, the piece of equipment or operation being investigated should pay for itself within the specified time period, based on the potential savings or profits realized through its use.

Collecting data: This begins with a complete review of published literature if available or of historical data in the firm's files. Often, the wheel gets reinvented only because someone did not bother to search out existing information. If not otherwise available, data can be obtained through private sources or roughly estimated through assumptions.

Analysis of data: This is the process of converting developed data into something meaningful and useful. The use of a computer is highly beneficial. Often the computer can generate maximum amounts of information at a minimum cost.

Interpretation of results: Interpretation of the results usually occurs upon completion of the analysis. The results must be well organized, stored properly, then carefully adapted and utilized in the evaluation phase.

Formulation of alternative solutions: Different avenues leading to the same final objective are to be investigated and proposed to management as alternative methods. Hence, in the case of a new product, for example, different methods of manufacturing would be proposed or different levels of automation suggested, then their effect on final project profitability examined.

Evaluation of alternatives: In evaluating the alternatives it is important to use uniform criteria for all, not different ones for each alternative.

If the return-on-investment concept is to be used on one alternative, then each alternative is to be evaluated by the return-on-investment concept. Furthermore, the method of calculation of the return on investment (ROI) must be uniform as well.

Identification of the best alternative(s): In most firms, this task is performed by top management; accordingly, the analyst must narrow the choice down to the two or three best possibilities. Top management can then identify the one that comes closest to meeting the objectives.

As soon as the analysis, evaluation, selection, and approval of the best alternative have been completed, the implementation process begins. The engineer or technologist will design, procure, and then install the equipment or assets called for in the project. He or she will often be present during the start-up of the operation and make revisions if necessary.

1.3 Capital Expenditure Policies

Wear and tear of productive facilities necessitates their eventual replacement. Industrial and consumer demands for more goods and services necessitate an increase in supply and hence an increase in productive facilities. Firms respond to these pressures through capital expenditures by investing new plants, equipment, and products. Often, capital spending can be minimized by sacrificing some output capabilities or through productivity improvement or cost reduction opportunities.

Basically, capital expenditures can be classified into five general groups:

1. Maintenance of productive facilities
2. Optimization of existing productive capacity
3. Mechanization or automation of existing facilities
4. Expansion of product lines or productive capacity
5. Necessities due to governmental regulations

For whichever purpose the expenditure is made, except in the case of number 5, the final criterion is the profit or savings to be realized through the modification.

1.4 Basic Concepts and Assumptions

In order to make an economic evaluation of a project, certain basic information must be established. More detailed techniques will be considered in later chapters.

REVENUE
Revenue (R) refers to any increase in the owner's equity resulting from sales or services of business.

GROSS PROFIT
Gross Profit G (also referred to as *gross income*) is the yearly earning from a venture throughout its operating life. It is equal to revenue minus raw material cost, operating expenses including overhead, maintenance, labor, and Social Security and unemployment taxes. It does not include deductions for depreciation and income tax. It can be expressed as $G = R - C$, where C is the various costs listed above.

BREAK-EVEN
Break-even is a situation at which gross profit G is equal to zero. Stated differently, break-even occurs where revenue, R, from sales or services just equals the costs C associated with doing business, the ones mentioned in the explanation of gross profit. Hence, $G = R - C = 0$, or $R = C$.

FIXED CAPITAL INVESTMENT
Fixed capital investment I consists of the investment in facilities and equipment.

WORKING CAPITAL
Working capital I_w is money tied up in raw materials, intermediate and finished-goods inventories, and accounts receivable, as well as cash needed to operate a given project.

INCOME TAX RATE
Income tax rate t is a government tool for controlling inflation. A high rate decreases the supply of money available for business investment and spending. The federal income tax rate can be taken at 48%, while the state income tax rate can be taken at an average of 5%.

DEPRECIATION
Depreciation d consists of a fixed annual charge on the facility or equipment investment which will result in recovery of the initial investment at the end of the useful life of the item. If the actual life of the facility or equipment is known, an exact rate of depreciation can be established where the sum of the rates will just equal the investment.

INTEREST
Interest i is the rental charge for the use of borrowed money. It is another inflation controller. High interest rates discourage borrowing, making new investments less desirable.

NET PROFIT

Net profit P is equal to gross profit minus depreciation, interest, and income tax. It can be expressed as

$$P = G - i(I + I_w) - t(G - dI) \tag{1-1}$$

where I = capital investment in facilities or equipment (fixed capital)
I_w = working capital
G = gross profit
i = interest rate
d = depreciation rate
t = income tax rate (federal and state)

RATE OF RETURN ON INVESTMENT

Rate of return on investment (ROI) is the annual rate of return on the original investment and can be expressed as

$$\text{ROI} = \frac{\text{net profit}}{\text{total investment}} = \frac{P}{I + I_w} \tag{1-2}$$

This ratio, often multiplied by 100 to yield a percentage, is the simplest and perhaps the most widely used index for measuring the attractiveness of a venture.

PAYOUT, OR PAYBACK, TIME

Payout, or payback, time (PT) is another form of measuring the attractiveness of a venture. It is the ratio of capital investment to yearly net profit and can be expressed as

$$\text{PT} = \frac{I}{P} \tag{1-3}$$

where PT is given in years. It should be noted that payout, or payback, time is based only on I rather than on total capital investment, that is, $I + I_w$.

DISCOUNTED RATE OF RETURN

The discounted rate of return is the rate at which the sum of future profits equals the total capital investment (fixed plus working). It can be expressed mathematically as follows:

$$(I + I_w) = \frac{P_1}{(1 + i)^1} + \frac{P_2}{(1 + i)^2} + \cdots + \frac{P_n}{(1 + i)^n} \tag{1-4}$$

where I = fixed capital investment
I_w = working capital

P_1 = net profit or saving at the end of first year
P_2 = net profit or saving at the end of second year
P_n = net profit or saving at the end of year n
i = after-tax interest rate, which is found by trial-and-error

Discounting is done because of the fact that future profits generated by a project will decrease in value over time due to inflation. This topic is discussed in detail in Chapter 5 and Appendix A.

MINIMUM RETURN RATE

This is the minimum acceptable rate of annual return on investment, or minimum return rate, ROI_m, set by the firm. New projects, no matter how technologically sound, must show at least that rate of return, after taxes, before they can be considered. The minimum return rate is established based on the following variables: (1) the cost of borrowed money or the interest the firm must pay for the use of someone else's money, (2) five year average return on shareholders' equity[2], (3) potential risk of failure associated with given projects. In general, most firms employ (1) plus (2) if a project or series of projects is relatively familiar to the firm. They add on (3) if the project is a totally new venture for the firm. Hence, if the going interest rate is 7% per year, and if the firm's average return on shareholders' equity is 13%, then the minimum acceptable return rate is set at 20%. On the other hand, if there is a substantial risk involved with a project, the ROI_m might be raised to 30% or 40%.

The following examples will illustrate these concepts.

Example 1-1

Management is considering whether to increase production in a plant producing antifreeze. The capital investment and working capital needed are $200,000 and $50,000, respectively. The interest on the borrowed capital is 10%, the depreciation rate is 10%, and the income rate is 50%. If the gross profit is $250,000 per year, determine the return on investment and payback time.

Solution:
By Equation 1-1,

$$P = G - i(I + I_w) - t(G - dI)$$
$$P = 250,000 - 0.10(200,000 + 50,000)$$
$$- 0.50[250,000 - 0.10(200,000)] = \$110,000$$

---

[2] Average return on shareholders' equity can be defined as the net income divided by the average shareholders' investment (stocks, bonds, etc.). Mathematically it can be expressed as

$$\frac{\text{net profit}}{\text{average shareholders' investment}} \times 100$$

Then, by Equation 1-2,

$$\text{ROI} = \frac{P}{(I + I_w)} = \frac{110,000}{200,000 + 50,000} = 0.44, \text{ or } 44\%$$

Now, by Equation 1-3, the payback time is

$$\text{PT} = \frac{I}{P} = \frac{200,000}{115,000} = 1.74 \text{ yrs.}$$

Example 1-2
A project has been proposed to replace and old truck with a new one costing \$25,000. Due to improved energy efficiency and more load capacity, the truck will realize a net saving of \$7000 per year. The truck will last four years and then will be sold for \$5000. Determine the discounted rate of return. Neglect income taxes, interest, and depreciation.

Solution:
We let $P_1 = P_2 = P_3 = P_4 = \$7000$, and $P_5 = \$5000$. Then by Equation 1-4,

$$(I + I_n) = \frac{P_1}{(1 + i)^1} + \frac{P_2}{(1 + i)^2} + \frac{P_3}{(1 + i)^3} + \frac{P_4}{(1 + i)^4} + \frac{P_5}{(1 + i)^5}$$

$$25,000 = \frac{7000}{(1 + i)^1} + \frac{7000}{(1 + i)^2} + \frac{7000}{(1 + i)^3} + \frac{7000}{(1 + i)^4} + \frac{5000}{(1 + i)^5}$$

We now substitute values for r and stop searching at a point where the left-hand side of the equation equals the right-hand side. At $i = 0.20$,

$$25,000 = \frac{7000}{(1.20)} + \frac{7000}{(1.20)^2} + \frac{7000}{(1.20)^3} + \frac{7000}{(1.20)^4} + \frac{5000}{(1.20)^5}$$

$$= \frac{7000}{1.20} + \frac{7000}{1.440} + \frac{7000}{1.728} + \frac{7000}{2.0736} + \frac{5000}{2.4883}$$

$$= 5833 + 4861 + 4051 + 3376 + 2010 = 20,131$$

which is short of 25,000 by 4869.
At $i = 0.15$,

$$25,000 = \frac{7000}{(1.15)^1} + \frac{7000}{(1.15)^2} + \frac{7000}{(1.15)^3} + \frac{7000}{(1.15)^4} + \frac{5000}{(1.15)^5}$$

$$= \frac{7000}{1.15} + \frac{7000}{1.3225} = \frac{7000}{1.5208} + \frac{7000}{1.7490} + \frac{5000}{2.0114}$$

$$= 6087 + 5293 + 4603 + 4002 + 2486 = 22{,}471$$

which is short of 25,000 by 2529.
At $i = 0.10$,

$$6363 + 5785 + 5260 + 4781 + 3104 = 25{,}293$$

We see that we exceed the 25,000 by 293, which indicates that the actual value for r is somewhere between 0.15 and 0.10, perhaps very close to 0.10. Hence, by interpolation.

$$i = 0.10 + 0.05 \left(\frac{293}{293 + 2529} \right) = 0.10 + 0.005 = 0.105$$

Hence, the discounted rate of return $= 0.105(100) = 10.5\%$

Example 1-3

Management is considering whether to purchase and install an automatic tape machine for its packaging line. It has been estimated that 3 hours of manual labor can be saved per day, at $3.99 per hour. The cost of the machine with installation is $2625. The annual costs associated with the use of this machine are as follows:

- Depreciation   at 5% on investment
- Insurance   at 3% on investment
- Maintenance   at 5% on investment
- Interest   at 10% on investment

If the provision for income tax is 51% and the minimum rate of return is 15%, should the machine be purchased and installed?

Solution:
- *Estimated Gross Savings*
- (3 h/day) ($3.99/h) (220 days/yr) $2633

- *Less expenses*
- Depreciation   at 5% on investment   131
- Insurance   at 3% on investment   79
- Maintenance   at 5% on investment   131
- Interest   at 10% on investment   263
- Total estimated expense $604

- Net savings before taxes $2029
- Provisions for taxes at 51% $1035
  Net savings after taxes   994

- Total investment required $2625
- ROI   37.9%
- ROI_m 15.0%
- Payback time   2.6 yr

As can be seen, the minimum rate of return is being met; hence, the venture should be undertaken.

1.5   Engineering Economics and Social Values

If engineers or technologists are to be more than just technicians they must look beyond the profitability of a venture. They must look forward to the possible social implications of the operation.

These social and ethical concerns, compared to technical matters, are not so readily formalized or calculated. Nevertheless, they should not be ignored, since the firm's reputation and image may be at stake. Degree of automation, for instance, should be carefully analyzed, for it may have an important bearing on labor problems. Pollution abatement, on the other hand, is just as essential as monetary return on investment and should always be incorporated when economic studies are performed: to neglect this is to neglect true engineering economics.

Summary

An engineering-economic analysis presents several different alternative means for carrying out a project. It also determines whether a project should be considered at all. The main objective of such an analysis is to predict the outcome of a proposed expenditure in measureable terms so that available funds are used to the best advantage.

An engineering-economic analysis involves three distinct phases: (1) preparation, (2) analysis, and (3) evaluation. These three phases break down further into eight steps: (a) understanding of the project, (b) defining the objectives; (c) collecting of data, (d) analyzing the data, (e) interpreting the results (f) formulating alternative solutions, (g) evaluating alternatives, and (h) identifying the best alternative(s).

The basic formulas used in an analysis are:

1.   Net profit $= P = G = i(I + I_w) - t(G - dI)$

where G = gross profit
I = fixed investment capital

I_w = working capital
i = interest rate
t = income tax rate
d = depreciation rate

2. Return on investment

$$\text{ROI} = \frac{\text{net profit}}{\text{total investment}}$$

$$= \frac{P}{(I + I_w)}$$

(This ratio is often multiplied by 100 to yield a percentage.)

3. Payback, or payout time

$$\text{PT} = \frac{\text{fixed capital investment}}{\text{net profit}}$$

$$= \frac{I}{P}$$

where PT is expressed in years

4. Discounted rate of return

$$(I + I_w) = \frac{P_1}{(1 + i)^1} + \frac{P_2}{(1 + i)^2} + \cdots + \frac{P_n}{(1 + i)^n}$$

where P_1, P_2, and P_n = profits at the end of years 1, 2, and n, respectively
i = after-tax interest rate, which is found by trial and error

Problems

1. You recently had a house constructed, which you plan to use for rental purposes. The following costs were incurred with this project:

		$
·	Legal fees, city permits	400
·	Purchase of lot	9,000
·	Survey of lot	70
·	Architect's fee	2,000
·	Construction costs	30,000
·	Fire and liability insurance for 1 year	300
·	Advertising for tenants	25

- Interest costs prior to completion of construction   3,000
- Grading, seeding, sodding   100
- Grass mowing and general preparation for showing   50

Which costs are capital investment and which are working capital?
2. Give examples of some current needs for which present designs meet functional but not economic criteria.
3. Suppose you are a manager of people and are faced with the decision whether to replace half your staff with machines. Comment on some of the advantages and disadvantages of automation.
4. A new chemical has just been invented, and the projected process involves an investment of $1,000,000 as well as the following yearly costs and revenue:

	$
· Raw materials	200,000
· Labor	130,000
· Maintenance	50,000
· Utilities	10,000
· Overhead	260,000
· Selling expense	100,000
· Revenue from sales	1,000,000

Assuming that the depreciation rate is 10% on investment, total income tax after allowable depreciation is 50%, and the interest rate is 7%, determine the following:
a. Gross profit
b. Net profit after taxes and depreciation
c. Return on investment
d. Payout time
e. If the minimum rate of return is 15%, should this chemical be produced?
5. The following information is available regarding possible alternatives:

	Alternative A	Alternative B	Alternative C
· Investment I, $	250,000	550,000	1,000,000
· Gross profit G, $/yr	300,000	500,000	700,000

If depreciation is 10% on investment and total income tax rate is 50%, which alternative will realize the quickest return on your investment?
6. A process for a new product can be expressed as follows:

$$A + B = C + D$$

where A and B = raw materials
C = final product
D = by-product

The by-product is a toxic liquid having no credit value and must be treated at a cost of $0.01 per pound.

The demand for the final product is 500,000 pounds per year and it can be sold at $2.00 per pound. The cost of *A* and *B* is $0.25 and $0.35 per pound, respectively. If capital investment is $2,000,000, working capital is $1,500,000, depreciation and interest are 10% each on investment, and total income tax rate is 55%:

a. Should the venture be undertaken if the minimum return rate is 15%?

b. Should it be undertaken if the selling price can be increased to $3.00 per pound, while the demand remains the same?

Cost Estimation and Analysis

2

We recall from Chapter 1 that the main objective of an economic feasibility study is to identify and evaluate the economic outcome of a proposed project so that whatever funds are assigned to it may be used to the best advantage. To have a viable output from such an economic study, a good input is essential. Because net profit equals total income minus all expenses incurred, understanding the many different types of costs that are generally associated with a given project or operation, and how to estimate them most efficiently, is a must for the engineer or technologist. Money is paid out for expenses incurred as a result of the project or operation, such as those for raw materials, labor, utilities, supervision, and equipment in the case of a manufacturing operation. Other indirect costs are incurred as well, which cannot be neglected if a complete analysis of the total cost is to be obtained. Examples of indirect expenses are administrative salaries, product distribution, and selling costs, to mention but a few.

The total quantity of funds required to put a project in operation is known as *capital investment*, which breaks down into two components, *fixed capital* and *working capital*. We recall from Chapter 1 that fixed capital I consists of investment in facility (factory, plant, office, warehouse) and equipment (machinery, reactors, boilers, computers, electrical generators, pumps, etc.). Working capital I_w refers to money tied up in raw materials, intermediate and finished-goods inventories, and accounts receivable, as well as cash needed to operate a given project. The expense involved in keeping a project or an operation producing is known as *operating cost*. Operating cost is a continuous cost, unlike capital investment, which is a one-time cost.

Since all three costs—capital investment, working capital and operating cost—are essential to project evaluation, it is the objective of this chapter to bring forth techniques available for sound cost estimation.

2.1   Types of Estimates and Their Costs

There are a number of methods available for cost estimation, ranging in accuracy from a rough estimate to a detailed estimate derived from drawings, blueprints, and specifications. The choice of method depends on the purpose of the estimate. In general, three types of estimate are employed by most industries:

1.   Order-of-magnitude
2.   Semidetailed (budget authorization estimate)
3.   Detailed (firm estimate)

These estimates are used for feasibility studies, selection among alternative investments, appropriation-of-funds requests, capital budgeting, and presentation of fixed-price bids, to name but a few.

Regardless of the estimating method being employed it is important to recognize that the level of detail carries a price tag directly proportional to its level of accuracy and to the time required to prepare the data as input for the estimate. Simultaneously, the level of detail and level of accuracy are directly proportional to the quality and quantity of the output which is the final estimate.

Table 2-1 depicts the relationship between the cost of the estimate as a percentage of total project cost and the probable accuracy of the estimate, based on total project costs of $500,000, $1,000,000, $5,000,000, $10,000,000, $15,000,000, and $20,000,000. As can be seen, estimates on larger projects require a lower expenditure per project dollar, while smaller projects require a higher percentage. Hence, from Table 2-1, an estimate accurate to within ± 10%[1] of a $500,000 project would be expected to be around 1.6% or $8,000. On a $20,000,000 project, an estimate accurate to within ± 10% would be expected to be around 0.30% of the total project cost, or $60,000. Similarly, on a $5,000,000 project, ± 10% accurate estimate would be about 0.46% of the total project, or $23,000.

---

[1] The plus (+) means that the estimate is below the actual costs while the minus (−) means that the estimate is above those costs.

TABLE 2-1   Estimation of the Cost of Cost Estimating as a Percentage of Total
             Project Cost

Level of accuracy, %	Total Cost of the Project					
	$500,000	$1,000,000	$5,000,000	$10,000,000	$15,000,000	$20,000,000
5	4.00	3.70	1.00	0.80	0.70	0.65
10	1.60	1.50	0.46	0.40	0.34	0.30
15	0.76	0.70	0.21	0.19	0.17	0.15
20	0.44	0.37	0.13	0.11	0.10	0.08
25	0.28	0.24	0.08	0.07	0.07	0.05
30	0.21	0.17	0.06	0.05	0.05	0.04
35	0.16	0.13	0.04	0.04	0.03	0.03
40	0.12	0.10	0.03	0.03	0.02	0.02
45	0.10	0.08	0.03	0.02	0.02	0.02
50	0.08	0.06	0.02	0.02	0.01	0.01

Used by permission of NL Industries, Inc.

2.2   Order-of-Magnitude Estimates

The order-of-magnitude cost estimates usually have an average accuracy level of $\pm 50\%$, often varying from ± 30 to $\pm 70\%$, depending on the size of the project. Such estimates, as mentioned previously, require much less detail than firm estimates, making them least costly to prepare but most risky in terms of over- or under-expenditure. Nevertheless, estimates of this type are extremely important for determining if a proposed project should be given further consideration or for screening a large number of alternative projects in a short period of time. With order-of-magnitude cost estimates, precision is sacrificed for speed; information quickly becomes available to show whether expected profit is sufficient to justify the risk of investment or, simply, whether the project warrants further consideration.

Order-of-magnitude estimates are usually derived from cost indexes, cost ratios, historical data, experience, or physical dimensions.

COST INDEXES

Most cost data which are available for immediate use in order-of-magnitude estimates are historical, that is, based on conditions at some time in the past. Since the value of money (Appendix A) depreciates continuously as a function of time, this means that all published cost data are out of date. Some method must be used for converting past costs to present costs. This can be done by the use of a cost index which gives the relative cost of an item in terms of the cost at some particular base period.

If the cost at some time in the past is known, the equivalent cost at the present time can be obtained by multiplying the original cost by the ratio of the present index value to the index value at the time of original cost. Mathematically, this can be expressed as follows:

$$\text{present cost} = (\text{original cost}) \frac{(\text{index value at present})}{(\text{index value at time of original cost})} \qquad \textbf{(2-1)}$$

Expressed differently,

$$\text{cost in year B} = \frac{(\text{index value at year B}) (\text{cost in year A})}{(\text{index value at year A})}$$

Example 2-1

A refrigeration unit was purchased in January of 1976 for $5,000. What is its equivalent cost in January of 1977, given that the idexes are 543.3 and 582.8 respectively?

Solution:

$$(\$5,000) \frac{(582.8, \text{index January 1977})}{(543.3, \text{index January 1976})} = (\$5,000) (1.0727) = \$5,364$$

This is a 7.27% increase in one year.

Cost indexes can be used to give a general estimate, but no index can account for all economic factors, such as changes in labor productivity or local conditions. The common indexes permit fairly accurate estimates, ±10% at best, if the period involved is less than 10 years. For periods greater than 10 years, the accuracy falls off rapidly.

There are many types of cost index[2] covering every area of interest: equipment, cost, labor, construction, raw materials, etc. The most common of these indexes are Marshall and Stevens equipment cost indexes, and *Chemical Engineering* plant cost indexes.[3] Table 2-2 presents a list of the values for both indexes for the years 1970 through 1976.

COST-CAPACITY RELATIONSHIP

Cost estimates can be rapidly approximated where cost data are available for similar projects of different capacity. In general, costs do not rise linearly; that is, if the size doubles the cost will not necessarily increase twofold. The reason for this is that the fabrication of a large piece of equipment usually involves the same operations as a smaller piece, but each operation does not take twice as long; further, the amount

---

[2] For a detailed summary of various cost indexes, see *Engineering News-Record,* vol. 180, pp. 77–88, 1968.

[3] Published every other Monday in *Chemical Engineering,* a McGraw-Hill publication.

TABLE 2-2   Major Cost Indexes

Year	Marshall and Stevens Installed Equipment 1926=100	Chemical Engineering Plant Cost 1957–1959=100
1970	303.3	125.7
1971	321.3	132.2
1972	332.0	137.2
1973	344.1	144.1
1974	398.4	165.4
1975	444.3	182.4
1976	472.1	192.1
1977	505.4	204.1

of metal used on a piece of equipment is more closely related to its area than to its volume. Accordingly, the relationship can be expressed mathematically as:

$$C_B = C_A \times \left(\frac{Q_B}{Q_A} \right)^X \qquad\qquad \text{(2-2)}$$

where C_B = cost at capacity B
     C_A = cost at capacity A
     Q_B = quantity or capacity B
     Q_A = quantity or capacity A
      X = cost-capacity factor

The component X in the above equation, the *cost-capacity factor,* varies according to the type of project being considered. The range is from 0.2 to 1.00, the average, however, being 0.6 to 0.8. Steam electric generating plants, for example, have a factor of about 0.8. Waste-treatment plants usually range between 0.7 and 0.8. Large public housing projects also average about 0.8. On the other hand, steel storage tanks have a cost-capacity factor as low as 0.4 or as high as 0.8, depending on their shape. In the absence of other information a factor of 0.75 can be used.

Example 2-3
    Determine the cost of a 60,000,000-kilogram synthetic rubber production plant, given that a 45,000,000 kilogram plant costs $80,000,000 and the cost-capacity factor is 0.63.

Solution:

C_A = $80,000,000
Q_A = 45,000,000 kilograms
Q_B = 60,000,000 kilograms
X = 0.63

Then, by equation (2-2):

$$C_2 = \$80,000,000 \times \frac{(60,000,000)^{0.63}}{(45,000,000)}$$
$$= \$95,896,240, \text{ or approximately } \$96,000,000$$

In general, the cost-capacity concept should not be used beyond a tenfold range of capacity, and care must be taken to make certain that the two capacities or equipments are similar with regard to construction, materials of construction, location, and other pertinent variables such as time reference. In industry it is a standard procedure to limit scaling to capacity ratios of 2:1 and in some extreme cases 3:1. Should two different time references be used, convert the cost of the previous project to a current basis, using an appropriate index to correct historical costs for time differential. The following example will illustrate.

Example 2-4

Consolidated Edison of New York is considering construction of a 300-megawatt steam-generating plant in Brooklyn. In 1971 a 100-megawatt plant built in Brooklyn cost $22,000,000. Given that this is 1976, estimate the cost of the new plant, given a capacity factor of 0.8.

Solution:

Chemical Engineering cost indexes from Table 2-2 are:

· 1971–132.2
· 1976–192.1

Then, by equation 2-2 (modified):

$$C_B (1976) = \$22,000,000 \times \frac{(192.1)}{(132.2)} \times \frac{(300)^{0.8}}{(100)}$$
$$= \$76,986,690, \text{ or approximately } \$77,000,000$$

2.3 Semidetailed Estimates

Semidetailed, or budget, estimates are on the average accurate to within $\pm$ 15%, ranging between 10 and 20%. For most projects this level of accuracy is quite adequate for decision making, giving the potential investor enough information to decide whether or not to proceed. During selection from among alternative investments, if order-of-magnitude estimates still yield two or more alternatives, semidetailed estimates are then employed for further screening.

Semidetailed estimates, which are most frequently applied for preparing definitive estimates, require more information than do order-of-magnitude estimates. Instead of using mathematical relationships, historical costs, or project similarity, the project must be considered on its own. Actual quotations are to be obtained on major equipment and major related items. Equipment installation labor is evaluated as a percentage of the delivered equipment costs. Preliminary design data are usually necessary along with some drawings from which costs for concrete, steel, piping, instrumentation, etc., are obtained. Unit costs are then applied to the measured units. For example, schedule 40 1-inch 316 stainless steel piping costs $5.16 per linear foot. A percentage of delivered equipment cost is often used instead of measured units to achieve the same goal.

Example 2-5
The principal equipment items for a highly automated waste-treatment plant are estimated to cost $500,000. Using historical information, it is possible to assign percentages to the various components other than principal equipment items and their installation and to generate a cost for these components.

Given the components and percentages in Table 2-3, prepare an estimate of the fixed capital investment for the waste-treatment plant.

Solution:

Components		Cost
· Purchased equipment (delivered)		$500,000
· Purchased equipment installation (34%)	(0.34)(500,000)	170,000
· Piping, installed (20%)		100,000
· Instruments, installed (5%)		25,000
· Electrical, installed (4%)		20,000
· Buildings (5%)		25,000
· Utilities, installed (5%)		25,000
· Raw materials storage, installed (2%)		10,000
· Engineering, overhead, etc. (15%)		75,000
· Contingencies (10%)		50,000
Fixed capital investment		$1,000,000

Estimating by percentage of delivered-equipment cost is commonly used for preliminary and budget estimates. The method yields highly accurate results when applied to projects similar in nature to *recently* completed ones.

It should be noted that in the above analysis a 10% contingency allowance has been added as a buffer to reflect possible inaccuracy or inflation. In general, for a project with engineering substantially completed and with major pieces of equipment priced (vessels, pumps, conveyors, heat exchangers, processing equipment, instrumentation and controls, etc.) a contingency allowance of 5% is added. For projects for which engineering is 15 to 25% completed and for which major items of equipment have been estimated with 50% covered by firm quotes, a con-

TABLE 2-3

Components	Percent of delivered equipment cost
Purchased (major) equipment installation	34
Piping, installed	20
Instruments, installed	5
Electrical, installed	4
Buildings	5
Utilities, installed	5
Raw materials storage, installed	2
Engineering, overhead, etc.	15
Contingencies	10
Total	100

tingency allowance of 10% is added. for projects for which engineering is less than 10% completed and for which major items of equipment have been estimated with quotes for less than 50%, a contingency allowance of 15% is added. Finally, for projects that have been scoped, for which only preliminary engineering has been completed, and for which major equipment items have been specified but substantially no design has been undertaken, a contingency allowance of 20% is added.

2.4 Detailed Estimates

Detailed cost estimates should have an accuracy of between 5 and 10%. They thus require careful determination of each individual item in the project, or detailed itemizing of each component making up the cost. Facilities, equipment, and material needs are determined from complete engineering drawings and specifications, and are priced either from up-to-date cost data or, preferably, from firm delivered quotations. Installation costs are computed from up-to-date labor rates, efficiencies, and worker-hour calculations. These estimates, however, as seen from Table 2-1, are time-consuming and costly to prepare and should be used only when absolutely necessary. In fact, they are almost exclusively prepared by contractors bidding for a given job; however, these bids are often accurate to within ± 5% or better. If the bid is too high, the job may not be awarded. If the bid is too low, the job, although awarded, will produce a loss to the contractor. Therefore, it is absolutely necessary to be as accurate as possible.

2.5 Capital Investment Cost Estimation

The fixed capital requirements of a new project can be broken down into three components for estimating purposes: (1) depreciable fixed investment, (2) expensed or amortized[4] investment, and (3) nondepreciable fixed investment. *Depreciable fixed investment* can be further broken down into buildings and services; equipment, including installation; and other items such as transportation, shipping and receiving facilities. The *amortized investment* consists of: research and development; engineering and supervision; start-up costs; and other things including franchises, designs, and drawings. The *nondepreciable fixed investment* also has identifiable parts. The two parts are land and working capital.

Most of the above components are self-explanatory. For some, further elaboration follows.

RESEARCH AND DEVELOPMENT

This usually pertains to new manufacturing plants, where expenditures for such activities are usually associated with process-improvement and cost-reduction efforts aimed at increasing productivity and profits. Research and development costs average 3 to 4% of sales or services associated with the project. For large pharmaceutical companies, these costs may be as high as 8 to 10%.

ENGINEERING AND SUPERVISION

This is the cost for construction design and engineering, drafting, purchasing, accounting, travel, reproduction, communications, and various office expenses directly related to the project. This cost, since it cannot be directly charged to equipment, materials, or labor, is typically considered as an indirect cost ranging from 30 to 40% of the purchased-equipment cost or 10 to 15% of the total direct costs of the project.

START-UP COST

After a project has been completed, a number of changes usually have to be made before the project can operate at an optimum level. These changes cost money for equipment, materials, labor, and overhead. They result in loss of income while the project is not producing or is operating at only partial capacity. These costs may be as high as 12% of the fixed-capital investment, though they usually stay under 10%. In general, an allowance of 10% for start-up cost is quite satisfactory.

LAND

This is the cost for land and the accompanying surveys and fees, which usually amounts to 4 to 8% of the purchased equipment cost or 1 to 2% of the fixed-capital investment. Because the value of land usually appreciates with time, this cost is not included in the fixed-capital in-

---

[4] Amortization is a form of depreciation applicable to intangible assets such as patents, copyrights, franchises, etc. Generally, straight-line depreciation methods must be used, and only certain items that are amortized can be deducted as expenditures for federal income tax purposes. Chapters 6 and 7 deal with depreciation and taxes, respectively.

vestment when estimating certain operating costs, such as depreciation. This topic is fully discussed in Chapter 6.

WORKING CAPITAL

This consists of the total amount of money invested in raw materials; intermediate and finished-goods inventories; accounts receivable; cash kept on hand for monthly payment of operating expenses such as salaries, wages, and raw materials purchases; accounts payable; and taxes payable.

The raw materials inventory usually amounts to a 1-month supply of the raw materials valued at delivered prices. Finished products in stock and intermediate products have a value approximately equal to the total manufacturing cost for 1 month's production or service. Credit terms extended to customers and from suppliers are usually based on an allowable 30- to 45-day payment period (accounts receivable and accounts payable, respectively). The cost of working capital varies from 10 to 25% of fixed-capital investment and may increase to as much as 50% or more for firms producing products of seasonal demand because of large inventories that must be carried for long periods of time.

2.6   Operating-Cost Estimation

Determination of the necessary capital investment (fixed and working) for a given project is only one part of a complete cost estimate. Another equally important part is the operating-cost estimation. Operating cost, production cost, or manufacturing cost is the cost of running a project, a manufacturing operation, or a service. In this section and throughout the book the three costs are considered together.

Accuracy is as important in estimating operating cost as it is in estimating capital investment. The largest cause of error in operating cost estimation is overlooking elements that make up the cost. Accordingly, it is very useful to break down operating cost into its elements, as shown below. This breakdown then becomes a valuable checklist to preclude omissions.

1.   Direct (variable) operating costs
    a.   Raw materials
    b.   Operating labor
    c.   Operating supervision
    d.   Power and utilities
    e.   Maintenance and repairs
    f.   Operating supplies
    g.   Others: laboratory charges, royalties, etc.
2.   Indirect (fixed) operating costs
    a.   Depreciation
    b.   Taxes (property)

    c. Insurance
    d. Rent
    e. Other: interest
3. General overhead costs
    a. Payroll overhead
    b. Recreation
    c. Restaurant or cafeteria
    d. Management
    e. Storage facilities
4. Administrative costs
    a. Executive salaries
    b. Clerical wages
    c. Engineering and legal costs
    d. Office maintenance
    e. Communications
5. Distribution and marketing costs
    a. Sales office
    b. Sales staff expenses
    c. Shipping
    d. Advertising
    e. Technical sales service

As can be seen, operating costs fall into two major classifications: direct and indirect. *Direct* costs (also called *variable* costs) tend to be proportional to production or service output. *Indirect* costs (also called *fixed* costs) tend to be independent of production or service output. Some costs are neither fixed nor directly proportional to output[5] and are known as *semivariable* costs. Direct and indirect costs are usually estimated on a basis of cost per unit of output or service and can generally be regarded as linear over a wide range of production or service volume. This concept is fully developed in Chapter 3 in connection with break-even analysis.

The other costs—overhead, administrative, and distribution and marketing—are expressed on a time basis, since they are related to the level of investment rather than to the level of output. The period is usually 1 year because: (1) the effect of seasonal variation is evened out, (2) this permits rapid calculations at less than full capacity, and (3) the calculations are more directly usable in profitability analysis.

The best source of information for an operating-cost estimation is data from similar or identical projects. Most firms have extensive records of their operations, permitting quick estimation from existing data. Adjustments for increased costs resulting from inflation must be made, and differences in size of operation and geographical location must be considered.

---

[5] For example, one supervisor is able to oversee the workers in a department up to a certain level of production. If additional workers are added to the department, the point is eventually reached where it is necessary to hire another supervisor.

Methods for estimating operating cost in the absence of specific information are discussed below.

DIRECT (VARIABLE) COSTS

Raw materials. The amount of raw materials required per unit of product can usually be determined from literature, experiments, or process material balances. Credit is usually given for by-products and salvageable scrap. In many cases, certain materials act only as an agent of production and may be recovered to some degree. Accordingly, the cost should be based only on the amount of raw materials actually consumed.

Example 2-6

A process for a new product can be expressed as follows:

$$A + B = C + D$$

where A and B = raw materials

C = final product

D = salable by-product

The costs of A and B are \$0.25 and \$0.35 per kilogram, respectively; D can be sold for \$0.05 per kilogram; and for every kilogram of C and D generated, 1 kilogram each of A and B is required. Determine the raw materials cost.

Solution:

$$\text{Raw materials cost} = 0.25 + 0.35 - 0.05 = \$0.55/\text{kg}$$

Example 2-7

Consider again the process given in Example 2-6. However, a 25% excess of B is now required, of which 90% is recycled for further use. Determine the raw materials cost.

Solution:

$$0.25 + 1.25(0.35) - 0.05 - (0.25)(0.90)\,(0.35) = \$0.55875/\text{kg}$$

Direct price quotations for raw materials from prospective suppliers are preferable to published market prices. For an order-of-magnitude cost estimate, however, market prices are often sufficient.

Freight or transportation charges should be included in the raw materials costs, and these charges should be relevant to where they are to be used. For example, if raw materials purchasing is centralized and then the materials are dispersed to various locations, the added freight cost from central point to final destination must also be included.

Operating labor. The average rate for labor in different industries at various locations can be obtained from the U.S. Department of Labor, Bureau of Labor Statistics, *Monthly Labor Review.* Depending on the industry, operating labor may vary from 5 to 25% of the total operating cost.

The most accurate way to establish operating labor requirements is to use a complete manning table, but shortcut methods are available and are quite satisfactory for most cost estimates. One technique suggests that labor requirements vary to about the 0.20 to 0.25 power of the capacity ratio when plant capacities are scaled up or down. Hence, Equation 2-2 (capacity relationship) can be employed. The equation recognizes the improvement in labor productivity as plants increase in output and the lowering of labor productivity as output decreases, and it can be used to extrapolate known worker hours or cost of labor from one operation to another of a different capacity. The operations must, however, be similar in nature.

Example 2-8

A 200,000-barrel-per-day petroleum refinery requires six operators per shift. Determine the labor requirement per shift for a similar refinery producing 500,000 barrels per day.

Solution:

By employing Equation 2-2 and a power factor of 0.25 (as a buffer), the labor requirement is

$$6\left(\frac{500,000}{200,000}\right)^{0.25} = 7.54, \text{ or 8 operators}$$

Example 2-9

A process plant generating 100 tons per day of a product requires 30,000 worker hours of operating labor per year. Determine the annual labor requirements for a plant generating 60 tons per day.

Solution:

The same equation is employed; this time, however, 0.20 is used as power factor, again as a buffer.

$$30,000\left(\frac{60}{100}\right)^{0.20} = 27,000 \text{ worker h/yr}$$

Operating supervision. The cost for direct supervision of labor is generally estimated at 15 to 20% of the cost of operating labor.

Power and utilities. The cost for utilities, such as steam, electricity, natural gas, fuel oil, cooling water, and compressed air, varies widely, depending on the amount of consumption, the location, and the source. In Niagara Falls, New York, for instance, electric power is relatively cheap compared to other locations. Natural gas is relatively cheap in the Gulf Coast states.

As a rough approximation, power and utility costs for a manufacturing facility amount to 10 to 20% of the operating cost. Utility consumption does not vary directly with output level, and variation to the 0.9 power of the capacity ratio is a good relationship.

Maintenance and repairs. Maintenance and repairs are necessary if a plant, an office, a warehouse, a manufacturing facility, etc., is to be kept in efficient operating condition. These costs include the cost for labor, materials, and maintenance supervision.

Records for the firm's existing operations are the only reliable source of maintenance cost, but with experience it can be estimated as a function of investment. Maintenance cost as a percentage of fixed-capital investment ranges between 3 and 15%, with the average between 8 and 10%.

For operating rates of less than full capacity (100%), the following is generally true: For a 75% operating rate, the maintenance and repairs cost is about 85% of its full-capacity cost; for a 50% operating rate, the maintenance and repair cost is about 75%.

Operating supplies. These are supplies such as charts, janitorial supplies, lubricants, etc., which are needed to keep a project functioning efficiently. Since these cannot be considered as raw materials or maintenance and repairs materials, they are classified as operating supplies. The annual cost for operating supplies is approximately equal to 2% of the total investment.

Others. Charges for laboratory facilities, patents, royalties, rentals (for copying machines, typewriters, and machinery), etc., can range between 2 and 10% of operating labor, selling price, or operating cost, depending on the particular situation.

INDIRECT (FIXED) COSTS

Depreciation. Equipment, buildings, and other material objects require an initial investment, which must be written off as an operating expense. In order to write off this cost, a decrease in value is assumed to occur throughout the useful life of the material assets. The decrease in value is termed *depreciation*. This concept is fully developed in Chapter 6.

The annual depreciation rate on a straight-line basis for machinery and equipment is generally about 5% of the fixed-capital investment; for buildings the rate is about 2.5%, while for equipment used for research and development the rate is 10%. For pollution-abatement equipment the rate is about 20%.

Property taxes. The amount of local property taxes is a function of the location of the operation and the regional laws. For highly populated areas, the range on an annual basis is 2 to 5% of the fixed-capital investment, while for less-populated areas local property taxes are about 1 to 2%. This concept is fully developed in Chapter 7.

Insurance. Insurance rates depend on the type of operation and the extent of available protection facilities. Generally, these rates annually amount to 1 to 2% of the fixed-capital investment.

Rent. Annual costs for rented land and buildings are about 8 to 12% of the value of the rented property.

Interest. Since borrowed capital (fixed and working) is usually used to finance a project, interest must be paid for its use. As seen in Chapter 5, fluctuations in interest rates are a function of the state of the economy and can range between 7 and 12%, depending on the borrower (size and type of firm), with the average being 8%.

OVERHEAD COSTS

General overhead. General overhead costs usually include payroll, recreation, restaurant or cafeteria, management, and storage facilities as a lump sum. The costs range between 40 and 70%, with the average being 50%, of the total cost for operating labor, operating supervision, and maintenance and repairs.

ADMINISTRATIVE COSTS

The salaries for top management, such as the director of manufacturing, the technical director, the vice-president for operations, etc., are not a direct manufacturing cost. Still, they must be charged to administrative costs along with clerical wages, engineering and legal costs, office maintenance expenses, and communications costs (telephone, teletype), which are all part of the operating cost. These costs may vary markedly from operation to operation and depend somewhat upon whether the operation is a new one or an addition to an existing one. In the absence of accurate cost figures from records, or for a quick cost estimate, the administrative costs may be approximated as 40 to 60% of the operating labor, with the average about 45%.

DISTRIBUTION AND MARKETING COSTS

The costs of selling a product or a service provided by a successful operation are charged to distribution and marketing costs. Included in this category are salaries, wages, supplies, and other expenses of sales offices; salaries, commissions, and travel expenses for salespeople; and expenses for shipping, containers, advertising, and technical sales service. As with administrative costs, for a quick estimate, the distribution and marketing cost can be approximated as 10% of *sales.*

Example 2-10
Management is considering whether to purchase and install an automatic bean-crushing machine for its vegetable oil extraction plant. The required capital investment is $200,000, all fixed. Estimate the added annual costs that will be realized from this expansion, given the following:

· Depreciation	5% of investment
· Insurance	1% of investment
· Maintenance and Repairs	8% of investment
· Property taxes	3.5% of investment
· Interest	8% of investment

Solution:
· Fixed capital investment = $200,000

· Depreciation at 5% of investment	$10,000
· Insurance at 1% of investment	2,000
· Maintenance and repairs at 8% of investment	16,000
· Taxes at 3.5% of investment	7,000
· Interest at 8% of investment	16,000
Total added annual cost	$51,000

Example 2-11
Management needs a quick cost estimate for a new product just developed. The demand for the product is estimated to be 400,000 pounds per year, and the product can be sold at $2.50 per pound. The engineering department has estimated that capital investment required is $400,000, of which 85% is depreciable while the remaining 15% is nondepreciable working capital. Of the depreciable investment, $40,000 is for an additional building while the remainder is for new equipment and machinery. Estimate the operating cost, given the following information from company records:

· Raw materials cost—$1.00 per pound of product
· By-product and scrap credit—none
· Utilities, Steam—$0.075 per pound of product
    Electricity—$0.010 per pound of product
· Labor—12,000 worker hours at $8.50/worker hour[6]
· Supervision—17% of labor cost
· Maintenance—8% of investment per year
· Operating supplies—1% of investment per year
· Depreciation—to be calcuated
· Taxes—2% of investment per year
· Interest—7% of investment per year
· Insurance—1% of investment per year

---

[6] Includes fringe benefits.

- Overhead costs—40% of labor, supervision, and maintenance
- Administrative cost—40% of labor
- Distribution costs—10% of total operating cost

Solution:

Table 2-4 depicts the procedure for calculating the operating cost step by step. Cost are figured on an annual basis and then converted to cost per pound of product. Of the $400,000 capital investment, the fixed capital is (0.85) (400,000) = $340,000, while the remaining $60,000 is working capital.

TABLE 2-4   Calculating Operating Cost

1.	*Direct operating costs*	*Annual Cost*
	a. Raw materials ($1.00/lb)(400,000 lb)	$400,000
	b. By-product and scrap credit	0
	c. Utilities, Steam (0.075)(400,000)	30,000
	Electricity (0.010)(400,000)	4,000
	d. Labor ($8.50/h)(12,000 h)	102,000
	e. Supervision (0.17)($102,000)	17,340
	f. Maintenance (0.08)($340,000)	27,200
	g. Operating supplies (0.01)($400,000)	4,000
	Subtotal Direct Operating Costs	$584,540
2.	*Indirect operating costs*	
	a. Depreciation, Building (0.025)($40,000)	1,000
	Equipment (0.05)($300,000)	15,000
	b. Taxes (0.02)($340,000)	6,800
	c. Insurance (0.01)($340,000)	3,400
	Subtotal Indirect Operating Costs	$26,200
3.	*Overhead costs*	
	(0.40)($102,000 + $17,340 + $27,200)	$58,616
4.	*Administrative costs*	
	(0.40)($102,000)	$40,800
	Subtotal Operating Cost	$710,156
5.	*Distribution costs*	
	(0.10)($1,000,000)	$100,000
	TOTAL OPERATING COST	$810,156
	OPERATING COST PER POUND OF PRODUCT	$2.0253

2.7   Shortcut Method for Operating-Cost Estimation

Given the information in Section 2.6 it is possible to assign average values to all the components that make up operating cost. For some components, an average value has been given already; for the remaining ones, a value is given in the outline below. The use of average values should be discouraged, however, since the results of such an estimate lack individuality. Averages make no allowance for differences between situations and do not challenge the true capability of the estimator. The outline is useful, nevertheless, in instances where a high level of precision is neither necessary nor possible, and sometimes no data at all are available. Any output may be considered better than no output, and the most expedient figures are often necessary.

Average Data for Order-of-Magnitude Operating-Cost Estimate
1. Direct operating costs
   a. Raw materials—estimate from price lists
   b. By-product and salvage value—estimate from price lists
   c. Operating labor—from literature or from similar operations
   d. Operating supervision—17.5% of operating labor
   e. Utilities—15% of operating cost or from similar operations
   f. Maintenance and repairs—9% of fixed capital investment
   g. Operating supplies—2% of total investment (fixed plus working)
   h. Others: Laboratory—10% of operating labor
       Royalties—2.5% of sales or service charges
       Contingencies—10% of direct operating cost
2. Indirect operating costs
   a. Depreciation—7% of fixed capital investment
   b. Property taxes—2.5% of fixed capital investment
   c. Insurance—1.5% of fixed capital investment
   d. Interest—8% of total investment
   e. Rent—10% of the rented property
3. Overhead cost—50% of operating labor, supervision, and maintenance and materials.
4. Administrative cost—45% of operating labor
5. Distribution and marketing costs—10% of sales

Summary

Cost estimates are an important component of economic analysis. Order-of-magnitude estimates, which are usually accurate to within ±50% are extremely useful in preliminary studies or rapid evaluation among alternatives. These are usually based on cost indexes, cost-capacity relationships, or physical dimensions. Semidetailed estimates are usually accurate to within ±15% and are used for budgeted purposes or for feasibility studies that require some precision; instead of using mathematical relationships between historical costs and estimated costs, the components of the project must be considered on their own as separate entities. Detailed estimates, accurate between ±5 and ±10%, are prepared almost exclusively by contractors making fixed-price bids; these require careful determination of each individual item in the project, and hence require more data than either of the methods discussed above.

The three basic types of estimating methods can be applied equally well to both capital investment and operating costs. The choice of method is solely dependent on the purpose and accuracy of the study. For most feasibility studies, either the order-of-magnitude or the semidetailed estimate is probably sufficient; however, both capital investment and operating costs should be determined with comparable precision.

Problems

1. The cost of a construction project in 1971 was $750,000. Estimate the cost in 1974.
2. Equipment for a chemical plant cost $250,000 in 1971. Estimate the cost in 1974.
3. The delivered cost of the major equipment for a nuclear energy plant is $5,000,000. Estimate the total cost of the plant using the concept of *percentage of delivered-equipment cost* and the percentages given in Example 2-5.
4. A waste-treatment plant with a capacity of 10,000 gallons per day costs $3,000,000. Estimate the cost for a plant with a capacity of 15,000 gallons per day.
5. Reestimate the cost in Problem 4, given that the years are 1972 (for the 10,000 gallons per day) and 1975 (for the 15,000 gallons per day).
6. A one-story warehouse 120 by 60 feet is to be added to an existing warehouse 60 by 30 feet, which was built in 1972 for $500,000. Estimate the cost of the project in 1975, given a cost-capacity factor of 0.88.
7. A new office building constructed in 1972 had a labor cost of $200,000. Estimate the labor cost for an identical building in 1975.
8. What does an operating cost include?
9. Why are average figures justified for depreciation expense even though it is not constant with time?
10. Estimate the total operating cost per year for a chemical plant, given the following: The total capital investment is $2,000,000, of which 80% is fixed. Of the 80%, 70% is invested in equipment. The labor cost is $200,000, and the raw materials cost is $250,000. Assume the distribution and marketing cost to be 15% of the *total operating cost*.
11. A two-story, 20,000-square-foot warehouse costs $300,000, with the following breakdown of the costs:

	Item	Percent
·	Lumber	14.2
·	Carpentry	10.0
·	Plumbing	13.6
·	Cabinets	7.2
·	Concerete	5.6

·	Wallboard	6.1
·	Electrical wiring	5.2
·	Flooring	9.2
·	Hardware	2.2
·	Heating	3.0
·	Insulation	2.0
·	Lighting	1.6
·	Painting	7.2
·	Roofing	3.2
·	Contingencies	9.7
	Total	100.0

a. What is the unit estimate for the next warehouse?

b. A 30,000-square-foot, two-level warehouse is to be built. Estimate the total cost of the project and item costs. $X = 0.88$.

12. The capital investment for a soap plant is $1,500,000, and the plant produces 3,000,000 bars annually. The selling price per unit is 40 cents. Working capital amounts to 13% of the total capital investment. The investment capital comes from company funds; hence there is no interest charge. The raw materials cost per bar of product is $0.05, labor $0.05, and utilities $0.03. The distribution and marketing cost is 7.5% of the selling price. Estimate the following:

a. Direct operating cost per bar of product

b. Total operating cost per year

c. Gross profit

13. Product F can be produced at a rate of 12,500 pounds per day, requiring the following raw materials:

	Raw material	Quantity/day, lb	Price, $/lb
·	A	11,750	0.34
·	B	3,500	0.05
·	C	2,500	0.03
·	D	200	0.06
·	E	1,200	0.88
	Total	19,150	

The labor cost is $0.075 per pound, the depreciation charge is $0.03 per pound, the laboratory charge is $0.002 per pound, and the distribution and marketing cost is 11% of the selling price. The selling price is $0.68 per pound, and the firm expects to sell 4,300,000 pounds this year. Determine the expected gross profit for the year, given that the scrap value of the by-product is $0.10 per pound.

14. A plating operation center consumes 1000 pounds per day of raw materials costing $7.50 per pound. Of the raw materials 80% are converted to the finished product while the remaining 20% (unconverted raw materials) have a scrap value of $2.00 per pound. The product output from this center is 500,000 pounds per day at a total

revenue of $12,125 per day. Given a variable cost (labor, supervision, maintenance, etc.) per day of $2500 and a fixed cost per day of $3,500, determine the daily gross profit for the center.

15. A rough rule of thumb for the chemical industry suggests that for every $1 of annual sales, $3 of fixed-capital investment is needed. If the total capital investment is $3,000,000, (of which 20% is working capital), the annual operating cost is $1,800,000, and the income tax rate is 50%, determine:

a. Gross profit

b. Net profit, ROI, and payback time.

Break-Even Analysis

3

The relationship of sales revenue, costs, and volume to profit and loss is fundamental to every business, and a basic understanding of these relationships is necessary before any project is carried out. Payback time, return on investment, or discounted-cash-flow analysis is not always a sufficient tool to demonstrate what happens to profit as changes occur in sales revenue, costs, and volume. Break-even analysis, particularly break-even charts, is useful in this regard, by exhibiting the relationship among the above variables and the degree of effect each has on the final profit.

This chapter deals with the cost-volume-profit relationship, development of break-even equations and charts, estimation of cost-volume relationships, and their application for effective decision making.

3.1 Terminology

In break-even analysis, the elements considered are total revenue from sales and total costs incurred; the latter is broken down into fixed cost, semivariable cost, and variable cost.

TOTAL REVENUE FROM SALES

This is an estimate of the dollars to be realized from the sales of products or services. It is the first figure to be established and is the most basic. One approach may be multiplying the number of units expected to be sold by the unit selling price to get the revenue figure. Another approach may be adjusting last year's dollar total upward or downward as the economy indicates.

Total revenue from sales, however, does not include fixed income or nonoperating income.

FIXED COSTS

These are indirect costs. They tend to remain constant in total dollar amount regardless of volume, or output. At zero volume and at 100% volume, the total dollar amounts are the same. Fixed costs may include rent, interest on investment, property taxes, property insurance, executive salaries, allowance for depreciation, and sums spent for advertising.

VARIABLE COSTS

Variable costs are those that vary directly with the level of output. Direct labor, materials, and certain supplies used are considered variable. If volume is halved, variable costs will be halved; if volume is doubled, variable costs will double. For example, if the production of one desk requires 10 worker hours at $5 per hour, then the production of two desks requires 20 worker hours ($100), or a variable cost per desk of $50.

TOTAL COSTS

Total cost is the sum of all fixed and variable costs incurred over a fiscal year.

GROSS PROFIT

Gross profit is total revenue less total costs, given that the former is greater than the latter. Gross profit is computed before income taxes.

LOSS

Loss is total costs less total revenue, given that the former is greater than the latter. On balance sheets and other tables, loss is usually enclosed in brackets or preceded by a minus sign. Brackets will be used in this book.

BREAK-EVEN POINT

The *break-even point* (BE) is the volume of output at which neither profit nor loss occurs, or where total revenue from sales is equal to total cost (fixed plus variable). Often, the break-even point is expressed as a percent of production or service capacity instead of as sales volume.

Example 3-1

The following information is available about a manufacturing operation:

- Selling price per unit = $10
- Variable costs per unit = $5
  - Fixed costs = $30,000
  - Output, units = 5000, 6000, and 7000

Determine the loss, break-even point, and profit as the sales of units increase.

Solution:

	For 5000 units	For 6000 units	For 7000 units
· Revenue from sales	$50,000	$60,000	$70,000
· Variable costs	25,000	30,000	35,000
· Fixed costs	30,000	30,000	30,000
· Total costs	$55,000	$60,000	$65,000
· Gross profit or [loss]	[$5,000]	$0 Break-even	$5,000

3.2 Mathematical analysis

The point in the operation of a project at which revenues and incurred costs are equal to each other is the break-even point. At this particular output or level of operation, a project will realize neither a profit nor a loss. The break-even point can be computed mathematically or can be ascertained graphically by presenting the relationship of revenue, costs, and volume of a productive capacity. Graphical analysis will be presented in Section 3-3.

If b is the variable cost per unit of output and C_v; is the total variable cost for the year; then for an annual output of x units the variable cost is

$$C_v = bx \qquad (3\text{-}1)$$

Let C_f equal the fixed cost per year, which remains relatively constant, and C_t the total annual cost; then for an annual output of x units, the total cost is:

$$C_t = C_f + bx = C_f + C_v \qquad (3\text{-}2)$$

C_t is a linear relationship, since b is assumed to be independent of x, and C_f is constant.

If p is the selling price per unit of output and G is the gross profit, then using Equation 3-2

$$G = px - C_t = px - (C_f + bx) \tag{3-3}$$

Since no profit or loss occurs at the break-even point, Equation 3-3 at $G = 0$ becomes

$$G = 0 = px - (C_f + bx)$$

or

$$px = C_f + bx$$

Finally,

$$\text{Break-even output or volume (BEV)} = \frac{C_f}{p - b} \tag{3-4}$$

In terms of break-even sales dollars (BES) the relationship is

$$\text{BES} = \frac{C_f}{1 - b/p} \tag{3-5}$$

Example 3-2
Given the information in Example 3-1, what are the break-even volume and break-even sales?

Solution:

$$\text{Since } b = \$5$$
$$p = \$10$$
$$C_f = \$30,000$$

then by Equation 3-4

$$\text{BEV} = \frac{C_f}{p - b} = \frac{30,000}{10 - 5} = 6000 \text{ units}$$

or by Equation 3-5

$$\text{BES} = \frac{C_f}{1 - b/p} = \frac{30,000}{1 - 5/10} = \$60,000$$

Referring back to Example 3-1, we see that these answers indeed agree.

Example 3-3

A project can produce 25,000 units per year. Fixed costs are $12,000 per year, the variable cost per unit is $4, and the selling price is $6 per unit. Find the break-even point and the gross profit at this maximum capacity.

Solution:

The break-even point by Equation 3-4 is

$$BEV = \frac{C_f}{p - b} = \frac{12,000}{6 - 4} = 6000 \text{ units}$$

and the gross profit by Equation 3-3 is

$$G = px - (C_f + bx) = 6(25,000) - 12,000 + 4(25,000)$$
$$= 150,000 - 112,000 = \$38,000$$

Example 3-4

Fixed costs of an operation are estimated to be $120,000 while the variable costs are expected to equal 40% of sales. Find the break-even sales volume.

Solution:

Since $b = 0.40p$, then by Equation 3-5

$$BES = \frac{120,000}{1 - 0.40p/p} = \frac{120,000}{1 - 0.40} = \$200,000$$

3.3 Graphical Analysis

The mathematical analysis for break-even points is relatively simple. Nevertheless, the use of a break-even chart provides a clearer idea of the firm's position vis-à-vis its break-even point by enabling a person to see several important cost relationships that would otherwise be difficult to visualize. As with the mathematical analysis, most break-even charts work with the idea that fixed costs do not change when sales volume increases or decreases but that variable or direct costs rise or fall proportionately with sales.

Figure 3.1 shows the essential features of a break-even chart, using Example 3-1 as reference.

In Figure 3.1, the vertical axis (or y axis) represents both sales revenue and costs, and the horizontal axis (or x axis) shows both production volume in units and sales volume in dollars. The vertical units of measurement on a break-even chart are always dollars while the horizontal

Figure 3-1

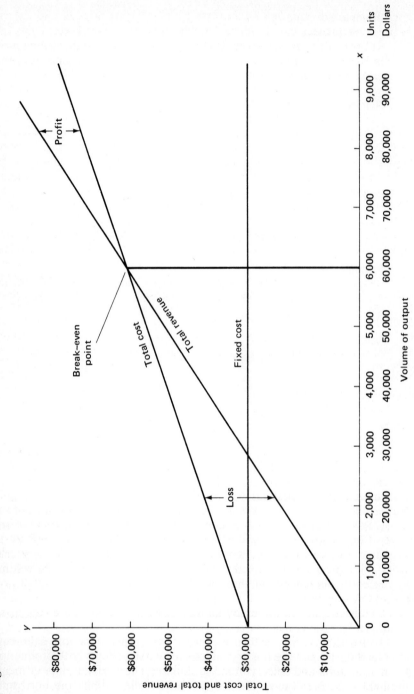

units of measurement can be units of production, dollars, percent of capacity, hours, etc.

At zero sales, revenue is also zero. Therefore, the total revenue line is a straight line passing through the origin, representing the sales revenue increasing as volume sold increases ($y = px$). If volume (the x axis) is expressed in terms of sales volume (dollars), the revenue line on the break-even chart is simply the straight line $y = x$.

Next, the total amount of fixed costs is plotted on the graph. Fixed costs in this case total $30,000 throughout the range of sales shown on the break-even chart. Variable costs are then added to fixed costs to arrive at total costs, which can be expressed in terms of y. Thus $y = C_t + bx$, with the slope of the variable cost line equal to b, or in this case $5 per unit. These variable costs are plotted above the fixed cost line, thereby summing the total cost of operations for any given level of sales or output.

The point at which the total cost line intersects the total income line, 6000 units or $60,000 in this example, is the break-even point. To the left of this point, the vertical distance between the total income and the total cost lines indicates a net loss; to the right, it represents the net profit. Hence, at sales volume of 4000 units, a net loss of $50,000 - $40,000 = $10,000 occurs. At a sales volume of 8000 units, $80,000 - $70,000 = $10,000 in a gross profits is realized.

Effect of changes in the various components. The revenue-cost-volume relationships suggest that there are three ways in which the profit of a project can be increased:

1. Increase the selling price per unit (p).
2. Decrease the variable cost per unit (b).
3. Decrease the fixed cost (C_f).

The separate effects of each of these possibilities are shown in Figure 3-2. Each starts from the current situation (Example 3-1 and Figure 3-1: $b = $5/unit, $p = $10/unit, $C_f = $30,000, BE = 6000 units = $60,000). The effect of a 10% change in each factor is calculated:

1. A 10% increase in selling price would decrease the break-even point to 5000 from 6000 units. At a sales volume of 8000 units the gross profit becomes $18,000, an increase in gross profit of $8000 ($18,000 - 10,000); while at 4000 units, the loss in profit becomes $6000 instead of original $10,000.
2. A 10% decrease in variable cost would shift the break-even point from 6000 to 5455 units. At a sales volume of 8000 units the gross profit becomes $14,000, an increase of $4000 ($14,000 - 10,000); while at 4000 units, the loss in profit becomes $8000 instead of original $10,000.
3. A 10% decrease in fixed cost would shift the break-even point from 6000 to 5400 units. At a sales volume of 8000 units the gross profit

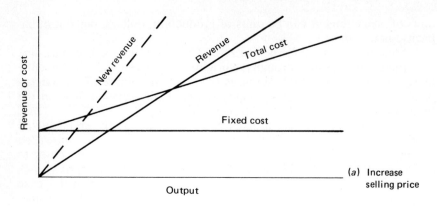

(a) Increase selling price

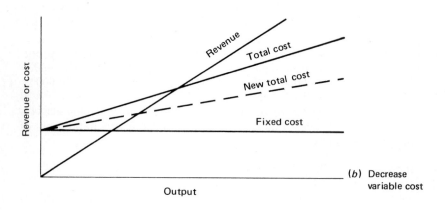

(b) Decrease variable cost

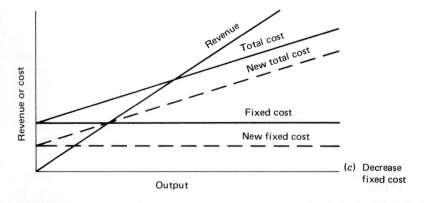

(c) Decrease fixed cost

Figure 3-2

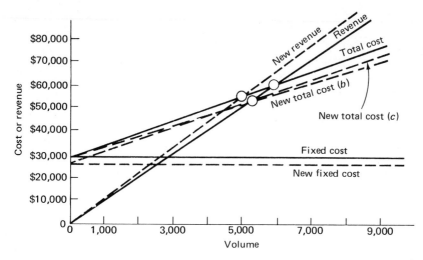

Figure 3-3

becomes $13,000, an increase of $3000 ($13,000 − 10,000); while at 4000 units the loss in profit becomes $7000 instead of the original $10,000. Figure 3-3 shows the three changes simultaneously.

If we look more closely at some of the relationships, we can calculate, for example, that a 10% increase in fixed cost could be offset by a 3.75% increase in selling price, a 7.5% decrease in variable cost, or a 7.5% increase in volume sold. This clearly shows that if one wanted to increase the profit of a given project, the sequence of actions should be (1) increase selling price, (2) sell more units, (3) decrease variable cost, and (4) decrease fixed costs.

Another important calculation made from the break-even chart is the *margin of safety*. This is the amount or ratio by which the current or operating volume exceeds the break-even volume. Assuming the current volume is 8000 units, and the break-even point in our illustrative situation is 6000 units, the margin of safety then is 33.33%. Sales volume can decrease by 25% before a loss is incurred, given that other factors remain constant.

3.4 Estimation of the Cost-Volume Relationship

In many practical situations, costs are expected to vary with volume or output in the straight-line relationship shown in Figure 3-4. The formula for this line of expected costs can be estimated by any of the following methods.

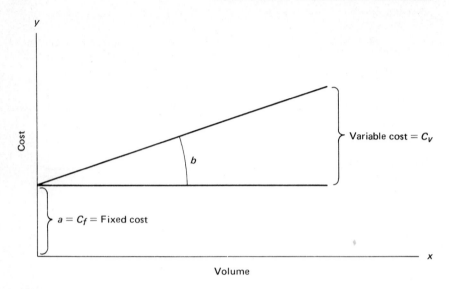

Figure 3-4

HIGH-LOW METHOD

Designating cost as y, volume as x, and the variable component as b, and letting fixed cost component $C_f = a$, the cost at any volume can be found from the formula $y = a + bx$, which is simply the general formula for a straight line.

If the values of a and b for a given line are unknown, they can be calculated, provided that total costs are known for any two points, or volume levels, on the line.

$$
\begin{aligned}
\text{Let } C_{TL} &= \text{total cost at the lower volume} \\
C_{TH} &= \text{total cost at the higher volume} \\
x_L &= \text{lower volume} \\
x_H &= \text{higher volume}
\end{aligned}
$$

The variable cost component b is then

$$b = \frac{C_{TH} - C_{TL}}{x_H - x_L} \tag{3-6}$$

and the fixed cost component a is

$$a = y_H - bx_H = C_{TH} - bx_H \tag{3-7}$$

Example 3-5

If production of 1000 kilograms of a specialty chemical costs $1500, while for 500 kilograms the cost is $1000, determine the cost-volume relationship.

Solution:

$$C_{TL} = \$1000$$
$$x_L = 500$$
$$C_{TH} = \$1500$$
$$x_H = 1000$$

Then by Equation 3-6

$$b = \frac{1500 - 1000}{1000 - 500} = \frac{500}{500} = \$1.00/kg$$

and by Equation 3-7

$$a = y_H - bx_H = \$1500 - 1(100) = \$500$$

Finally, the relationship is estimated as

$$y_e = 500 + 1x$$

where y_e designates estimated y.

SCATTER DIAGRAM METHOD

Another way to estimate a and b is to plot actual costs recorded in the past periods against the volume levels in those periods, such as illustrated in Figure 3-5, and then draw a straight line through the points so that the vertical deviation of the points above and below the line are exactly equal. In the event the points in the scatter diagram are numerous or widely scattered, the average values of the groups of data should be plotted to serve as guidepoints in drawing the line.

First, the data should be divided into several groups according to values of x, with each group having the same number of data points. An average is then taken of each group with respect to both x and y, these averages are then replotted, and a straight line is fitted as described above. The criterion of goodness of fit in the above method is a visual one and rather subjective.

Example 3-6

The cost of manufacturing electrical components can be expressed as follows:

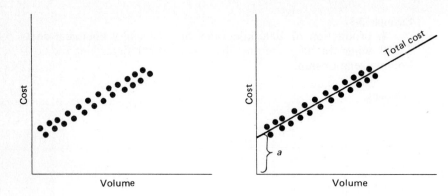

Figure 3-5

No. of components	10	20	30	40	50
Total cost (dollars)	100	130	150	190	210

Determine the cost-volume relationship and illustrate this relationship graphically. What is the cost of manufacturing 45 components?

Solution:
    In Figure 3-6 we plot the points, then fit a straight line through the points as shown. We see that a = fixed cost = $80. We then pick any x, go up to the fitted line and find the accompanying y_e as shown by the dotted line in Figure 3-6. Then by Equation 3-7

$$a = y_e - bx$$

Figure 3-6

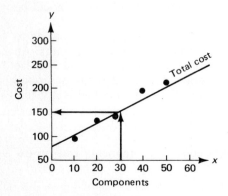

or

$$b = \frac{y_e - a}{x} = \frac{150 - 80}{30} = \$2.33/\text{component}$$

Finally the relationship can be expressed as follows:

$$y_e = 80 + 2.33x$$

Then the cost of manufacturing 45 components is

$$y_e = 80 + 2.33(45) = \$184.85, \text{ or } \$185$$

Example 3-7
    Consider the following table relating x and y:

x	6	14	5	8	8	15	7	6	3	10	4	13	9	7	2	11	12	11	3	2	1
y	8	11	6	7	9	12	6	4	1		9	7	10	8	8	5	10	11		9	6	4	3

a. Construct a scatter diagram.
b. Find the straight-line relationship between y and x.

Solution:
    We plot the values for x and y as shown in Figure 3-7, then fit a straight line through the points to yield $a = 3.5$. Then by Equation 3-7:

$$b = \frac{y_e - a}{x} = \frac{9 - 3.5}{10} = 0.55$$

Hence, $y_e = 3.5 + 0.55x$.
    We could have also arranged the above table in ascending order for x as follows:

x	1	2	2	3	3	4	5	6	7	7	8	8	9	10	11	11	12	13	14	15
y	3	4	5	4	6	7	6	8	6	8	7	9	8	9	9	10	11	10	11	12

Then we would have obtained an average value for each of the five groups of x and y to yield

x	2	4.5	7.5	10.25	13.5
y	4	6.75	7.5	9	11

Then the above values for x and y could be plotted and a straight

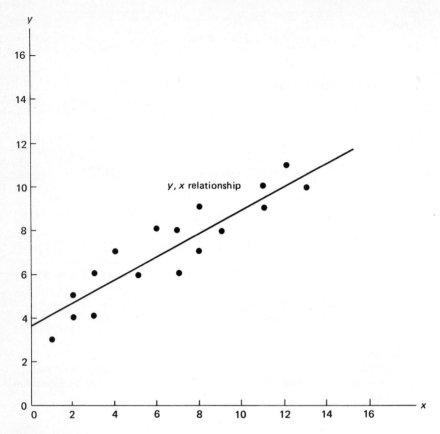

Figure 3-7

line fitted through the five points, as shown in Figure 3-8. We see that a still equals 3.5 while b is

$$b = \frac{y_e - a}{x} = \frac{8 - 3.5}{8} = 0.5625$$

Hence $y_e = 3.5 + 0.5625x$.

If we wish to estimate the value of y at $x = 16$, then by the first equation, derived

$$y_e = 3.5 + 0.55(16) = 12.3$$

while by the latter equation

$$y_e = 3.5 + 0.5625(16) = 12.5$$

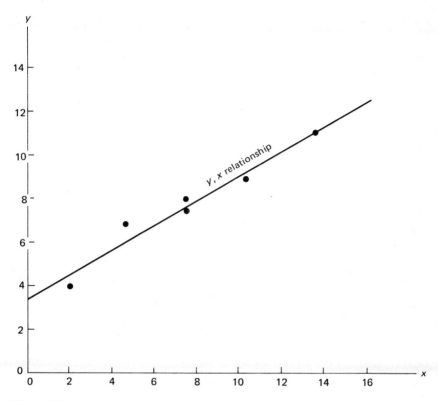

Figure 3-8

The error can be computed as follows:

$$\frac{12.5 - 12.3}{12.3} \times 100 = 1.63\%$$

which indicates that the shortcut method is quite accurate.

LEAST SQUARES METHOD

Another method, often yielding better estimates of a and b, is the method of *least squares*. That is, those values of a and b are best that, for a given set of data, minimize the sum of squares of the difference between the values of y and those given by the relationship equation with the selected values of a and b.

We write down in two adjacent columns every value of x and the corresponding actual value of y. In the third column each value of x is squared, and in the fourth column the product of each x is multiplied by the actual corresponding value of y. Each column is summed and the symbols Σx^2 and Σxy are used. (Σ means "sum of.") Then a and b are determined by solving the following two simultaneous equations.

$$Na + b(\Sigma x) = \Sigma y \tag{3-8}$$
$$a(\Sigma x) + b(\Sigma x^2) = \Sigma xy \tag{3-9}$$

where N is the number of pairs of items in a sample, that is, the number of x, y pairs. The following example will illustrate this concept.

Example 3-8

Consider the relationship between the number of tons of product produced and the total cost associated with the quantity produced, shown in Table 3-1

TABLE 3-1   Relationship between Amount of Product and Total Cost

Tons (x)	Total cost (dollars-y)
0	100
1	120
2	130
3	150

Determine the straight-line equation by the method of least squares. How many tons can be produced for $140?

Solution:

We create a table 3-2, as instructed above.

TABLE 3-2

x	y	x^2	xy
0	100	0	0
1	120	1	120
2	130	4	260
3	150	9	450
$\Sigma x = 6$	$\Sigma y = 500$	$\Sigma x^2 = 14$	$\Sigma xy = 830$

Then substituting the above results into Equations 3-8 and 3-9 yields

$$4a + 6b = 500$$
$$6a + 14b = 830$$

To solve for a and b, we multiply the first equation by 3 and the second by 2 to yield

$$12a + 18b = 1500$$
$$12a + 28b = 1660$$

Subtracting the first equation from the second, we get:

$$10b = 160$$
$$b = 16$$

then substituting the value for b into either of the equations:

$$4a + 6b = 500$$
$$4a + 6(16) = 500$$
$$a = 101$$

Therefore, the equation of the straight line is:

$$y_e = 101 + 16x$$

At $y = 140$:

$$140 = 101 + 16x$$
$$x = 2.438 \text{ tons}$$

Example 3-9

Reconsider Example 3-8 and let us obtain the equation of the straight line by fitting a straight line through the plotted points, Figure 3-9.

By inspection we see that at $x = 0$, a (the fixed cost) is equal to y_e, or \$100. Then, using the fitted line as reference, we pick any x, find the corresponding y_e, and determine b. Hence at $x = 1$, $y_e = 117$; therefore

$$b = \frac{y_e - a}{x} = \frac{117 - 100}{1} = \$17 \text{ per ton}$$

Our estimated equation is then

$$y_e = 100 + 17x$$

At $y = 140$:

$$x = \frac{140 - 100}{17} = 2.353 \text{ tons}$$

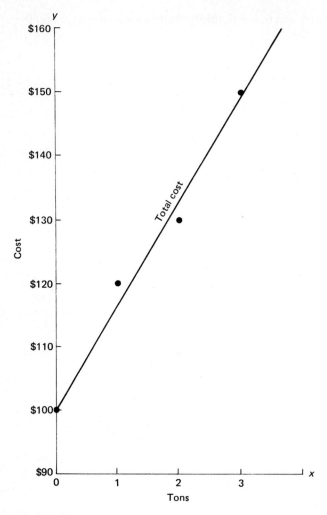

Figure 3-9

The error could have been

$$\frac{2.438 - 2.353}{2.353} (100) = 3.61\%$$

The usefulness of these equations for predictions and control depends on the extent of the scatter of the data. The measure of the scatter about the straight line, fitted or computed via the least squares, is called the *standard error of the estimate (Syx)* and is expressed as

$$Syx = \sqrt{\frac{[\Sigma y^2 - (\Sigma y)^2/N] - b(\Sigma xy - \Sigma xy/N)}{N - 2}} \qquad \textbf{(3-10)}$$

where N = pairs of items considered
  b = variable rate, or slope, of the line

Example 3-10
  Given the data in Example 3-9, calculate the standard error of the estimate.

Solution:
  We reproduce the table generated in Example 3-8 (Table 3-2) and add the y^2 component as shown in Table 3-3.

TABLE 3-3

x	y	x^2	xy	y^2
0	100	0	0	10,000
1	120	1	120	14,400
2	130	4	260	16,900
3	150	9	450	22,500
$\Sigma x = 6$	$\Sigma y = 500$	$\Sigma x^2 = 14$	$\Sigma xy = 830$	$\Sigma y^2 = 63,800$

Then by Equation 3-10, $b = 16$, $N = 4$:

$$Syx = \sqrt{\frac{[63,800 - (500)^2/4] - 16[830 - (6)(500)/4]}{4 - 2}}$$

$$= \sqrt{\frac{(63,800 - 62,500) - 16(830 - 750)}{2}}$$

$$Syx = \sqrt{\frac{1300 - 1280}{2}} = \sqrt{10} = 3.16$$

Hence one can predict that if 2.5 tons of product are produced the cost will be

$$y = 101 + 16(2.5) = 141 \pm 3.16$$

or between $137.84 and $144.16 with an absolute error of

$$\frac{\pm 3.16}{141} \times 100 = \pm 2.24\%$$

At 1.5 tons, however, the cost can be estimated to be

$$y = 101 + 16(1.5) = 125 \pm 3.16$$

and the absolute error is

$$\frac{3.16}{125} \times 100 = \pm 2.53\%$$

It should be noted from the above calculations that as the value of output (x) increases, the absolute error in cost estimation decreases accordingly.

At this point it would be useful to devise a numerical measure of the degree of relationship, or correlation, between the volume of output and the cost associated with the level of output. In other words, how well does the generated equation $y_e = a + bx$ approximate the true relationship between volume of output and total cost?

The correlation coefficient r is the relative measure of the relationship between two variables. It varies from 0 to ± 1, where 0 is no correlation, and ± 1 is perfect correlation. The sign of r is the same as that of b (variable cost rate) in our cost equation. Thus, if $r = -1$, all data points on a cost volume line are sloping down to the right, as shown in Figure 3-10a. Figure 3-10b shows positive correlation, or $r = +1$.

The correlation coefficient can be expressed mathematically as follows:

$$r = \frac{\Sigma xy - (\Sigma x \Sigma y / N)}{\sqrt{[\Sigma x^2 - (\Sigma x)^2/N][\Sigma y^2 - (\Sigma y)^2/N]}} \tag{3-11}$$

or in terms of the standard error of estimate

$$r = \sqrt{1 - \frac{S^2 yx\,(N - 1)}{\Sigma y^2 - [(\Sigma y)^2/N]}} \tag{3-12}$$

where $S^2 yx$ is the variance of the estimate or a measure of the variability of a set of data. Hence using data from Example 3-10

$$Syx = 3.16, \quad N = 4, \quad \Sigma y^2 = 63,800, \quad \Sigma y = 500$$

$$r = \sqrt{1 - \frac{3.16^2(4 - 1)}{63,800 - (500)^2/4}}$$

$$= \sqrt{1 - \frac{29.9568}{1300}} = \sqrt{0.9769} = 0.9884$$

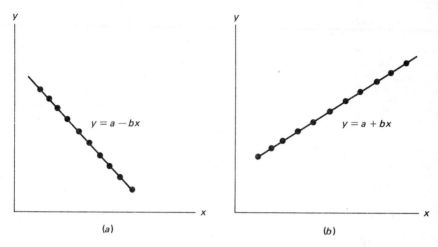

Figure 3-10

Since $r = 1.0$ is a perfect correlation we can see that in the above illustration 0.9884 is quite close to perfect, which indicates that the variable output is nearly completely responsible for the variability in cost. Stated differently, it shows that the equation $y_e = 101 + 16x$ is a very good estimation of the relationship between the tons of product produced and the total cost associated with the number of tons produced.

Now that we have learned the technique for computing r for a given set of data, the following question arises: How do we tell whether a particular correlation coefficient is or is not significant? Is the 0.9884 generated above a sufficient value to claim genuine relationship? Would $r = 0.6500$ have been sufficient? Statistical tests for significance are beyond the scope of this book; however, we can use a rule of thumb. If computed r is 0.75 or greater, then a good relationship exists. If r is below 0.75, there is a poor relationship or there is a relationship not necessarily linear. Figure 3-11 illustrates both points.

Example 3-11

The following information is available about an assembly-line operation:

1. The cost-volume relationship (total cost to produce versus volume assembled) is as follows:

Cost, $	1000	1500	2000	2250
Units	100	300	500	600

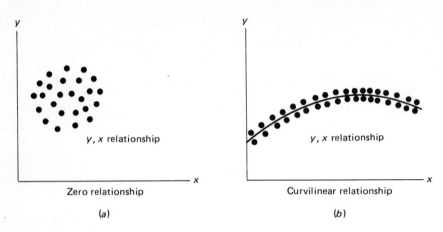

Figure 3-11

2. The selling price = \$4 per unit.

Given the above information, determine the following:

a. Cost equation as a function of volume
b. Goodness of fit
c. Break-even point
d. Is the operation profitable if only 400 units are sold?

Solution:
(See Table 3-4)

TABLE 3-4

x	y	x^2	xy	y^2
100	1000	10,000	100,000	1,000,000
300	1500	90,000	450,000	2,250,000
500	2000	250,000	1,000,000	4,000,000
600	2250	360,000	1,350,000	5,062,500
$\Sigma x = 1500$	$\Sigma y = 6750$	$\Sigma x^2 = 710,000$	$\Sigma xy = 2,900,000$	$\Sigma y^2 = 12,312,500$

a. By Equations 3-8 and 3-9

$$4a + \quad 1500b = 6750$$
$$1500a + 710,000b = 2,900,000$$

We multiply the first equation by 375, then subtract the first from the second to yield

$$1500a + 562,500b = 2,531,250$$
$$1500a + 710,000b = 2,900,000$$
$$147,500b = 368,750$$
$$b = \$2.50/\text{unit}$$

and

$$4a + 150(2.5) = 6750$$
$$a = \$750$$

Hence

$$y_e = 750 + 2.5x$$

b. By Equation 3-11

$$r = \frac{2,900,000 - [(1500) \times (6750)/4]}{\sqrt{[710,000 - (1500^2/4)]\,[12,312,500 - (6750^2/4)]}}$$

$$= \frac{368,750}{\sqrt{(147,500)\,(921,875)}} = \frac{368,750}{368,782} = 0.9999$$

which indicates that the relationship is linear and that $y_e = 750 + 2.5x$ describes the relationship quite well. The relationship is shown in Figure 3-12.

c. Since the selling price is \$4 per unit, the total revenue line $= 4x$, as shown in Figure 3-12. The break-even point is 500 units. We

Figure 3-12

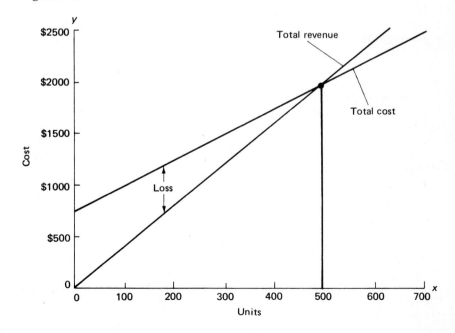

could also have calculated it by using Equation 3-4:

$$x_{\text{BEV}} = \frac{C_f}{p - b} = \frac{750}{4 - 2.5} = \frac{750}{1.5} = 500 \text{ units}$$

d. If only 400 units are sold, the gross profit will be

$$\begin{aligned} G = \text{R} - \text{C} &= 4x - (750 + 2.5x) \\ &= 4(400) - [750 + 2.5(400)] = -150 \end{aligned}$$

or a loss of \$150.

Inspection of Figure 3-12 would yield the same result.

NONLINEAR COST-VOLUME RELATIONSHIPS

Up to this point, we have assumed that the cost-volume equation was linear in form (that is, $y = a + bx$). In many practical problems the linear model, although perhaps not exact, yields an approximation close enough to the true form of the equation so that we need not concern ourselves with alternative, more complicated analysis. There are instances, however, when inspection of the scatter diagram may clearly indicate a nonlinear relationship or when one's theory has predicted such a relationship. Whenever such a nonlinear relationship does exist, the correlation coefficient for linear relationship will obviously underestimate the true degree of relationship since this particular coefficient measures only the goodness of fit of the best single straight line. We can see in Figure 3-13 that it is possible to have a strong relationship even though if a straight line is fitted through the points as shown, r can be less than 0.75. However, it would be incorrect to conclude that no relationship exists. If the scatter diagram indicates a more-or-less random distribution of points, such as shown in Figure 3-11a, we may then conclude that no relationship between y and x exists, but we must also be on the lookout for a nonlinear relationship. This is, of course, all the more reason why one should form the habit of always drawing scatter diagrams before proceeding with the analysis.

Another important reason why nonlinear relationships should be considered can be illustrated in the following example. Consider the data points given in Figure 3-14. A straight line can be fitted through the points as shown (solid line) and total cost estimated as a linear relationship.

Then given a revenue line, as shown, the break-even point (BE) can be determined. On the other hand, if the data points provided are connected as shown (dashed line), a new total-cost relationship is generated. This time, however, it is nonlinear or curvilinear, and a different outcome with respect to break even is realized.

We clearly see that there are two break-even points, low and high volume, indicated by BE_L and BE_H, respectively. Furthermore, it can be

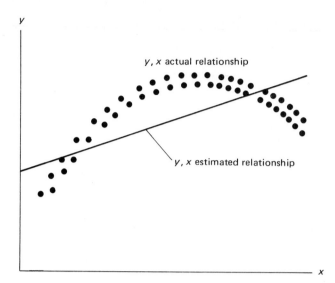

Figure 3-13

seen that at the initial break-even point as generated by the linear estimation, profit now occurs. Actually, close inspection of Figure 3-14
shows that midway between the new break-even points (BE_L and BE_H),
maximum profit occurs. The above example clearly illustrates that a correct estimation of the cost-volume relationship is essential for viable
break-even analysis.

The general topic of nonlinear cost-volume relationship estimation
is too complex to be covered here, but discussions can be found in a
number of intermediate texts. Several of the texts are suggested in Appendix B. The reason for the complexity of nonlinear analysis is that
once we get beyond the equation of the straight line, there are numerous
types of equations representing the different possible forms that a nonlinear relationship can take. There are polynomial, logarithmic, reciprocal, power, and exponential functions, to name just a few, available for
analysis. However, the degree of success in fitting a mathematical relationship depends upon how carefully the functional form of the equation
is picked.

Graphical methods, on the other hand, have a certain flexibility in
that the line can be drawn to fit the data as closely as desired with the
aid of a French curve. By this method, obviously, the relationship fitted
cannot be described by an equation. This makes it somewhat difficult to
summarize the relationships, evaluate the results, and predict new ob-
servations. Fortunately, the graphical method for nonlinear estimation is
usually quite adequate for graphical break-even analysis.

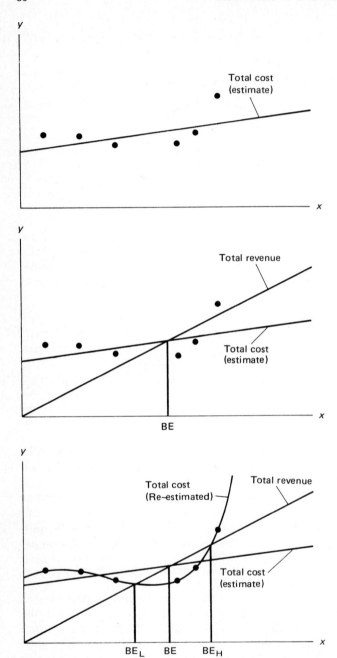

Figure 3-14

Example 3-12

A fertilizer manufacturer has the following data relating volume of output to production cost:

Cost (dollars)	18	74	106	504
Volume (kilograms)	0	40	80	126

Illustrate the cost-volume relationship graphically.

Solution:

A scatter diagram is generated in Figure 3-15a using the above values, then a "freehand" curve is fitted through the four points with the aid of a French curve. This is illustrated in Figure 3-15b.

From Figure 3-15b we can see that a, the fixed cost, is equal to $18 (at $x = 0$, $a = y_e$); however, we can not determine b, the variable cost, without resorting to mathematical analysis. As will be illustrated below, the lack of knowledge is not necessarily a handicap.

Example 3-13

The SEK Manufacturing company has found that in one of their manufacturing plants, the following relationship exists between units produced and the average manufacturing cost per unit.

Average cost (000)	28	34	48	56	64	72	76	80	86	90	92
Units produced	5	10	20	30	40	50	60	70	80	90	100

Estimate the cost-volume relationship and the break-even volume, given that the selling price is $1500 per unit. What profit will be realized next month if 60 units are sold at the above price?

Solution:

We proceed to plot the above data, as shown in Figure 3-16, and fit a curve through the points to generate the total cost. The revenue line is then drawn in and the break-even point determined. BE equals 46 units, or a sales volume of $68,000. By inspection, we can see that the fixed cost a is equal to $20,000.

Before we leave this chapter, it should be mentioned that in the event the points in the scatter diagram are numerous or widely scattered, the average value of the groups of date should be plotted, as before, to serve as guide points in drawing the curvilinear line. The method of averaging has been presented already.

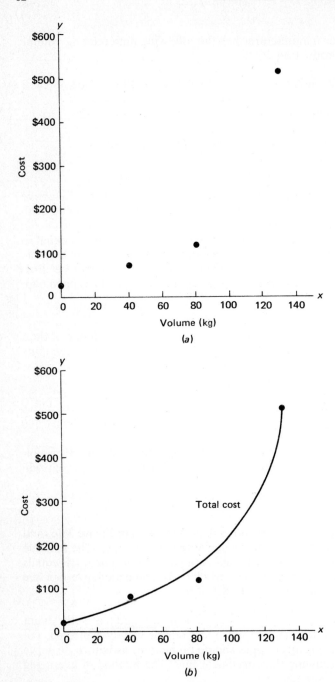

Figure 3-15

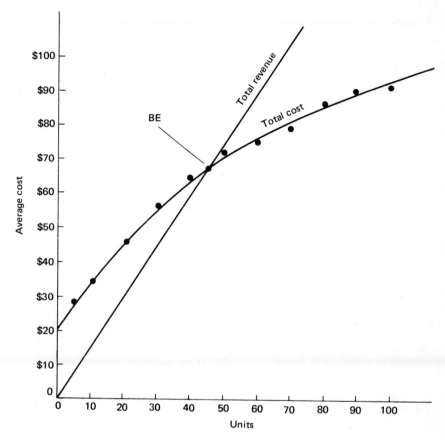

Figure 3-16

Summary

Break-even analysis is a useful tool in defining and describing the relationships between a firm's sales revenues, fixed and variable costs, and profits.

The break-even point is expressed in terms of units of volume as

$$\text{BEV} = \frac{C_f}{p - b}$$

or in terms of sales volume in dollars as

$$\text{BES} = \frac{C_f}{1 - b/p}$$

where p = selling price per unit
    b = variable cost
    C_f = fixed cost

The above relationship can also be expressed graphically as shown in Figure 3-1.

    In estimating the cost-volume relationship for linear functions (that is, $y_e = a + bx$), the three methods most widely used are (1) high-low, (2) line fit through scattered points, and (3) least squares. The least-squares method can also be used to express numerically the goodness of fit in terms of the correlation coefficient r. For a linear relationship r can be obtained by

$$r = \frac{(\Sigma xy - \Sigma x \Sigma y}{\sqrt{[\Sigma x^2 - (\Sigma x)^2/N][\Sigma y^2 - (\Sigma y)^2/N]}}$$

    In the case of a nonlinear relationship, the graphical method (free-hand curve fitting through the four points with the aid of a French curve) is usually adequate for effective break-even analysis.

    Typically, a reduction in fixed cost lowers the break-even point; and a reduction in variable costs per unit of product lowers the break-even point. Therefore, typically, a simultaneous reduction in both types of costs causes a quick and significant drop in the break-even point. If an increase in selling price can be achieved with no change in the other variables, once again there is a lowering of the break-even point.

    Finally, break-even should be viewed as a guide to decision-making about a project or operation—not a substitute for judgment, logical thinking, or common sense.

Problems

1. The Edwards Manufacturing Company produces calculators. An analysis of their accounting data reveals:

   Fixed costs = $500,000/y
   Variable costs = $20/calculator
   Capacity = 20,000 calculators/y
   Selling price = $70/calculator

   a. Compute the break-even point in number of calculators.
   b. Find the number of calculators Edwards must sell to show a profit of $50,000.
   c. What is the fixed cost per calculator at 80% capacity? What is the break-even point?

2. The annual fixed costs for a production unit operating at 75% capacity are $60,000, and the direct costs are $150,000 for annual net sales of $250,000. What is the break-even point?

3. The net sales of a certain company amount to $6,000,000 annually. When the fixed costs are $3,400,000 and the variable costs are 32% of sales dollars:
   a. What is the gross profit?
   b. What is the break-even point in terms of sales dollars?
   c. What sales volume is required to realize a profit of $800,000?
4. If the ratio of variable costs to sales dollars is 0.38 and the fixed costs are $250,000 annually, what is the break-even point?
5. The Ziggy Feed Company produces four types of feeds for dogs. From available records, the information in Table 3-5 is known. Determine the break-even point in dollars, given that the annual fixed cost is $80,000.

TABLE 3-5

Feed Type	Selling Price per Ton	Variable Cost per Ton	Percent of Sales Volume
A	30	15	40
B	40	16	20
C	36	16	25
D	32	12	15

6. The Holmes Publishing Company must set a price for a new book. The sales manager is considering three prices—$10, $8, and $6.50. Fixed costs associated with the book are $10,000, while the variable cost per book is $4.50. The sales forecast are as follows:

   · 4000 books at $10 per book
   · 6000 books at $8 per book
   · 10,000 books at $6.50 per book

   What should the book be priced at?

7. The following table shows a relationship between inventory cost and the amount of product stored in a certain warehouse.

y (Inventory cost)	6	12	19	16	9	10	11	15	20
x (Lots stored)		1	2	3	4	5	6	7	8	9

   a. Graph the above set of data.
   b. Determine the number of lots stored to minimize costs.

8. The cost to operate a small project can be expressed as follows:

y ($ Cost per day)		17	40	79	115	195	545
x (Units produced per day)		5	10	15	20	30	50

  a. Estimate the fixed cost a.
  b. Predict the cost of operation at a level of 40 units produced per day.
  c. Determine the break-even point, given that the selling price is $6.50 per unit.
9. The Icale Manufacturing Company produces floor polishes for industrial application. The data in Table 3-6 relate output per year (in pounds) to total cost (production, overhead, and selling) and to total revenue.

TABLE 3-6

Output per year (in pounds)	Total cost	Total revenue
100,000	52,480	69,800
120,000	62,440	82,800
140,000	72,060	95,480
160,000	81,700	107,840
180,000	91,660	119,880
200,000	101,600	131,600
220,000	111,360	143,000

  a. Determine the break-even point.
  b. How many pounds of floor polish should Icale produce in the forthcoming year to realize maximum profit?
10. The Tracy Company is considering an advertising campaign which will add $70,000 to fixed costs. Their product, now selling for $100, has variable costs of $30. Current fixed costs are $350,000. How many additional units must be sold to cover the added advertising cost?
11. A large chemical company now recovers 10,000 pounds of by-product per day at a cost of $0.90 per ton. A plant costing $90,000 with a life of 20 years must be built to recover an additional 10,000 pounds of the by-product per day because of air pollution.
  a. Neglecting interest and taxes, what selling price per ton would be required for the by-product to break even, given that the variable cost would be $0.80 per ton and a market could be developed?
  b. What would the selling price have to be for the investment to pay out in 5 years?
12. Economic analysis of a plant operation has generated the following empirical relations, where b is the variable cost per unit, p is the selling price per unit, and x is the units of production.

$$\text{Average sales price } p = A - Bx^2$$
$$\text{Average variable cost } b = Cx^3 + Dx^2$$

If C_f is the fixed cost and A, B, C, and D above are constants, determine the break-even point in terms of the constants.

13. The Wingo Motor Company currently buys starters for its motors at $2.50 each. An estimate of the cost to the company to manufacture these starters reveals that the fixed cost will be $5000 per year and the variable cost will be $1.25 per starter. Each motor requires one starter, and Wingo's annual production capacity is 6500 motors per year. At what percent of capacity does it pay for Wingo to manufacture its own starters?

14. The data in Table 3-7 represent a production cost of a specific motor, where x is the units produced and y is the cost in dollars associated with the number of units produced. Determine the break-even point in units if the selling price is $7.50 per unit.

TABLE 3-7

x (Units)	y (Dollars)
10	80
20	110
30	170
40	260
50	380
60	570
70	850

15. The XYZ Railroad operates a train daily over an established route. The railroad accountants have gathered the cost figures shown in Table 3-8 for the different train lengths. The operation is currently profitable at an average train length of 35 cars where it receives $100 per carload of goods. How can XYZ Railroad improve its profits given the above information?

TABLE 3-8

Number of cars	Total cost, $
10	2250
20	2600
30	2900
40	3500
50	5000
60 (maximum)	6250

16. The Goodbuy Shoe Company operates a chain of retail stores. As an efficiency expert, you are asked to study the relationship between the number of employees x and the average monthly operating cost

y for all the stores it owns, over the past year. When the data were plotted, the relationship was found to be approximately linear, with the points having a uniform scatter about the line. The data can be summarized as follows:

$$\Sigma x = 600 \qquad \Sigma y = 1,600$$
$$\Sigma x^2 = 5,200 \qquad \Sigma x^2 = 37,700$$
$$\Sigma xy = 13,600 \qquad N = 100$$

a. Determine the relationship between y and x.
b. Calculate the standard error of the estimate and the coefficient of correlation.
c. Store No. 85 has 10 employees and a $20,000 monthly operating cost. Is the performance of this store out of line with the performance of the other stores? How can you justify?

Evaluating
Investments

4

This chapter concerns itself with some of the different methods being employed to evaluate venture decisions. Years ago, intuition was an adequate tool for making such decisions. Today, however, due to pressures of competition, quantitative techniques have replaced intuition, reducing the risk of failure. A decision to undertake a venture involves careful analysis of capital requirements and other resources for profit maximization within the framework of social responsibilities. Right timing of the venture is critical as well since a product or process remains profitable for a limited time only, the average life cycle being five years.

Because of these life cycles, investments and costs must be carefully controlled. Among factors to be evaluated in an investment analysis are the uncertainties of the state of economy, the possibility of operating failures, and technological changes. With quantitative evaluations, making an investment decision is a matter of weighing anticipated profits against the minimum profitability standard set by a firm. The company must make profitable investments and refrain from making unprofitable ones.

Investment evaluation must be objective, realistic, appropriate to the situation, and easily understood by management. This responsibility lies in the hands of the evaluating engineer or technologist.

There are many methods in use for evaluating investments. Some incorporate the time value of money; that is, they consider the fact that profits to be realized from a given project decrease in value in the future as a result of inflation. Or, stated differently, the dollar will have a lower purchasing power next year and even lower the year after, and so on. Other methods, on the other hand, neglect the time value of money, which make them inefficient if a project has a long useful life. Chapter 5 deals with the former, while this chapter deals with the latter methods. Of these, the basic and most important methods are:

1. Payback Time (PT)
2. Return on Investment (ROI)
3. Benefit/cost analysis (B/C)

The most widely used of the above is payback time; however, return on investment is the most logical and theoretically acceptable means of determining investment feasibility. Since no single method is best for all cases, the engineer or technologist should understand the basic concepts involved in each method and be able to choose the best one suited to the situation.

Before proceeding to describe each of the above listed methods, there are investments to which none of them can be applied for measure of worth yet such investments are carried out regardless. Such investments are classified as *investments due to necessity*.

4.1 Investment Due to Necessity

Investments of this type are not very popular in view of the fact that they have no direct effect on cost reduction (saving) or on sales or profit increase, but are necessary for uninterrupted operations, to satisfy social or legal requirements, or to satisfy intangible but very important goals. The following are typical investments due to necessity:

1. Replacement of worn-down equipment
2. Investments made to conform to governmental regulations, such as anti-pollution measures
3. Replacement of facilities after disasters
4. Investment in research and development in order to remain competitive

The above investments, although not necessarily directly exhibiting tangible savings or profits, nevertheless do influence future profits, since shutting down a given operation may mean that no profits or savings will be realized from the operation. The following example will illustrate.

Example 4-1
    The lack of an exhaust system in the drum-filling area of a processing plant creates nearly unbearable conditions during the drumming of a volatile product. In addition, the existing exhaust fan lo-

cated in one corner of the area has only one narrow duct leading into it, which insufficiently draws fumes outside. Since this condition is in violation of the Occupational Safety and Health Act (OSHA) requirements, the government has ruled that unless the situation is corrected within 30 days, the area will be shut down until the requirements are met. In compliance, a new exhaust system has been installed at a cost of $3000.

Solution

As can be seen, capital had to be invested out of necessity. Although there will be no direct profits realized from this investment, indirect profits will be realized since production can be continued.

4.2 Payback Time

For studies involving the design of components (equipment) for processing plants, it is often convenient to evaluate capital expenditures in terms of *payback time* (other equivalent terms are *payback period, payout time, payoff period,* and *payoff time*). It is the number of years over which capital expenditure (not including working capital) will be recovered, or paid back, from profits made possible by the investment; that is, the project or piece of equipment will "pay for itself" in this number of years. It is a quick and convenient but crude method of identifying projects that are apt to be either highly profitable or unprofitable during their early years. If the payback time is equal to or only slightly less than the estimated life of the project or piece of equipment, then the proposal is obviously a poor one. If, on the other hand, the payback time is considerably less than the estimated life, then the proposal begins to look attractive.

Another attractive feature of payback time is its usefulness in selecting acceptable proposals out of several investment alternatives having similar characteristics.

The major disadvantage of payback time is its failure to consider profits after the investment has been recovered.

There are several ways to determine payback time. The three most widely used are *payback time based on average yearly gross profit, payback time based on average yearly net profit, and payback time based on average yearly cash flow.*

PAYBACK TIME BASED ON AVERAGE YEARLY GROSS PROFIT

$$PT = \frac{\text{capital invested}}{\text{average yearly gross profit}} = \frac{I}{G} \tag{4-1}$$

where PT is expressed in years. It should be noted that the invested capital does not include working capital.

PAYBACK TIME BASED ON
AVERAGE YEARLY NET PROFIT

$$\text{PT} = \frac{\text{capital invested}}{\text{average yearly net profit}} = \frac{I}{P} \qquad \textbf{(4-2)}$$

where $P = G - i(I + I_w) - t(G - dI)$
  G = gross profit
  I = Capital invested in equipment or facilities, or fixed capital invested
  I_w = working capital
  i = interest rate on all borrowed capital
  d = depreciation rate on fixed capital invested
  t = income tax rate (federal and state)

As can be seen, Equation 4-2 includes the interest charged on borrowed capital.

PAYBACK TIME BASED ON
AVERAGE YEARLY CASH FLOW

$$\text{PT} = \frac{\text{capital invested}}{\text{average yearly cash flow}} = \frac{I}{P + dI} \qquad \textbf{(4-3)}$$

Cash flow, which is the total amount of money generated by an investment, is found by adding the annual depreciation charge to net profit.

As in Equation 4-2, the above expression includes the interest charged on borrowed capital, fixed and working.

The following set of examples will illustrate the use and application of the above concepts.

Example 4-2
A piece of equipment costing $50,000 can replace a manual operation and save $20,000 per year in labor costs. It is estimated that repair costs associated with this equipment are $5000 per year. Assuming that the depreciation rate is 10% on investment, total income tax after allowable depreciation is 50%, and the interest rate is 8% per year, compute the following:

a. Payback time based on gross profit
b. Payback time based on net profit
c. Payback time based on cash flow

Solution:
Since the above values (excluding investment) are constant each year, they are the same as averages. Hence,

$$\text{Gross profit} = \text{revenue} - \text{cost}$$
$$= \$20,000 - \$5000$$
$$= \$15,000/\text{y}$$

Then by Equation 1-1

$$P = G - i(I + I_w) - t(G - dI)$$
$$= 15,000 - 0.08(50,000) - 0.50\,[15,000 - 0.10(50,000)]$$
$$= 15,000 - 4000 - 5000 = \$6000/\text{y}$$

a. By Equation 4-1

$$\text{PT} = \frac{I}{G} = \frac{50,000}{15,000}$$
$$= 3.33 \text{ yr}$$

b. By Equation 4-2

$$\text{PT} = \frac{I}{P} = \frac{50,000}{6000}$$
$$= 8.33 \text{ yr}$$

c. By Equation 4-3

$$\text{PT} = \frac{I}{P + dI} = \frac{50,000}{6000 + 0.10(50,000)}$$
$$= \frac{50,000}{11,000} = 4.55 \text{ yr}$$

Example 4-3
    A proposed investment requires $120,000. The project's esti-
mated life is 8 years, and the investment (proposed) can be fully
depreciated over the 8 years on a straight-line basis; that is, the
yearly expenses due to depreciation are equal. If the total gross profit
at the end of 8 years is $500,000, income tax after allowable depre-
ciation is 50%, and interest rate is 10% per year, compute:

a. Payback time based on average yearly net profit
b. Payback time based on average yearly cash flow

Solution:

$$\text{Average yearly gross profit } G = \frac{\text{total gross profit}}{\text{life of project}}$$
$$= \frac{500,000}{8} = \$62,500$$

$$\text{Yearly depreciation expense} = \frac{\text{capital investment}}{\text{life of project}}$$

$$= \frac{120,000}{8} = \$15,000$$

$$\text{Yearly depreciation rate} = \frac{\text{yearly depreciation expense}}{\text{capital investment}}$$

$$= \frac{15,000}{120,000} = 0.125$$

Hence by Equation 1-1, where P is average yearly net profit,

$$P = G - i(I + I_w) - t(G - dI)$$
$$= 62,500 - 0.10(120,000) - 0.50[62,500 - 0.125(120,000)]$$
$$= 62,500 - 12,000 - 23,750 = \$26,750$$

a. By Equation 4-2

$$PT = \frac{I}{P} = \frac{120,000}{26,750} = 4.5 \text{ yr}$$

b. By Equation 4-3

$$PT = \frac{I}{(P + dI)} = \frac{120,000}{26,750 + 15,000} = 2.9 \text{ yr}$$

Example 4-4

Consider a project requiring a capital investment of $120,000. The project's estimated life is 8 years. Using the data in Table 4-1, compute payback time based on net profit and cash flow.

TABLE 4-1

Year (1)	Gross Profit (2)	Deprecia-tion Charges (3)	Net Taxable Income (4)	Income Taxes (5)	Net Profit (6)	Net Cash Flow (6)+(3)
1	$ 20,000	$ 15,000	$ 5,000	$ 2,500	$ 2,500	$ 17,500
2	30,000	15,000	15,000	7,500	7,500	22,500
3	40,000	15,000	25,000	12,500	12,500	27,500
4	50,000	15,000	30,000	17,500	17,500	32,500
5	50,000	15,000	30,000	17,500	17,500	32,500
6	50,000	15,000	30,000	17,500	17,500	32,500
7	50,000	15,000	30,000	17,500	17,500	32,500
8	50,000	15,000	30,000	17,500	17,500	32,500
Sum	340,000	120,000	220,000	110,000	110,000	230,000

Solution:

$$\text{Average yearly net profit } P = \frac{\text{total net profit}}{\text{life of project}}$$

$$= \frac{110,000}{8}$$

$$= \$13,750$$

$$\text{Average yearly cash flow} = \frac{\text{total cash flow}}{\text{life of project}}$$

$$= \frac{230,000}{8}$$

$$= \$28,750$$

Then by Equation 4-2

$$PT = \frac{120,000}{13,750} = 8.9 \text{ yr}$$

and by Equation 4-3

$$PT = \frac{120,000}{28,750} = 4.2 \text{ yr}$$

Example 4-5
In example 4-4, based on net profit, should the investment be considered?

Solution:
The investment should not be considered since payback time based on net profit exceeds the estimated life of the project.

As mentioned previously, one of the most useful features of payback time is its ability to determine quickly which of several proposals is the most attractive venture and should be considered. The following example will illustrate such an evaluation.

Example 4-6
Two alternative machines with similar characteristics have been suggested to replace designated portions of manual operation. The following information applies to the two proposals:

	Machine A	Machine B
· Capital investment, $	600,000	400,000
· Maintenance and repairs, $/yr	16,000	40,000

· Insurance and taxes, $/yr	18,000	14,000
· Interest charge, $/yr	60,000	40,000
· Income tax rate, %	50	50
· Service life, yr	20	18
· Saving in labor costs, $/yr	604,000	432,000

Which proposal should be considered?

Solution:

$$G_A = 604,000 - 16,000 - 18,000$$
$$= \$570,000/\text{yr}$$
$$G_B = 432,000 - 40,000 - 14,000$$
$$= \$378,000/\text{yr}$$
$$\text{where } G_A = \text{gross profit for machine } A$$
$$G_B = \text{gross profit for machine } B$$

Then by Equation 4-1

$$PT_A = \frac{I_A}{G_A} = \frac{600,000}{570,000} = 1.050 \text{ yr}$$

$$PT_B = \frac{I_B}{G_B} = \frac{400,000}{378,000} = 1.058 \text{ yr}$$

Although machine A has a lower payback time, the analysis is not complete since interest, depreciation, and income tax have not been included. Therefore, net profits realized with each machine must be computed. Hence

$$dI_A = \frac{\text{capital investment}}{\text{service life}}$$

$$= \frac{600,000}{20} = \$30,000$$

$$dI_B = \frac{400,000}{18} = \$22,000$$

Similarly

where dI_A = yearly depreciation expense for machine A
dI_B = yearly depreciation expense for machine B

Then by Equation 1-1

$$P = G - i(I + I_w) - t(G - dI)$$
$$P_A = 570,000 - 60,000 - 0.50(570,000 - 30,000)$$

$$= \$240,000/\text{yr}$$
$$P_B = 378,000 - 40,000 - 0.50(378,000 - 22,000)$$

Then by Equation 4-2

$$PT_A = \frac{I_A}{P_A} = \frac{600,000}{240,000} = 2.5 \text{ yr}$$

$$PT_B = \frac{I_B}{P_B} = \frac{400,000}{160,000} = 2.5 \text{ yr}$$

We can see that both machines have equal payback times based on net profits. Hence, we must continue the analysis and compute payback times in terms of cash flow. Hence by Equation 4-3

$$PT_A = \frac{I_A}{P_A + dI_A} = \frac{600,000}{240,000 + 30,000}$$

$$= 2.22 \text{ yr}$$

$$PT_B = \frac{400,000}{160,000 + 22,000} = 2.20 \text{ yr}$$

It is interesting to note that machine *A* is no longer the attractive one but machine *B* is.

It is important to understand, from the last example, that a payback analysis or any other analysis must include all known variables. If it does not, often the alternative chosen is not the best one (from an economic point of view).

MAXIMUM PAYBACK TIME
This is the maximum acceptable payback time (PT_M), which is set by the firm, based on minimum acceptable return rate. It is expressed as

$$PT_M = \frac{1}{d + [ROI_m/(1 - t)]} \qquad (4\text{-}4)$$

where d = depreciation rate
ROI_m = minimum acceptable return rate
t = income tax rate (federal and state)

Equation 4-4 establishes a parameter for payback time; that is, projects must "pay for themselves" within a period that is equal to or less than the time set by the firm, using a minimum acceptable return rate.

Example 4-7
A proposed project will require a fixed-capital investment of $100,000. If the annual gross profit will be $30,000, depreciation and interest rates are each 10%, income tax rate is 50%, and minimum rate of return is 15%, determine the following:

a. Maximum payback time
b. Should the project be undertaken?

Solution:

a. By Equation 4-4

$$PT_M = \frac{1}{d + [ROI_m/(1 - t)]}$$

$$= \frac{1}{0.10 + [0.15/(1 - 0.50)]} = 2.5 \text{ yr}$$

b. By Equation 1-1

$$P = G - i(I) - t(G - dI)$$
$$= 30,000 - 0.10(100,000) - 0.50[30,000 - 0.10(100,000)]$$
$$= \$10,000/yr$$

Then by Equation 4-2

$$PT = \frac{I}{P} = \frac{100,000}{10,000} = 10 \text{ yr}$$

Therefore, the project should not be considered since it exceeds the maximum payback time set by the firm.
If payback time is being considered in terms of cash flow, by Equation 4-3

$$PT = \frac{I}{(P + dI)} = \frac{100,000}{10,000 + 10,000} = 5 \text{ yr}$$

The project should still not be considered.

4.3   Return on Investment

The return-on-investment approach relates the project's anticipated net profit to the total amount of capital invested. The total capital invested consists of that actually expended for facilities or equipment as well as working capital (see Chapter 1 for definitions of fixed and working capital).

To obtain reliable estimates of investment returns, it is necessary to make accurate calculations of net profits at the required capital expenditure. To compute net profit, estimates must be made of direct production costs; fixed expenses such as interest, depreciation, and overhead; and general expenses.

The main disadvantage of the return-on-investment approach is its complexity as compared with payback time, but this disadvantage allows increased precision and thoroughness.

The two most widely used approaches in determining return on investment are *return on original investment* and *return on average investment*.

RETURN ON ORIGINAL INVESTMENT

This is the percentage relationship of the average annual net profit to the original investment (which includes nondepreciable items such as working capital). It can be expressed as

$$\text{ROI} = \frac{\text{net profit} \times 100}{\text{capital invested} + \text{working capital}} = \frac{P}{I + I_w} \times 100 \quad \textbf{(4-5)}$$

RETURN ON AVERAGE INVESTMENT

Because equipment is depreciated over its useful life, it is often convenient to relate net profit after depreciation and taxes to the average estimated investment during the life of the project. With this method, the return on investment is determined by dividing the average annual net profit or net savings by one-half the fixed-capital investment plus the working capital, or

$$\text{ROI} = \frac{\text{net profit} \times 100}{\text{capital invested}/2 + \text{working capital}} = \frac{P}{I/2 + I_w} \times 100 \quad \textbf{(4-6)}$$

Example 4-8

A proposed manufacturing plant requires $900,000 worth of equipment plus $100,000 of working capital. It is estimated that the annual gross profit will be $800,000. If depreciation and interest are 10% on investment and income tax is 50%, determine

a. Return on original investment
b. Return on average investment

Solution:
By Equation 1-1

$$P = G - i(I + I_w) - t(G - dI)$$
$$= 800,000 - 0.10(900,000 + 100,000)$$
$$- 0.50[800,000 - 0.10(900,000)]$$
$$= 800,000 - 100,000 - 355,000$$
$$= \$345,000/\text{yr}$$

a. By Equation 4-5

$$\text{ROI} = \frac{345,000}{900,000 + 100,000} \times 100 = 34.5\%$$

b. By Equation 4-6

$$\text{ROI} = \frac{345,000}{900,000/2 + 100,000} \times 100 = 62.72\%$$

As mentioned in Chapter 1, most firms set a minimum acceptable rate of return, which a project must meet or exceed before it can be considered, no matter how technologically sound the project may be.[1] Setting such rates reduces the number of projects that are presented to top management for evaluation.

Example 4-9
Given the data in Example 4-4, should the project be considered based on original investment if the minimum rate of return is 10%.

Solution

$$\text{Average annual gross profit} = \frac{\text{total gross profit}}{\text{project's estimated life}}$$
$$= \frac{340,000}{8}$$
$$= \$42,500$$

$$\text{Average annual depreciation charge} = \$15,000$$

$$\text{Average annual income tax} = \frac{\text{total income tax}}{\text{project's estimated life}}$$
$$= \frac{110,000}{8}$$
$$= \$13,750$$

---

[1] This rate in general equals the interest rate plus 5% as a buffer.

Then

$$\text{Average annual net profit} = \text{average annual gross profit}$$
$$- \text{depreciation cost}$$
$$- \text{average annual income tax}$$
$$= 42,500 - 15,000 - 13,750$$
$$= \$13,750$$

Thus

$$\text{ROI} = \frac{13,750}{120,000} \times 100 = 11.5\%$$

As can be seen, the project or investment should be undertaken, since ROI exceeds ROI_m.

4.4 Benefit/Cost Analysis

There are capital expenditure projects to which payback time or ROI cannot be applied as measures of project worth. Governmental expenditures for public works in the areas of flood control, environmental protection, conservation, highways, public health, and urban renewal are a few examples of such projects. Since no cash flows are realized, that is, no cash receipts are available throughout the life of such projects, there is no basis for an economic evaluation. Nevertheless, since nearly all federal projects are financed from a common pool of tax funds, a project's worth must be assessed by some means and weighed against an estimate of the project's cost to make sure that whatever limited funds are available are allocated and spent wisely. This is where benefit/cost (B/C) analysis comes in.

The term *benefit* in benefit-cost analysis refers to the savings from projects such as public works. Examples of such benefits are: reduced destruction of property from flooding; reduced demand for medical and hospital services due to a cleaner environment; reduced accident costs by elimination of hazardous intersections or improvement of guard rails; reduced vehicle wear and tear due to improved road surfaces; reduced travel time due to shorter routes, higher speeds, or elimination of unnecessary stops; and reduced crime and looting due to urban renewal.

It should be mentioned, however, that the positive benefits mentioned above often yield negative benefits simultaneously. These negatives must be incorporated into the analysis as well; that is, the negative benefits must be subtracted from the positive benefits to yield a net positive benefit. An example of a negative benefit would be longer distances to travel because a highway improvement proposed for safety reasons will restrict access to a highway. Accordingly, additional wear and tear on a car or bus will be realized as well as an increase in energy consumption.

The costs considered are similar to those of private enterprises, that is, costs for engineering, construction, and maintenance, plus less obvious costs for the survey; design inspection of the construction; bid evaluation; transportation; contract negotiation, award, and management; supervision; personnel; accounting; and other applicable services.

The above definitions of benefit/cost permit measurable benefits to be weighed against measured costs. For a project to be economically acceptable, it must yield user benefits which meet or exceed the cost of providing those benefits; that is, the ratio of benefit to cost must equal or exceed 1. Expressed mathematically:

$$\frac{\text{positive user benefits minus negative user benefits}}{\text{initial investment plus annual operating costs}} = \frac{B}{C} \geq 1 \quad \textbf{(4-7)}$$

The following series of examples will illustrate this concept.

Example 4-10

Four alternative highway improvements are being considered. If each will have a useful life of 20 years, which alternative should be chosen, given the data in Table 4-2?

TABLE 4-2

Alternative	Capital investment	Annual operating cost	Annual User benefits
A	$100,000	$20,000	$22,500
B	130,000	15,000	27,950
C	150,000	12,000	28,275
D	200,000	10,000	32,000

Solution:
Alternative A

$$\text{Total benefit} = 22,500(20) = \$450,000$$
$$\text{Total cost} = 100,000 + 20,000(20) = \$500,000$$
$$\frac{B}{C} = \frac{450,000}{500,000} = 0.90$$

Alternative B

$$\text{Total benefit} = 27,950(20) = \$559,000$$
$$\text{Total cost} = 130,000 + 15,000(20) = \$430,000$$
$$\frac{B}{C} = \frac{559,000}{430,000} = 1.30$$

Alternative C

$$\text{Total benefit} = 28,275(20) = \$565,000$$
$$\text{Total cost} = 150,000 + 12,000(20) = \$390,000$$
$$\frac{B}{C} = \frac{565,500}{390,000} = 1.45$$

Alternative D

$$\text{Total benefit} = 32,000(20) = \$640,000$$
$$\text{Total cost} = 200,000 + 100,000(20) = \$400,000$$
$$\frac{B}{C} = \frac{640,000}{400,000} = 1.60$$

As can be seen, Alternative *D* appears to be the most attractive.

4.5 Incremental Analysis

Incremental analysis is the evaluation of the profitability of a project and its alternatives, on the basis of the effects specifically caused by each project. Thus, incremental cash flows, incremental operating costs, or incremental investments are those which occur (or do not occur) as a direct result of a particular project or course of action.

For example, consider a project to replace a 10,000-liter chemical reactor with an identical 25,000-liter unit. The only relevant factors which can be considered are productivity improvement per unit of time and costs that will be reduced or incurred, such as reduction in energy consumption per unit of output, or increase or decrease in maintenance costs. Reduction in labor cost would only be counted if an operator could be laid off because of the slack time generated by the productivity improvement. The analysis would not include such plant costs as overhead, supervision, quality control, floorspace occupancy, etc., since these would not increase or decrease as a result of this project.

Example 4-11
You are faced with a "make-versus-buy" decision. You are planning to purchase a specific item but are considering the possibility of making it instead, knowing that you have available capacity to do so. What costs should you consider and which should you ignore?

Solution:
The incremental costs that should be considered will be *only* the direct costs of labor and materials plus any actual net additions to other costs such as energy and inventory. The machinery, building,

and supervisory staff already exist; the cost of these does not change in manufacturing this item. Hence the accountant's concept of average cost does not apply here. Only the incremental costs can be considered.

When doing an incremental analysis on a project, it is frequently necessary to stand back and carefully take an overall view of the situation. For each situation, the relevant costs and profits must be isolated from the irrelevant ones. The next example will illustrate.

Example 4-12
The cost data in Table 4-3 are available regarding owning and operating a 1977 eight-cylinder Chevrolet Impala four-door hardtop (equipped with air conditioning, radio, automatic transmission, power steering, and power brakes). Which costs are relevant to answering each of the following questions?

TABLE 4-3

Variable costs	Average per kilometer, c
Gasoline and oil	2.83
Maintenance	0.80
Tires	0.47
Total	4.10
Nonvariable costs	Annual, $
Insurance*	300
License and registration	34
Depreciation	1400
Total	1734

*For married male, 25 years of age or older, or for a married female, 21 years of age or older. Otherwise the insurance rates are higher than given.

a. Should one buy the automobile or use public transportation?
b. Should an owner register the automobile for another year or should public transportation be used?
c. Should a proposed trip be taken?

Solution:
a. The relevant costs are $1734 plus 4.10c per kilometer of expected travel distance.
b. The relevant costs are for insurance, license, and registration ($334) plus 4.10c per kilometer times the anticipated distance to be traveled by the automobile during the year.

c. Given that the person owns and has registered the automobile already, the relevant cost is 4.10c per kilometer times the estimated distance of the proposed trip.

The basic point of the above example is that the relevant costs for a given decision are the costs affected by that decision. All other costs can be ignored.

DECIDING BETWEEN ALTERNATIVES WITH INCREMENTAL ANALYSIS

The concept of incremental analysis finds its greatest use and application in decision-making between alternative investments. Investments and profits of mutually exclusive projects are compared incrementally (occurrence of one excludes the occurrence of the others), then, depending on the resultant ROIs, a decision is reached as to which of the alternatives is the best.

When comparing one alternative with another the first task is to determine the incremental profit representing the difference between the two profits, that is, between projects A and B, A and C, B and C, etc. The second task is to determine the difference between the two investments, for A and B, A and C, B and C, etc. The incremental investment is considered desirable if it yields an ROI greater than or equal to the minimum rate of return (ROI_m) as set by the firm. In simple terms, the incremental ROI can be expressed mathematically as follows:

$$\text{ROI}_{\text{incremental}} = \text{ROI}_{B-A} = \frac{P_B - P_A}{(I + I_w)_B - (I + I_w)_A} \qquad \textbf{(4-8)}$$

To apply the rate of return on an incremental basis for a group of independent projects, it is first necessary to rank the projects in ascending order of their total investment, fixed plus working capital $(I + I_w)$. Then Equation 4-8 is employed to yield the incremental rates of return. The following examples will illustrate.

Example 4-13

The following information is available regarding two investment alternatives. It is also known that one of the alternatives must be selected.

· Alternative	Investment $(I + I_w)$, $	New profit (P), $
· A	30,000	3300
· B	40,000	5200

Given that ROI_m = 15%, which alternative should be chosen?

Solution:
    Using Equation 4-5, the individual ROIs for each project are calculated first, then the incremental analysis is applied using Equation 4-8. Hence

$$\text{ROI}_A = \frac{P_A}{(I + I_w)_A} = \frac{3300}{30000} = 0.11 \text{ or } 11\%$$

$$\text{ROI}_B = \frac{P_B}{(I + I_w)_B} = \frac{5200}{40000} = 0.13 \text{ or } 13\%$$

then,

$$\text{ROI}_{B-A} = \frac{P_B - P_A}{(I + I_w)_B - (I + I_w)_A} = \frac{5200 - 3300}{40,000 - 30,000} = 0.19 \text{ or } 19\%$$

We can see from the above computations that individually, both projects would be rejected since both ROIs are below 15%, the minimum rate of return. However, recall that one of the two alternatives must be selected; that is, rejection of both is not permitted. Hence alternative B is chosen, based on the incremental ROI of 19%, which exceeds the minimum rate of return.
    Before a decision is made, it is recommended that the results be summarized in tabular form as shown below, making them clearer and easier to compare.

Alternative	Investment	Net profit	ROI	Incremental ROI compared to A	B
A	$30,000	$3300	11%	—	—
B	$40,000	$5200	13%	19%	—

Example 4-14
    We must choose one of four alternatives, A, B, or C, or do nothing. Alternative A costs $500,000 and produces an after-tax cash flow of $125,000; B costs $800,000 and produces a cash flow of $170,000; C costs $1,000,000 and produces a cash flow of $225,000. Given a minimum rate of return of 20%, determine which alternative should be chosen.

Solution:

$$\text{ROI}_A = \frac{125,000}{500,000} = 0.25, \text{ or } 25\%$$

$$\text{ROI}_B = \frac{170,000}{800,000} = 0.2125, \text{ or } 21.25\%$$

$$\text{ROI}_C = \frac{225,000}{1,000,000} = 0.225, \text{ or } 22.5\%$$

$$\text{ROI}_{B-A} = \frac{170,000 - 125,000}{800,000 - 500,000} = 0.15, \text{ or } 15\%$$

$$\text{ROI}_{C-A} = \frac{225,000 - 125,000}{1,000,000 - 500,000} = 0.20, \text{ or } 20\%$$

$$\text{ROI}_{C-B} = \frac{225,000 - 170,000}{1,000,000 - 800,000} = 0.275, \text{ or } 27.5\%$$

Our summary table looks as follows:

Alternative	Total Investment	Cash flow	ROI	Incremental ROI compared to A	B
A	$ 500,000	$125,000	25%	—	—
B	800,000	170,000	21.25%	15%	—
C	1,000,000	225,000	22.5%	20%	27.5%

From the above information we see clearly that the "do-nothing" alternative can be dropped immediately from further consideration since the individual ROIs for all three projects exceed the minimum rate of 20%. Since alternative A yields the highest ROI, 25%, this alternative becomes the initial "current best" alternative.

Comparing alternative B and A, we see that for an additional investment of $300,000 our return is only 15%, which is below the minimum rate of 20%. Hence alternative B is rejected from further consideration.

We next compare alternative C with A, and we see that for an additional investment of $500,000 our return is 20%. This being equal to the minimum rate, alternative C becomes the "current best" alternative, and alternative A is removed from consideration. Since alternative B has been rejected already, no incremental analysis is needed between C and B. Hence alternative C is the best solution, yielding maximum profit for the corporation. It is important to recognize that even though the incremental ROI between C and B is 27.5%, which exceeds the minimum rate of 20%, this is no longer relevant since B did not meet the criteria initially.

Another important point to recognize from the above example is that selecting the alternative with the highest ROI on its profit *does not* necessarily lead to the alternative that will maximize profit. As we clearly saw, even though alternative A has the highest ROI, the profit will not be maximized for a minimum rate of return of 20%. The reason is that it is always desirable to continue investing additional funds for a project as long as their earnings are more than or equal to the minimum rate of return set by the firm.

4.6   Application of Break-Even Analysis to Investment Alternatives

In the previous sections of this chapter we concerned ourselves with the different methods employed in evaluating investment alternatives. We made use of payback time, return on investment, and benefit/cost analysis to screen out the best projects among mutually exclusive alternatives.

But what about investments due to necessity where none of the above methods can be employed, yet an investor has a choice between two courses of action? To illustrate, consider a pollution-abatement investment. The investor has the following two options: invest $100,000 for a waste-treatment plant of type A which will require $1000 a year to maintain, or invest $50,000 for a waste treatment plant of type B which will require $1500 a year to maintain. Both plant types will be approved by the Environmental Protection Agency. Which investment should be undertaken? Since none of the methods employed so far (PT, ROI, or B/C) is applicable (because there is no quantitative measure in savings or profit), break-even analysis becomes very useful in such situations. The concept can be applied as follows.

Let the output, or volume (x axis) be measured in terms of time units n (years, months, days, etc.) while the y axis, or cost, remains as before. Then the break-even point can be expressed as:

$$n_{BE} = \frac{I_A - I_B}{I_{wB} - I_{wA}} \tag{4-9}$$

where I_A = initial outlay for project A
I_B = initial outlay for project B
I_{wA} = working capital (cash needed to operate project A)
I_{wB} = working capital (cash needed to operate project B)
n_{BE} = break-even point as a function of *time*

This relationship can also be expressed graphically as shown in Figure 4-1. As can be seen, the break-even point occurs where the total costs for the individual projects are equal. This simply means that at the break-even point it takes n years for project A (higher initial outlay and lower yearly operating expense) to catch up to project B's lower initial outlay and higher yearly operating expense.

The following example will illustrate this concept.

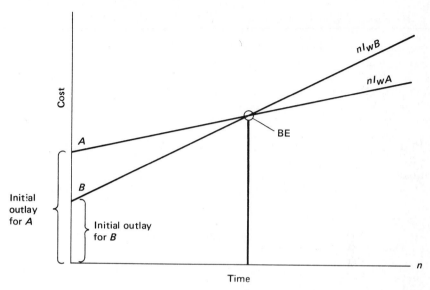

Figure 4-1

Example 4-15

The following information is available about two competing proposals:

$$
\begin{aligned}
\text{Initial investment for project } A &= \$10,000 \\
\text{Initial investment for project } B &= \$\ 5,000 \\
\text{Yearly expense for project } A &= \$\ 1,000 \\
\text{Yearly expense for project } B &= \$\ 1,500
\end{aligned}
$$

Determine what investment should be considered.

Solution:
By Equation 4-9

$$
n_{\text{BE}} = \frac{I_A - I_B}{I_{wB} - I_{wA}} = \frac{10,000 - 5,000}{1,500 - 1,000} = 10 \text{ years}
$$

Hence, they will break even in 10 years. If the project will last 10 years or more, A is more attractive because of its lower yearly operating expense. However, if the project will not last 10 years, for foreseen reasons, then B is more attractive because of its lower initial investment.

4.7   Sunk Costs

We saw in the previous section that it is the increment (or difference) between alternatives that is relevant in a comparison of them and that the only possible differences between alternatives for the future are differences in the future. Since only the future impact of investment alternatives can be affected by current decisions and actions, whatever has already occurred with a given project cannot be changed by any choice among alternatives for the future. This simply means that costs incurred in the past must be disregarded. Past cost that cannot be altered by future actions is called *sunk cost*. Sunk cost is irrelevant in engineering-economic studies even though it may have a slight influence on future cash flows or investments. Although this principle seems simple to understand, most people have difficulty applying this concept when making decisions between alternatives. To illustrate, suppose that 5 years ago you purchased 100 shares of a particular stock at $100 per share for a sum of $10,000. The stock is now worth $50 per share. In all probability you will try to recover your loss by holding on to the stock until the price per share is equal to what you originally paid. Your decision is not necessarily a correct one. Rather than holding on to the stock and anticipating recovery, a better choice might be to unload the stock at a loss of $5000 (sunk cost) and use the money recouped ($5000) more productively now and in the future. However, it is the emotional pain of losing the $5000 that makes the loss difficult to ignore in practice.

Example 4-16
Consider a machine that was purchased 5 years ago for $10,000, having a useful life of 10 years. A new process is being proposed, however, which would make this machine obsolete. The new process requires additional labor and other costs equal to $500 per year. The machine in question, being a highly specialized piece of equipment has no salvage value; the cost of removing it just equals its value as scrap metal. Would adoption of the new process result in a gain or a loss to the firm?

Solution:
Since the machine has a useful life of 10 years and no salvage value, the depreciation charge on it was set at 10,000/10 = $1000 per year for a total of $5000 to date. the book value remaining on the machine is still $5000, or $1000 a year for the remaining 5 years.
If the new process has an added cost of $500 per year, one might argue that in spite of this increase, adoption of the new process will save $500 per year ($1000 − $500), since the depreciation charge of $1000 a year would no longer be a cost. This argument is incorrect, however, since the book value must still be written off at the rate of $1000 a year for the next 5 years, which is the remaining life of the machine. Thus the depreciation charge of $1000 per year is not a

relevant cost to this problem. It is a sunk cost associated with past actions. The adoption of the new process would in fact, result in a $500-a-year *loss* to the firm.

Example 4-17

A total of $200,000 has been spent for research and development leading to a new product. Introduction of this product into manufacturing will require an additional investment in new facilities of $20,000, and it is expected to generate $10,000 a year in profits over the next 5 years. Which cost is relevant to the profitability of this project?

Solution:

The relevant cost is $20,000 not the $200,000. The $200,000 is a sunk cost having no effect on the profitability of this project. The investment in research and development cannot be depreciated or recouped.

4.8 Screening and Analysis of New Projects

Most firms would like to invest in new opportunities that may come along. Often, however, there are several different opportunities under consideration at the same time, of which 90% are not worth following up and 10% may be profitable, with 1% occasionally very rewarding. Accordingly, it is highly advantageous to be able to screen out as rapidly as possible the worthwhile from the others.

In the earliest stages of feasibility investigation, it is essential to keep the analysis simple at first, to determine whether or not the overall concept is worthy of further evaluation. If potential is recognized, the data can be refined and additional details filled in later. Since the percentage of profitable projects is relatively low, elaborate analysis very early is seldom desirable.

The limited analysis described above is the *screening test*. Its objective is to indicate at an early stage whether a specific proposal is worth pursuing further or recognize which of several available alternatives would warrant further consideration.

During the analysis of new projects, it is important to consider the many uncertainties that accompany them. For instance, the capital investment required could be miscalculated by as much as 50%. In addition, estimates of the useful life, as will be seen in Chapter 6, are always uncertain since they heavily depend not only on the firm's leadership and policies and on the state of the economy, but also on possible technological changes. Accordingly close examination of the elements making up the analysis is very important. For example, in Example 4-8, a 10% decrease in the net profit will decrease the return on investment 8.6%, given that everything else remains constant.

The study of the relative magnitude of the change in one or more of the elements that make up the economic analysis, as just shown, is termed *sensitivity analysis*. With it, one element at a time can be varied over a predetermined range of values while holding the other elements constant. Thus, if the element can be varied without significantly affecting the criterion employed, (for example, ROI, B/C, or PT), then the analysis is said to be insensitive to uncertainties regarding that particular element. On the other hand, if a small change (usually 5%) in the estimate of one of the elements will reduce the criterion significantly, the analysis is said to be very sensitive to changes in the estimates of that element. The level of significance is usually determined by the firm.

Example 4-18

Given the data in Examples 4-4 and 4-9, should the project be undertaken, given that the gross profit will decrease by 5% and the required capital investment will increase by 5%?

Solution

$$G = \$42,500(0.95) = \$40,375$$

Then

$$P = \$40,375 - \$15,000 - \$13,750 = \$11,625$$

and

$$ROI = \frac{\$11,625}{\$120,000}(100) = 9.7\%$$

which is below the minimum rate of return of 10%. Hence, the project should not be undertaken unless higher profits can be realized. Then,

$$ROI = \frac{\$13,750}{\$132,000}(100) = 10.4\%$$

This ROI is still above the minimum rate. Hence, it is insensitive to a 5% increase in the capital investment requirement.

Summary

The attractiveness of any proposed investment depends upon the value the investor (firm or individual) places on its money and the way in which that value is defined. The most widely used methods for investment evaluation that disregard the time value of money are the following:

1. Payback time
    a. $\dfrac{\text{capital invested}}{\text{gross profit}} = I/G$

    b. $\dfrac{\text{capital invested}}{\text{net profit}} = I/P$

    c. $\dfrac{\text{capital invested}}{\text{cash flow}} = \dfrac{I}{P + dI}$

2. Return on investment
    a. $\dfrac{\text{net profit}}{\text{capital invested} + \text{working capital}} (100) = \dfrac{P}{I + I_w} (100)$

    b. $\dfrac{\text{net profit}}{\text{average capital invested} + \text{working capital}} (100) = \dfrac{P}{I/2 + I_w} (100)$

Most firms utilize minimum return on investment (ROI_m) as a criterion for evaluating proposed investments. Projects must meet or exceed this before they can be considered.

For capital expenditure projects to which payback time and ROI cannot be applied as measures of project worth, the benefit/cost concept can often work. The concept enables measurable benefits for the public to be weighed against measured costs that the taxpayer will have to bear.

$$\frac{\text{positive user benefits} - \text{negative user benefits}}{\text{initial investment} + \text{annual operating costs}} = \frac{B}{C} \geqq 1$$

Incremental costs and benefits are those which are incurred if a project is undertaken but will not be incurred if a project is not undertaken. One should always remember that it is prospective increments that are relevant to the comparison of alternatives.

In decision-making between alternative investments, incremental analysis finds its greatest use.

$$ROI_{\text{incremental}} = \frac{P_A - P_B}{(I + I_w)_A - (I + I_w)_B}$$

where the difference in profits is measured against the difference between the required investments.

Sunk costs are irrelevant in economic studies unless they affect future profits or investments or other future events. The only relevant differences between alternatives are future, not past, differences.

Problems

1. A proposed manufacturing plant will require $5,000,000 in equipment and facilities and $1,250,000 in working capital. If the annual profit will be $1,500,000, the annual depreciation and interest rates are 10% each, and the income tax rate is 50%, determine
   a. Payback time
   b. Return on original investment
   c. Return on average investment

2. An investigation of a proposed investment is being made. If the minimum rate of return set by the firm is 15%, the depreciation rate is 9%, and the income tax rate is 50%, what is the minimum payback time required before the proposed investment can be fully considered?

3. If the interest rate is 11% per year, what is the minimum payback time required in Problem 2 before the investment can be made on a 10-year project?

4. The heat loss of a bare steam pipe costs $2000 per year. An insulation that will reduce the heat loss by 95% costs $1500, and an insulation that will reduce the heat loss by 90% costs $600. If the estimated life of the pipe is 8 years and the interest rate is 10% per year, which alternative is more desirable?

5. A pipe to carry steam has been designed, and insulation is being considered for the pipe. The insulation can be obtained in thicknesses of 1, 2, 3, or 4 inches. The following data pertain to each insulation thickness:

	1 in	2 in	3 in	4 in
Btu/day saved	7,200,000	8,400,000	8,880,000	9,120,000
Cost of installed insulation, $	1,200,000	1,600,000	1,800,000	1,900,000

   If the value of heat is $0.30 cents per 1000 Btu and steam is used 300 days per year, what thickness of insulation should be used?

6. An engineer must choose either a batch or a continuous system for manufacturing a particular chemical. The batch system requires a lower capital investment but a higher operating cost because of high labor requirements. The costs and profits associated with the system are as follows:

	Batch system	Continuous system
Capital investment, $	20,000	30,000
Cash flow, $/yr	5,600	7,700
Useful life, yr	10	10

   If the company requires a minimum rate of return of 10%, which system is more attractive?

7. A firm purchases 250,000 kilograms per year of a product at $0.63 per kilo and resells it at $0.70 per kilo to its customers. It is possible, however, for the firm to manufacture the product at $0.36 per kilo with $100,000 in processing equipment and $25,000 in working capital. The useful life of the equipment is 15 years. If the firm is in the 52% tax bracket and money is worth 10.75% per year, should the firm continue buying the product or make its own?

8. Additional instrumentation has been suggested to improve the quality of a product. The capital expenditure needed for the instrumentation is $70,000, and it will cost $6000 per year to operate the instruments; however, the improved quality control will realize a savings of $30,000 per year because of a decrease in reworked material. Depreciation and interest rates are 10% per year each, and the income tax rate is 50%. Should the instrumentation be installed, given the requirement that any investment return at least 15% per year?

9. During the construction of a storage tank, a decision must be made regarding whether the tank should have a cone top or a floating roof. The cone top costs $100,000, but a vapor loss of $25,000 will occur. The floating roof costs $200,000 and will eliminate the vapor losses. If the tank will last 15 years, money is worth 10% per year, and the income tax rate is 50%, which roof should be installed?

10. A utility company is considering two alternative power plants having the same capacity. One plant uses a boiler and steam turbine while the other uses a gas turbine. The data in Table 4-4 pertain to each proposal.

TABLE 4-4

	Boiler and steam turbine	Gas turbine
Capital investment, $	1,380,000	920,000
Fuel costs, $/yr	36,800	52,900
Maintenance & repairs, $/yr	27,600	34,500
Insurance & taxes, $/yr	41,400	27,600
Service life, yr	20	10

If all other costs are the same for either type of power plant and the interest rate is 15% per year, which power plant should be recommended?

11. The following cost data are based on a process for the manufacture of 20,000 transistorized components.

· Sales income—$2,185,000/yr
· Manufacturing costs—$1,955,000/yr

- Investment required—$517,000
- Economic life of project—7 yr

Would this project be a profitable venture for the engineering and business talent of a firm? Why?

12. A project requires an investment of $100,000, of which $40,000 will be used as working capital. The estimated net profits that will be realized each year throughout its estimated economic life are the following: −$10,000, −$500, $10,000, $30,000, $60,000, and $15,000 for years 1 through 6, respectively. If the minimum return rate is 15%, should th project be considered?

13. A company has three alternative investments which are being considered. Company policies dictate that the minimum return rate (ROI_m) be 15% and that straight-line depreciation be used. If the three investments have similar characteristics, money is worth 15% per year, the company is in the 50% tax bracket, and the data in Table 4-5 are given, determine which investment (if any) should be made, utilizing:
   a. Payback time
   b. Return on investment

TABLE 4-5

	Investment A	Investment B	Investment C
Fixed capital investment, $	100,000	170,000	210,000
Working capital, $	10,000	10,000	15,000
Useful life, yr	5	7	8
Annual cash flows, $	*	52,000	59,000

*For investment **A,** the variable cash flow to the project is $30,000, $31,000, $36,000, $40,000, and $43,000, for each year, respectively.*

14. Consider the three alternatives in Table 4-6. Determine the benefit/cost ratio for each alternative.

TABLE 4-6

Alternative	Annual user benefits, $	Annual Maintenance cost, $	Investment, $	Useful life, yr
A	1,900	8,000	100,000	30
B	7,000	5,000	120,000	30
C	25,000	−12,500	150,000	30

15. The annual costs for the upkeep of a proposed bridge will be $200,000. The costs begin the same year the bridge is made available for public use. The savings resulting from this project have been

estimated at $25 per vehicle per year. The first-year traffic load is expected to be 300,000 vehicles, growing by 50,000 vehicles each year for the next 20 years, then remaining constant at 1,300,000 per year. Initial investment will be $100,000,000.

a. Determine the annual benefit to cost ratio.
b. Compare prospective savings with expected costs on a year-by-year basis to determine when the bridge should be opened.

16. Consider the three alternative projects listed in Table 4-7. Compute the benefit/cost ratio.

TABLE 4-7

Alternative	Annual user benefits, $	Annual Operating costs, $	Initial investment, $	Useful life, yr
A	9,000	6,000	100,000	30
B	15,000	12,000	200,000	30
C	25,000	15,000	300,000	30

17. For a project to connect two cities with a highway, two alternative routes have been proposed. The data in Table 4-8 have been compiled. The travel cost would be $0.05 per passenger car kilometer and $0.10 per truck kilometer. Without either alternative, these costs are $0.10 and $0.20 per kilometer, respectively, because of the wear and tear on the old road. The cost of travel *time* is estimated to be $0.06 per kilometer for commercial vehicles nad $0.00 for noncommercial vehicles. These costs on the present road are $0.10 and $0.00 per kilometer, respecitvely, because of the lower speed limit. Determine which, if either, of the alternatives should be considered.

TABLE 4-8

	Alternative A	Alternative B
Length, k	10	12
Cost of land, $	200,000	250,000
Other investments, $	1,800,000	1,500,000
Annual maintenance cost, $	30,000	20,000
Useful life, yr	20	20
Estimated noncommercial passenger cars/yr	500,000	400,000
Estimated commercial passenger cars/yr	120,000	100,000
Estimated commercial trucks/yr	70,000	60,000

18. In Table 4-9 is information regarding four mutually exclusive projects you are to evaluate. You may choose one of them or reject all. Given $ROI_m = 15\%$, which alternative, if any, will you choose?

TABLE 4-9

		Incremental ROI, %		
Alternative	ROI, %	A	B	C
A	10			
B	15	25		
C	12	15	4	
D	16	20	19	31

19. Given the information in Table 4-10 regarding five mutualy exclusive projects, determine which alternative is the proper choice if the minimum rate of return is 14%. Repeat for 24%, 34%, and 45%.

TABLE 4-10

		Incremental ROI, %			
Alternative	ROI, %	A	B	C	D
A	35				
B	33	26			
C	30	25	25		
D	27	20	17	10	
E	25	20	18	16	20

20. EDP Packaging Company, which has been custom packaging an industrial oil for a single customer for several years with a manual drum-filling operation, has decided to automate its filling line at a substantial saving in labor cost. Because of this saving, EDP also expects to cut the cost to its customer (toll charge) by $0.50 per gallon. Given the cost datain Tabel 4-11, does this look like a good investment? Illustrate your reasoning graphically and mathematically.

TABLE 4-11

	Fixed cost, $	Variable cost, $/gal.	Toll charge, $
Old system	100,000	$1.00	2.00
New system	200,000	$0.75	1.50

21. The Balock Paint Company is considering the installation of one of two types of filling machine. A long-run forecast predicts that sales

will not fall below 10,000 gallons per month for the next 5 years, the expected life of each machine. Machine A will increase fixed costs by $20,000 per year but will reduce variable costs by $4000 per year. Variable costs now amount to $4 per gallon. At what point would the company be indifferent as to which machine it pruchases? Which machine should be purchased?

Evaluating Investments Using the Time Value of Money

5

Since many economic feasibility studies extend over a long period of time or deal with projects having long useful lives, it is necessary to recognize that future cash flows or profits generated by these projects will decrease in value over time because of inflation. As stated in the introductory section of Chapter 4, today's dollar will have less purchasing power next year and even less the year after, and so on.

This chapter, then, concerns itself with methods of comparing cash flows or profits at various points in time. These take into account the time value of money, which is interest. The basic and most important methods are:

1. Maximum payback time (PT_M)
2. Discounted cash flow analysis (DCF)
3. Benefit/cost analysis (B/C)

The most widely used of the above methods is DCF; however, since no single method is best for all cases, the engineer or technologist should understand the basic concepts involved in each method and be able to choose the one best suited to the needs of the particular situation.

Before proceeding to the methods listed above, it is necessary to define *interest* and to present the mathematical relationships which permit conversion of money at a given point in time to an equivalent amount at some other point in time.

5.1 Interest and the Time Value of Money

Interest is defined as the compensation paid for the use of borrowed money. Since most firms have to borrow capital in order to expand, interest expense plays a significant role in an economic analysis. The rate at which the interest is to be repaid is usually determined at the time the capital is borrowed, along with a scheduled time of repayment. To the lender, interest represents compensation for not being able to use the money elsewhere right now. That is, interest in most respects is the compensation for the decrease in value of the money between now and when the loan is repaid, this decrease being due to inflation. The borrower, on the other hand, must invest the borrowed capital in an activity that will yield a return higher than the penalty (interest) for borrowing the capital.

How interest rates are determined and the effect of interest rates on the national economy are given in Appendix A, along with the impact of frequency compounding, continuous compounding, and average interest rate determination.

5.2 Interest Formulas and Interest Tables

In economic terms, *principal* is defined as capital on which interest is paid while *interest rate* is defined as the cost per unit of time of borrowing a unit of principal. The time unit most commonly taken is 1 year.

INTEREST FORMULA SYMBOLS

Let PW = principal, or present worth
i = interest rate per period
n = number of interest periods
m = interest periods per year
S = principal plus interest due, or future worth
R = uniform periodic payment

COMPOUND INTEREST

Compound interest can be defined as interest earned on interest, that is, interest is earned, not only on the principal, but also on all previously accumulated interest. If a payment is not made, the interest due is added to the principal, and interest is charged on this converted principal during the following year. To illustrate, consider the following example. An individual borrows $1000 at 10% annual interest rate and fails to pay back the loan and the interest at the end of the year. Accordingly, $100, which is the unpaid interest, gets added on to the principal at the beginning of the second year, for a sum of $1100. The second year interest payment is then $1100(0.10) = $110. Hence, the total *compound interest* due after the second year is:

$$\$1100 + (\$1100)(0.10) = \$1210$$

Such compounding can be expressed mathematically. At the end of year 1:

$$S_1 = PW + PW \cdot i = PW(1 + i) \tag{5-1}$$

and at the end of year 2:

$$S_2 = PW(1 + i) + PW(1 + i)i = PW(1 + i)^2 \tag{5-2}$$

and at the end of year n:

$$S_n = PW(1 + i)^n \tag{5-3}$$

In Equation 5-3, $(1 + i)^n$ is commonly referred to as the *compound-amount factor* of a single payment.

Example 5-1
    A firm wishes to borrow $10,000 at an annual interest rate of 10%. What would be the total compound amount due after 5 years?

Solution:
    By Equation 5-3

$$\begin{aligned} S &= PW(1 + i)^n \\ &= 10,000(1 + 0.10)^5 \\ &= 10,000(1.61051) \\ &= \$16,105.10 \end{aligned}$$

Without a hand calculator or a table of logarithms, computation of the compound-amount factor (1.61051) would take a great deal of time. As we move further on in the chapter, interest computations become even more difficult. For that reason, interest tables have been developed. Even though they only give four significant figures, these are adequate for most economic analysis studies.

Table 5-1 represents a section of a typical interest table. This table uses the 10% compound-interest factor for $n = 5$ years and can be used for all typical interest problems having this rate and number of interest periods. Other rates can be found in Appendix B.

Example 5-2
    Repeat Example 5-1 using the interest table given in Table 5-1.

Solution:
    Using Table 5-1, looking under column 1, *compound-amount factor*, at $n = 5$ the value is 1.6105. This factor is then multiplied by 10,000 to yield $16.105.

TABLE 5-1 10% Compound-Interest Factors

	Single Payment		Uniform Annual Series			
	(1) Compound-Amount Factor, Given PW, to Find S	(2) Present-Worth Factor, Given S to Find PW	(3) Compound-Amount Factor, Given R, to Find S	(4) Sinking-Fund Factor, Given S, to Find R	(5) Present-Worth Factor, Given R, to Find PW	(6) Capital Recovery Factor, Given PW, to Find R
n	$(1+i)^n$	$\dfrac{1}{(1+i)^n}$	$\dfrac{(1+i)^n-1}{i}$	$\dfrac{i}{(1+i)^n-1}$	$\dfrac{(1+i)^n-1}{i(1+i)^n}$	$\dfrac{i(1+i)^n}{(1+i)^n-1}$
1	1.1000	0.9091	1.0000	1.0000	0.9090	1.1000
2	1.2100	0.8264	2.1000	0.4762	1.7355	0.5762
3	1.3310	0.7513	3.3100	0.3021	2.4869	0.4021
4	1.4641	0.6830	4.6410	0.2155	3.1699	0.3155
5	1.6105	0.6209	6.1051	0.1638	3.7908	0.2638

It should be noted that the error between both computations is:

$$\frac{16,105.10 - 16,105}{16,105.10}(100) = 0.00062\%$$

which is quite close enough.

Equation 5-3 can be rewritten in terms of *present worth* (PW) and is referred to as the *single-payment present-worth factor:*

$$PW = \frac{1}{S(1 + i)^n} \qquad \text{(5-4)}$$

where S = future worth

$\frac{1}{(1 + i)^n}$ = present-worth factor

Equation 5-4 shows that future amount is reduced when converted to present amount. This is known as *discounting*. It merely means that future worth of money is less than present worth, because of inflation.

Example 5-3
   If a loan has a maturity of $14,600 at an annual interest rate of 10%, what would be its value 4 years before it reaches maturity?

Solution:
   By Equation 5-4,

$$PW = S\left(\frac{1}{(1 + i)^n}\right) = 14,600\left(\frac{1}{(1 + 0.10)^4}\right) = 14,600\left(\frac{1}{1.4641}\right)$$

$$= 14,600(0.683013) = \$9971.99$$

Example 5-4
   Repeat Example 5-3 using the interest table given in Table 5-1.

Solution:
   Looking at Table 5-1, column 2, *present-worth factor*, at $n = 4$ the value is 0.6830. Hence

$$14,600(0.6830) = \$9971.80$$

The error then becomes

$$\frac{9971.99 - 9971.80}{9971.99}(100) = 0.0019\%$$

which once again is extremely low.

Example 5-5
   If a $10,000 debt compounds to $14,641 in 4 years, what is the annual interest rate?

Solution:
   By Equation 5-3

$$14,641 = S = PW(1 + i)^n = \$10,000(1 + i)^4$$

Dividing both sides of the equation by $10,000 yields

$$1.4641 = (1 + i)^4$$

Then i can be obtained by taking logarithms of both sides (see Appendix C if you are not familiar with logarithms or if a hand calculator is not available).

$$\log 1.4641 = 4 \log (1 + i)$$
$$0.1656 = 4 \log (1 + i)$$

(Note that 0.01656 is obtained using a hand calculator. From the logarithmic table in Appendix C we would get 0.1644. Then dividing both sides by 4 yields

$$0.0414 = \log (1 + i)$$

Taking antilogarithms yields

$$(1 + i) = 1.10$$
$$\text{and } i = 1.10 - 1 = 0.10, \text{ or } 10\%$$

The above tedious computation can be avoided with the use of interest tables. The next example will illustrate.

Example 5-6
   Repeat Example 5-5 using Table 5-1.

Solution:

$$\frac{14,641}{10,000} = 1.4641 = \text{compound-amount factor}$$

Now looking under Column 1 of Table 5-1, at $n = 4$ we find 1.4641, which means that $i = 10\%$.

Example 5-7

If $10,000 compounds to $12,624 in 4 years, what is the annual interest rate? Use Appendix B.

Solution:

$$\frac{12,624}{10,000} = 1.2624 = \text{compound-amount factor}$$

Going to Appendix B, under Column 1 we zero in on the table where the above factor is equal or as close as possible to the compound-amount factor at $n = 4$. Hence, going through the table we locate 6% as the annual interest rate.

ANNUITIES

An *annuity* is a series of equal payments occurring at equal time intervals. Payments of this type are used to pay off debt or depreciation. In the case of depreciation, the decrease in the value of equipment with time is accounted for by an annuity plan. For the uniform periodic payments made during n discrete periods at $i\%$ interest to accumulate an amount S

$$S = R\left[\frac{(1 + i)^n - 1}{i}\right] \tag{5-5}$$

Equation 5-5 is termed the *annuity compound-amount factor* and $\dfrac{(1 + i)^n}{i}$ is the *compound-amount factor*.

The reciprocal of Equation 5-5 is known as the *annuity sinking-fund factor* and can be used to determine yearly depreciation cost. It is expressed as follows:

$$R = S\left[\frac{i}{(1 + i)^n - 1}\right] \tag{5-6}$$

where $\dfrac{i}{(1 + i)^n - 1} = \text{sinking-fund factor}$

An analysis of Equation 5-6 shows that equal amounts of R, when invested at $i\%$ interest, will accumulate to some specified future amount S over a period of n years. In terms of depreciation expense, it shows that equal yearly depreciation costs invested at an $i\%$ interest rate for n years will accumulate to an amount equal to the original cost of the equipment.

Example 5-8
What would be the total amount received after 5 years if $1000 were invested each year at 10% annual interest rate?

Solution:

$$R = \$1000$$
$$i = 10\%, \text{ or } 0.10$$
$$n = 5 \text{ years}$$

Then by Equation 5-5

$$S = R\left[\frac{(1+i)^n - 1}{i}\right] = 1000\left[\frac{(1+0.10)^5 - 1}{0.10}\right] = 1000\left[\frac{1.61-1}{0.10}\right]$$
$$= 1000\,[6.1051]$$
$$= 6105.10$$

In this example, $5000 is the principal; $1105.10 is the interest.

The same answer can be obtained using Table 5-1. Looking under Column 3, *compound-amount factor*, at $n = 5$ the value is 6.1051. Multiplying this value by 1000 yields $6105.10.

Example 5-9
Consider a piece of equipment costing $10,000 with installation. Its useful life is estimated to be 5 years; hence, it can be depreciated over 5 years. The depreciation will be charged as a cost by making equal charges each year, the first payment being made at the end of the first year. If the annual interest rate is 10%, determine the yearly depreciation cost.

Solution:
Equal payments must be made over each of 5 years at an annual interest rate of 10%. After 5 years, the total amount of annuity must equal the total amount depreciated. Hence,

S = amount of annuity = total amount to be depreciated = $10,000
n = number of payments = 5
i = annual interest rate = 10%, or 1.10
R = equal payments per year = yearly depreciation cost

Then by Equation 5-6,

$$R = S\left[\frac{i}{(1+i)^n - 1}\right] = 10,000\left[\frac{0.10}{(1+0.10)^5 - 1}\right] = 10,000\left[\frac{0.10}{1.61 - 1}\right]$$
$$= 10,000(0.16393) = \$1639.30$$

Using Table 5-1, Column 4, *sinking-fund factor*, at $n = 5$ the value is 0.1638. Multiplying by 10,000 yields $1638.

The *present worth* (PW) of an annuity is the principal which would have to be invested at the present time at compound interest i to yield a total amount at the end of the annuity term equal to the amount of the annuity. In other words, it is the present amount (PW) that can be paid off through equal annual payments of R over n years at $i\%$ interest. Combining Equation 5-3 with Equation 5-5 gives

$$PW(1 + i)^n = S = R\left[\frac{(1 + i)^n - 1}{i}\right]$$

(5-7)

or

$$PW = R\left[\frac{(1 + i)^n - 1}{i(1 + i)^n}\right]$$

Equation 5-7 is known as the *annuity present-worth factor*, where $\dfrac{(1 + i)^n - 1}{i(1 + i)^n}$ is the *present-worth factor*.

Example 5-10

A loan is being repaid at $1705 per year at a 10% annual interest rate. If the length of the annuity is 5 years, what is the present worth of this annuity?

Solution

By Equation 5-7,

$$PW = R\left[\frac{(1 + i)^n - 1}{i(1 + i)^n}\right] = 1705\left[\frac{(1 + 0.10)^5 - 1}{(1 + 0.10)^5}\right]$$

$$= 1705\left[\frac{1.61 - 1}{0.10(1.61)}\right]$$

$$= 1705(3.78882) = \$6459.93$$

Using Table 5-1, Column 5, *present-worth factor*, at $n = 5$ the value is 3.7908. Multiplying by 1705 yields $6463.31.

The reciprocal of Equation 5-7 is known as the *annuity capital-recovery factor*. It is the annual payment R required to pay off some present amount PW over n years at $i\%$ interest. It can be expressed as follows:

$$R = PW\left[\frac{i(1 + i)^n}{(1 + i)^n - 1}\right]$$

(5-8)

Example 5-11
   What would be the annual repayment required to cover a $10,000
loan borrowed for 5 years at 10% annual interest rate?

Solution:
   By Equation 5-8, and from Example 5-10,

$$R = PW \left[\frac{i(1 + i)^n}{(1 + i)^n - 1} \right]$$

$$= 10,000 \left[\frac{0.10(1 + 0.10)^5}{(1 + 0.10)^5 - 1} \right]$$

$$= 10,000 \left[\frac{0.161}{0.61} \right]$$

$$= 10,000(0.26393) = \$2639.30$$

Using Table 5-1, column 6, *capital-recovery factor*, at $n = 5$ that
value of 0.2638. Multiplying by 10,000 yields $2638, of which $10,000
is the principal and $3190 will be the interest.

   Equations 5-3, 5-4, and 5-8 will be employed in the three methods
of evaluation (PT_M, DCF, and B/C) which recognize the time value of
money. Equation 5-6 will be employed in Chapter 6, which deals with
depreciation.

5.3   Maximum Payback Time

This is the maximum acceptable payback time (PT_M) which is set by the
firm, based on minimum acceptable return on investment and the on time
value of money. Accordingly, employing Equation 5-8, Equation 4-4 rear-
ranges to

$$PT_M = \frac{1 - t}{\left[\dfrac{i(1 + i)^n}{(1 + i)^n - 1} \right] + (ROI_m - i) - d} \tag{5-9}$$

   where $n = $ is the length of useful life of the project
      $ROI_m = $ minimum acceptable return on investment
         $d = $ depreciation rate
         $t = $ income tax rate (federal plus state)

Example 5-12
   Consider Example 4-7 again. If money is worth 10% per year,
determine the maximum payback time allowed and whether the project should be considered.

5-9 and from Appendix B,

$$= \cfrac{1 - t}{\left[\cfrac{i(1 + i)^n}{(1 + i)^n - 1}\right] + (ROI_m - i) - d}$$

n = 10 years
ROI_m = 15%, or 0.15
i = 10%, or 0.10
d = 10%, or 0.10
t = 50%, or 0.50
capital-recovery factor = 0.1627   (Appendix B)

$$PT_M = \frac{1 - 0.50}{0.1627 + 0.15 - 0.10 - 0.10} = \frac{0.50}{0.1127} = 4.44 \text{ yr}$$

The project still should not be considered.

5.4   Discounted-Cash-Flow Analysis

The most popular method for evaluating investment alternatives, taking into account the time value of money, is the *discounted-cash-flow* (DCF) method. It includes all cash flows over the entire life of the project and adjusts them to one point fixed in time, usually the time of the original investment. The method requires a trial-and-error calculation to determine the compound interest rate at which the sum of all the time-adjusted cash outflows (investment) equals the sum of all the time-adjusted cash inflows (net profit plus depreciation). The main attractiveness of this technique is that unlike the other methods in Chapter 4, it considers both the amount and the timing of all cash inflows and outflows.

The discounted-cash-flow rate of return is the *after-tax interest rate*, i, at which capital could be borrowed for the investment and just break even at the end of the useful life n of the project. To determine the DCF rate of return the present worth PW of the project—or *net cash flow* (NCF) (net profit plus depreciation) compounded on the basis of end-of-year income—is expressed as:

$$PW = NCF_1\left[\frac{1}{(1 + i)^1}\right] + NCF_2\left[\frac{1}{(1 + i)^2}\right] \qquad \text{(5-10)}$$

$$+ \cdots + NCF_n\left[\frac{1}{(1 + i)^n}\right]$$

where $\dfrac{1}{(1 + i)^1}$ = present worth at the end of year 1

$\dfrac{1}{(1 + i)^2}$ = present worth at the end of year 2

$\dfrac{1}{(1 + i)^n}$ = present worth at the end of the project

Then the present worth of the fixed investment I, compounded at interest rate i, plus working capital (I_w) is expressed as

$$PW = (I + I_w)_0\left[\frac{1}{(1 + i)^0}\right] + (I + I_w)_1\left[\frac{1}{(1 + i)^2}\right] \tag{5-11}$$
$$+ \cdots + (I + I_w)_n\left[\frac{1}{(1 + i)^n}\right]$$

where $\dfrac{1}{(1 + i)^0}$ = present worth at the start of the project

If only one time investment is made, at the beginning of the project, then Equation 5-11 becomes

$$PW = (I + I_w)_0\left[\frac{1}{(1 + i)^0}\right] = \frac{I + I_w}{1} = I + I_w$$

The present worth of the investment must be equal to the present worth of the cash flows; that is, investment (cash outflows, or O) must equal the sum of all the time adjusted cash inflows. Therefore, we set Equation 5-10 equal to Equation 5-11:

$$(I + I_w) = \frac{NCF_1}{(1 + i)^1} + \frac{NCF_2}{(1 + i)^2} + \cdots + \frac{NCF_n}{(1 + i)^n} \tag{5-12}$$

or expressed differently:

$$O = -(I + I_w) + \frac{NCF_1}{(1 + i)^1} + \frac{NCF_2}{(1 + i)^2} + \cdots + \frac{NCF_n}{(1 + i)^n} \tag{5-13}$$

A trial-and-error calculation is required to determine the DCF rate of return i. The following example will illustrate the basic principles involved in DCF calculation.

Example 5-13
    A project having a useful life of 5 years requires $100,000 in fixed capital investment and $10,000 in working capital. The cash

flow (net profit plus epreciation) that will be realized each year from the project is shown below. What is the rate of return?

· Year	Cash flow, $
· 1	30,000
· 2	31,000
· 3	36,000
· 4	40,000
· 5	43,000

Solution:
The values of i that will be used are 15% and 20%, and Appendix B and Equation 5-13 will be utilized. For $i = 15\%$, or 0.15,

$$O = -110,000 + \frac{30,000}{(1 + 0.15)^1} + \frac{31,000}{(1 + 0.15)^2} + \frac{36,000}{(1 + 0.15)^3}$$

$$+ \frac{40,000}{(1 + 0.15)^4} + \frac{43,000}{(1 + 0.15)^5}$$

$$= -110,000 + 26,087 + 23,440 + 23,671 + 22,870 + 21,379$$

$$= -110,000 + 117,447 = +7447$$

For $i = 20\%$, or 0.20,

$$O = -110,000 + 25,000 + 21,528 + 20,883 + 19,290 + 17,280$$
$$= -110,000 + 103,931 = -6069$$

Hence, by interpolation the DCF rate is equal to

$$0.15 + 0.05\left(\frac{7447}{7447 + 6069}\right) = 0.15 + 0.028 = 0.178, \text{ or } 17.8\%$$

Since the discounted-cash-flow rates of return are only approximated by the process of interpolation, a slight error is introduced. To keep the error to a minimum, interpolation should only be attempted between adjacent tabled values, for example between 10% and 11%. Interpolation between, say, 2% and 10% wold increase the error greatly.

Example 5-14
Repeat Example 5-13 with the following change: Of the $100,000 in fixed capital investment needed, $50,000 will be required initially, followed by $25,000 at the *beginning* of year 2 and $25,000 at the *beginning* of year 3. What is the rate of return?

Solution:

At $i = 15\%$, or 0.15, utilizing Appendix B and results from Example 5-13:

$$O = -60,000 - \frac{25,000}{(1 + 0.15)^1} - \frac{25,000}{(1 + 0.15)^2} + 26,000 + 23,440$$
$$+ 23,671 + 22,870 + 21,379$$
$$= -60,000 - 21,739 - 18,904 + 26,000 + 23,440$$
$$+ 23,671 + 22,870 + 21,379$$
$$= -100,643 + 117,447 = +16,804$$

At $i = 20\%$, or 0.20,

$$O = -60,000 - 20,833 - 17,361 + 25,000 + 21,528$$
$$+ 20,883 + 19,290 + 17,280$$
$$= -98,194 + 103,931 = +5737$$

At $i = 25\%$, or 0.25

$$O = -60,000 - 20,000 - 16,000 + 24,000 + 19,840$$
$$+ 18,432 + 16,384 + 14,090$$
$$= -96,000 + 94,746$$
$$= -1254$$

Hence, by interpolation

$$0.20 + 0.05 \left(\frac{5737}{5737 + 1254} \right) = 0.241, \text{ or } 24.1\%$$

5.5 Benefit/Cost Analysis

This section is a continuation of Section 4.4. However, we now incorporate the time value of money into the analysis. The difference, as will be seen shortly, is significant enough for projects of long useful life to warrant careful consideration before actual decision making among alternatives.

In consideration of the time value of money, Equation 4-7 is rearranged, in terms of present worth, to read

$$\frac{\left(\begin{array}{c} \text{annual positive} \\ \text{user benefits} \end{array} \right) - \left(\begin{array}{c} \text{annual negative} \\ \text{user benefits} \end{array} \right)}{\left(\begin{array}{c} \text{initial} \\ \text{investment} \end{array} \right) + \left[\left(\begin{array}{c} \text{annual operating} \\ \text{cost} \end{array} \right) \left(\frac{(1 + i)^n - 1}{i(1 + i)^n} \right) \right]} = \frac{B}{C} \geq 1 \quad \textbf{(5-14)}$$

where $\dfrac{(1 + i)^n - 1}{i(1 + i)^n}$ = the present-worth factor

In terms of annual equivalent cost, Equation 4-7 becomes

$$\frac{\left(\begin{array}{c}\text{annual positive}\\ \text{user benefits}\end{array}\right) - \left(\begin{array}{c}\text{annual negative}\\ \text{user benefit}\end{array}\right)}{\left(\begin{array}{c}\text{initial}\\ \text{investment}\end{array}\right)\left[\dfrac{i(1 + i)^n}{(1 + i)^n - 1}\right] + \left(\begin{array}{c}\text{annual operating}\\ \text{cost}\end{array}\right)} = \frac{B}{C} \geq 1 \quad \textbf{(5-15)}$$

where $\left[\dfrac{i(1 + i)^n}{(1 + i)^n - 1}\right]$ = the capital-recovery factor

Example 5-15

Repeat Example 4-10, given that i is 8% and minimum acceptable B/C is 1.0.

Solution:

From Appendix B, at $i = 8\%$ and $n = 20$, the present-worth factor is 9.8181. hence by Equation 5-14, for alternative A:

$$\frac{B}{C} = \frac{22,500(9.8181)}{100,000 + 20,000(9.8181)}$$

$$= \frac{220,907}{296,362}$$

$$= 0.75$$

For alternative B:

$$\frac{B}{C} = \frac{27,950(9.8181)}{100,000 + 15,000(9.8181)}$$

$$= \frac{274,416}{247,272}$$

$$= 1.11$$

For alternative C:

$$\frac{B}{C} = \frac{28,275(9.8181)}{100,000 + 12,000(9.8181)}$$

$$= \frac{277,607}{217,817}$$

$$= 1.27$$

For alternative D:

$$\frac{B}{C} = \frac{32,000(9.8181)}{100,000 + 10,000(9.8181)}$$

$$= \frac{314,179}{198,181}$$

$$= 1.59$$

As can be seen, alternatives B, C, and D exceed the minimum B/C. Note the effect of the time value of money on the final benefit/cost ratio.

Example 5-16

Repeat Example 4-10, comparing by annual equivalent cost.

Solution:

From Appendix B, at $i = 8\%$ and $n = 20$, the capital-recovery factor $= 0.1019$. For alternative A:

$$\frac{B}{C} = \frac{22,500}{100,000(0.1019) + 20,000}$$

$$= 0.75$$

For alternative B:

$$\frac{B}{C} = \frac{27,950}{100,000(0.1019) + 15,000}$$

$$= 1.11$$

For alternative C:

$$\frac{B}{C} = \frac{28,275}{100,000(0.1019) + 12,000}$$

$$= 1.27$$

For alternative D:

$$\frac{B}{C} = \frac{32,000}{100,000(0.1019) + 10,000}$$

$$= 1.59$$

As can be seen, the annual-equivalent-cost method is simpler than the present-worth method for determining the benefit/cost ratio.

Example 5-17
Because occasional floods have caused damage to property around a specific area of the East River, a proposal has been made to build a dam and a reservoir up the river at a cost of $15,000,000. The dam, however, will cause damage to fisheries valued at $65,000 per year and cause $250,000 per year loss in agriculture including grazing and crop raising. If annual operating and maintenance costs for the dam will be $100,000, determine the B/C ratio given $i = 8\%$.

Solution:
From Example 5-16, the capital-recovery factor is 0.1019. Hence, by Equation 5-15

$$\frac{B}{C} = \frac{2,500,000 - 65,000 - 250,000}{15,000,000(0.1019) + 100,000}$$
$$= \frac{2,185,000}{1,628,500} = 1.34$$

5.6 Comparison among the Three Popular Methods (PT, ROI, and DCF)

As mentioned in the introduction to this and the previous chapter, no single method for evaluating investment alternatives is best for all cases. It is important for the engineer or engineering technologist to understand the basic ideas involved in each method and to be able to choose the one best suited to the needs of a particular situation.

For example, a firm decides to skimp on the original investment and shift some of the burden to excessive start-up costs (working capital). Analyzed by the payback time method, the investment may appear attractive, because with no working capital being incorporated into the analysis the value is low. In such a situation, return on investment or discounted cash flow would be a much better criterion for analysis since all the variables are incorporated into the calculation. On the other hand, if the project involves the replacement of equipment only, payback time would seem to be the most attractive method. Why? In the case of a broker selling the products of others, however, payback time will be zero (no fixed capital investment) and only return-on-investment or discounted-cash-flow methods should be used. Why?

The following example will compare three projects by the three popular methods.

Example 5-18
A company has three alternative investments which are being considered. Each project requires the same fixed-capital investment

of $10,000 and working capital of $1000. Based on the data given in Table 5-2,[1] determine

a. Payback time
b. Return on original investment
c. Discounted cash flow

TABLE 5-2

	Project A		Project B		Project C	
Year	Net profit	Cash flow	Net profit	Cash flow	Net profit	Cash flow
1	$2750	$4750	$1550	$3550	$ 0	$2000
2	2000	4000	1550	3550	1000	3000
3	1300	3300	1550	3550	2000	4000
4	700	2700	1550	3550	2500	4500
5	0	2000	1550	3550	3000	5000
Average	1350	3350	1550	3550	1700	3700

Solution:
a. By Equation 4-2

$$PT_A = \frac{I}{P_A} = \frac{10,000}{1350} = 7.41 \text{ yr}$$

$$PT_B = \frac{I}{P_B} = \frac{10,000}{1550} = 6.45 \text{ yr}$$

$$PT_C = \frac{I}{P_C} = \frac{10,000}{1700} = 5.88 \text{ yr}$$

b. By Equation 4-5:

$$ROI_A = \frac{P_A}{(I + I_w)} (100) = \frac{1350}{(10,000 + 1000)} (100) = 12.27\%$$

$$ROI_B = \frac{1550}{11,000} (100) = 14.09\%$$

$$ROI_C = \frac{1700}{11,000} (100) = 15.45\%$$

[1] Depreciation expense for each project is $2000 per year.

c. By Equation 5-13 and by trial and error, for alternative A, at i = 0.15,

$$O = -10,000 + \frac{4750}{(1 + 0.15)^1} + \frac{4000}{(1 + 0.15)^2} + \frac{3300}{(1 + 0.15)^3}$$

$$+ \frac{2700}{(1 + 0.15)^4} + \frac{2000}{(1 + 0.15)^5}$$

$$= -10,000 + 4130 + 3025 + 2170 + 1544 + 994$$
$$= -10,000 + 11,863$$
$$= +1863$$

At i = 0.20

$$O = -10,000 + 3958 + 2778 + 1910 + 1302 + 804$$
$$= -10,000 + 10,752$$
$$= +752$$

At i = 0.25

$$O = -10,000 + 3800 + 2560 + 1690 + 1110 + 655$$
$$= -10,000 + 9815$$
$$= -185$$

Then, by interpolation,

$$i_A = 0.20 + 0.05 \left(\frac{752}{752 + 185} \right)$$

$$= 0.2400, \text{ or } 24.00\%$$

For alternative B, at i = 0.15,

$$O = -10,000 + 3087 + 2684 + 2334 + 2030 + 1765$$
$$= -10,000 + 11,900$$
$$= +1900$$

At i = 0.20

$$O = -10,000 + 2958 + 2465 + 2054 + 1712 + 1427$$
$$= -10,000 + 10,616$$
$$= +616$$

At i = 0.25

$$O = -10,000 + 2840 + 2272 + 1818 + 1454 + 1163$$

$$= -10,000 + 9547$$
$$= -453$$

Then, by interpolation,

$$i_B = 0.20 + 0.05 \left(\frac{616}{616 + 453} \right)$$

$$= 0.2290, \text{ or } 22.90\%$$

For alternative C, at $i = 0.15$,

$$O = -10,000 + 1739 + 2268 + 2630 + 2572 + 2486$$
$$= -10,000 + 11,696$$
$$= +1696$$

At $i = 0.20$

$$O = -10,000 + 1667 + 2083 + 2315 + 2170 + 2009$$
$$= -10,000 + 10,244$$
$$= +244$$

At $i = 0.25$

$$O = -10,000 + 1600 + 1920 + 2048 + 1843 + 1638$$
$$= -10,000 + 9049$$
$$= -951$$

Then, by interpolation,

$$i_C = 0.20 + 0.05 \left(\frac{224}{224 + 951} \right)$$

$$= 0.2010, \text{ or } 20.10\%$$

To summarize:

$$i_A = 24.00\%,$$
$$i_B = 22.90\%,$$
$$i_C = 20.10\%$$

Table 5-3 summarizes the answers obtained with each method. As can be seen, the first and fourth methods rank alternative A as the best choice while the ROI concept ranks alternative C as the best one.

TABLE 5-3

	Project A		Project B		Project C	
		Rank		Rank		Rank
Payback time, yr	2.99	1	2.82	2	2.70	3
Return on original investment	12.27%	3	14.09%	2	15.45%	1
Return on average investment	22.50%	3	25.83%	2	28.33%	1
Discounted cash flow	24.00%	1	22.90%	2	20.10%	3

The above example clearly shows that all methods presented in this chapter should be considered in a proper evaluation study, since no single index number can show all relevant factors.

5.7   Incremental Analysis

This section is a continuation of Section 4.5. However, we now incorporate the time value of money into the analysis. Accordingly, Equation 5-13 now becomes

$$O_{\text{incremental}} = -\left[(I + I_w)_B - (I + I_w)_A\right] + \left[\frac{(\text{NCF}_B - \text{NCF}_A)_1}{(1 + i)^1}\right]$$

$$= \left[\frac{(\text{NCF}_B - \text{NCF}_A)_2}{(1 + i)^2}\right] + \cdots + \left[\frac{(\text{NCF}_B - \text{NCF}_A)_n}{(1 + i)^n}\right]$$

Example 5-19
A company has three alternative investments which are being considered. With the data in Table 5-4, determine which alternative should be selected, if any, using discounted-cash-flow analysis. The minimum rate of return is 15%.

Solution
By Equation 5-13, for alternative A, at $i = 0.15$,

$$O = -11,000 + 4130 + 3025 + 2170 + 1544 + 995$$
$$= -11,000 + 11,864$$
$$= +864$$

TABLE 5-4

	Cash Flow, $		
Year	Project A	Project B	Project C
1	4750	3550	2000
2	4000	3550	3000
3	3300	3550	4000
4	2700	3550	4500
5	2000	3550	5000
Investment	11,000	12,000	10,000

At $i = 0.20$,

$$O = -11,000 + 3958 + 2778 + 1910 + 1302 + 804$$
$$= -11,000 + 10,752$$
$$= -248$$

So,

$$i = 0.15 + 0.05\left(\frac{864}{864 + 248}\right) = 0.189, \text{ or } 18.9\%$$

For alternative B, at $i = 0.15$,

$$O = -12,000 + 3087 + 2684 + 2335 + 2030 + 1765$$
$$= -12,000 + 11,902$$
$$= -98$$

At $i = 0.10$,

$$O = -12,000 + 3227 + 2934 + 2667 + 2425 + 2204$$
$$= -12,000 + 13457$$
$$= +1457$$

So,

$$i = 0.10 + 0.05\left(\frac{1457}{1457 + 98}\right) = 0.147, \text{ or } 14.7\%$$

For alternative C, at $i = 0.20$,

$$O = -10,000 + 1667 + 2083 + 2315 + 2170 + 2009$$
$$= -10,000 + 10,244$$
$$= +244$$

At $i = 0.25$,

$$O = -10,000 + 1600 + 1920 + 2048 + 1843 + 1638$$
$$= -10,000 + 9048$$
$$= -951$$

So,

$$i = 0.20 + 0.05\left(\frac{244}{244 + 951}\right) = 0.210, \text{ or } 21.0\%$$

Hence,

$$i_A = 18.9\%,$$
$$i_B = 14.7\%,$$
$$i_C = 21.0\%$$

Now, by incremental analysis (Equation 5-16), between alternatives B and A:

$$O = -(12,000 - 11,000) + \frac{(3550 - 4750)}{(1 + i)^1}$$
$$+ \frac{(3550 - 4000)}{(1 + i)^2} + \cdots + \frac{(3550 - 2000)}{(1 + i)^5}$$

At $i = 0.15$,

$$O = -1000 - 1043 - 340 + 164 + 486 + 776$$
$$= -1000 + 43 = -957$$

At $i = 0.10$,

$$O = -1000 - 1091 - 372 + 188 + 520 + 962$$
$$= -1000 + 207$$
$$= -793$$

At $i = 0.05$,

$$O = -1000 - 1143 - 408 + 216 + 700 + 1215$$
$$= -1000 + 580$$
$$= -420$$

At $i = 0.02$,

$$O = -1000 - 1176 - 433 + 236 + 786 + 1409$$
$$= -1000 + 822$$
$$= -178$$

At $i = 0.01$,

$$O = -1000 - 1188 - 441 + 243 + 817 + 1475$$
$$= -1000 + 906$$
$$= -94$$

Consider, then, $i_{B-A} = 0.05$. Between alternatives C and A, at $i = 0.15$,

$$O = -(10,000 - 11,000) - 2391 - 756 + 460 + 1492$$
$$= +1000 - 166$$
$$= +834$$

At $i = 0.20$,

$$O = +1000 - 2292 - 695 + 405 + 868 + 1206$$
$$= +1000 - 508$$
$$= +492$$

At $i = 0.25$,

$$O = +1000 - 2200 - 640 + 358 + 737 + 983$$
$$= +1000 - 762$$
$$= +238$$

At $i = 0.30$,

$$O = +1000 - 2115 - 592 + 318 + 630 + 806$$
$$= +1000 - 953$$
$$= +47$$

which is close enough to zero. Consider $i_{C-A} = 30\%$.

No incremental analysis is needed between C and B. Project B is rejected because of a DCF of 0.05%, which is lower than the minimum rate of 15%.

We now construct a summary table, Table 5-5. Alternative C is the best choice since the incremental DCF exceeds the minimum rate of return.

TABLE 5-5

			Incremental DCF, %		
Alternative	Investment, $	DCF, %	A	B	C
A	11,000	18.9	—	—	—
B	12,000	14.7	0.05	—	—
C	10,000	21.0	30.00	—	—

5.8   Application of Break-Even Analysis to Investment Alternatives Using the Time Value of Money

Equation 4-9 does not consider the time value of money. If the time value of money is to be considered, then it must be incorporated in the equation. Equation 4-9 then becomes, in terms of present worth of an annuity

$$\frac{(1 + i)^n - 1}{i(1 + i)^n} = \frac{I_A - I_B}{I_{wB} - I_{wA}} \tag{5-17}$$

where n is the break-even point as a function of *time* and can be obtained from Appendix B for a given value i.

Example 5-20

Consider the data given in Example 4-15; however, the initial investment for project B is now $5500. If money is worth 10% per year and the useful life of the project is only 20 years, which alternative should be chosen?

Solution:

By Equation 5-17,

$$\frac{(1 + i)^n - 1}{i(1 + i)^n} = 9.0$$

And from Appendix B at $i = 10\%$, $n = 20$ years, which is the break-even point. Hence alternative B should be chosen because of its lower initial capital investment.

Example 5-21

Consider the data given in Example 5-20; however, the useful life of the project is now 26 years instead of 20. Prove that alternative A is now superior to alternative B.

Solution:

The total cost of the project for the 26 years ($n = 26$), converted to present worth and using $i = 10\%$, is, for alternative A (from Appendix B):

$$\text{Present worth} = 10{,}000 + 1000 \left[\frac{(1 + i)^n - 1}{i(1 + i)^n} \right]$$

$$= 10{,}000 + 1000(9.161) = \$19{,}161$$

For alternative B:

$$\text{Present worth} = 5500 + 1500(9.161) = \$19{,}244$$

As can be seen, at the end of 26 years the total cost for alternative A will be \$81 less than that for alternative B.

Finally, if the project has an infinite life (for our purposes, 40 years or more), then the present-worth factor of an annuity is equal to $1/i$, or

$$\frac{(1 + i)^n - 1}{i(1 + i)^n} = \frac{1}{i} \text{ for } n \geq 40 \text{ yr} \tag{5-18}$$

and the break-even point is now expressed in terms of i

$$i_{BE} = \frac{I_{wB} - I_{wA}}{I_A - I_b} \tag{5-19}$$

Example 5-22

Consider the data in Example 5-20; however, the useful life of the project is now 60 years. If the minimum rate of return is 15%, which alternative is more attractive? What about if $ROI_m = 10\%$?

Solution:

By Equation 5-19,

$$i_{BE} = \frac{1500 - 1000}{10,000 - 5500} = 0.1111, \text{ or } 11.11\%$$

Hence alternative B is more attractive since it will take a long time for A to catch up to B. On the other hand, if $ROI_m = 10\%$, then A is more attractive. Why?

Summary

Interest is the amount charged for the use of borrowed money. The amount of interest associated with the time value of money can be calculated by using any one of the following mathematical relationships:

$$S = PW(1 + i)^n \qquad \text{single-payment compound amount}$$

$$PW = \frac{S}{(1 + i)^n} \qquad \text{single-payment present worth}$$

$$S = R\left[\frac{(1 + i)^n - 1}{i}\right] \qquad \text{annuity compound amount}$$

$$R = S\left[\frac{i}{(1 + i)^n - 1}\right] \qquad \text{annuity sinking fund}$$

$$PW = R\left[\frac{(1 + i)^n - 1}{i(1 + i)^n}\right] \qquad \text{annuity present worth}$$

$$R = PW\left[\frac{i(1 + i)^n}{(1 + i)^n - 1}\right] \qquad \text{annuity capital recovery}$$

Most firms use maximum payback time (PT_M) as a criterion for evaluating proposed investments if the payback-time method is being employed:

$$PT_M = \frac{1 - t}{\left[\dfrac{i(1 + i)^n}{(1 + i)^n - 1}\right] + (ROI_m - i) - d}$$

Although payback time and ROI are the most widely used methods for evaluating investment feasibility, the DCF method, in general, yields the best results, since it considers profitability in terms of the time value of money:

$$O = -(I + I_w) + \frac{NCF_1}{(1 + i)^1} + \frac{NCF_2}{(1 + i)^2} + \cdots + \frac{NCF_n}{(1 + i)^n}$$

The above equation is solved by trial and error to determine the i (interest rate) at which the sum of all the time-adjusted cash outflows (investment plus working capital) equals the sum of all the time-adjusted cash inflows (net profit plus depreciation).

For benefit/cost calculations, where the time value of money is being considered, the following relationship can be used:

$$\frac{\left(\begin{array}{c}\text{annual positive}\\\text{user benefits}\end{array}\right) - \left(\begin{array}{c}\text{annual negative}\\\text{user benefits}\end{array}\right)}{\left(\begin{array}{c}\text{initial}\\\text{investment}\end{array}\right)\left[\dfrac{i(1 + i)^n}{(1 + i)^n - 1}\right] + \left(\begin{array}{c}\text{annual}\\\text{operating cost}\end{array}\right)} = \frac{B}{C} \geqq 1$$

In decision making between alternatives, taking into consideration the time value of money, incremental DCF is used:

$$O_{\text{incremental}} = -\left[(I + I_w)_B - (I + I_w)_A\right] + \left[\frac{(NCF_B - NCF_A)_1}{(1 + i)^1}\right]$$

$$+ \left[\frac{(NCF_B - NCF_A)_2}{(1 + i)^2}\right] + \cdots + \left[\frac{(NCF_B - NCF_A)_n}{(1 + i)^n}\right]$$

Problems

1. How long will it take for $10,000 to double if it is compounded annually at 7% interest?

2. What will $20,000 amount to in 3 years at 9% per year if it is compounded annually? Semiannually? Quarterly?
3. If money is worth 7% per year, what is the present worth of a $14,000 receipt due in 4 years?
4. What is the effective rate of interest if the interest is compounded semiannually at 6% per year?
5. What will $15,000 amount to in 5 years if it is compounded continuously at 5% per year?
6. What is the present worth of a series of equal end-of-year payments of $1500 for 10 years, if the interest rate is 6% per year?
7. If $25,000 is owed, and if the interest rate is 7% per year, how long will it take to discharge a debt if equal end-of-year payments of $3500 are made?
8. A boy is celebrating his thirteenth birthday. His parents want to have $10,000 for his college education when he turns eighteen. They decide to set aside a certain amount now and each year until the boy enters college. If money is worth 7% per year, what is his parents' yearly contribution?
9. An original loan of $5000 was made at an annual interest rate of 5% for 5 years. At the end of the fifth year, the loan was extended for another 5 years at a new interest rate of 7%. If no interest was paid on the original loan or on the extended one, what is the total amount owed at the end of the 10 years?
10. If $50,000 is owed, and if equal payments of $9500 at the end of each year for 9 years will discharge the debt, what is the annual interest rate?
11. An operation can be performed manually at an annual cost of $15,000. How much can be spent for a machine to perform the same operation if the machine lasts 10 years, the operating cost of the machine is $4000 per year, and the interest rate is 11% per year?
12. Repeat Problem 4-13 using the DCF method.
13. Repeat Problem 4-14 and compare the three alternatives by the annual-equivalent-cost method at $i = 7\%$.
14. Solve Problem 5-13 using $i = 10\%$.
15. Solve Problem 4-15 using a saving of $30 per year per vehicle and $i = 5\%$.
16. A project requires an investment of $200,000, of which $80,000 will be used as working capital. The estimated cash flows (net profit and depreciation) that will be realized are: $-$20,000, $-$1000, $5000, $10,000, $40,000, and $50,000, for years 1 through 6, respectively. The project's useful life is 6 years. If $ROI_m = 15\%$ should the project be undertaken, on the basis of the DCF analysis?
17. Prove in Example 5-17 that alternative B should be chosen.
18. In Problem 4-13, determine which alternative should be chosen using the DCF method and incremental analysis.

Depreciation

6

Most fixed assets (to be defined shortly), with the exception of land, have a limited useful life; that is, their benefit to the firm is used up and they must be replaced with either identical or technologically more advanced assets. Accordingly, the Internal Revenue Service permits this loss in value to be charged off gradually (over the period of useful life) against the revenues from employment of these assets.

Depreciation is an extremely important concept in view of its impact on income taxes (recall Equation 1-1) and the net profits and cash flows that can be realized from a given project.

6.1 The Nature of Depreciation

Analyzing the costs and profits of a proposed project warrants recognition of the fact that fixed assets (buildings and services; equipment, including delivery and installation; shipping and receiving facilities; furniture; and fixtures; among others) decrease in value with age and use. This decrease in value may be attributed to *deterioration*, which is the physical process of wearing out, and *obsolescence*, which is the loss of usefulness as a result of technological changes not related to the physical condition of the asset. This reduction in value resulting from any of the above causes is known as *depreciation*. Depreciation due to deterioration is *physical depreciation;* while depreciation due to obsolescence is *functional depreciation.* The economic function of depreciation, therefore, is to expense out the original investment over the asset's useful life so that plans can be made for its continual replacement. Accordingly, *depreciation* can be defined as "the systematic conversion of fixed or tangible assets (previously defined) into expense." Systematic conversion of intangible assets (patents, copyrights, franchises, etc.) into expense is called *amortization.* Finally, the systematic conversion of the cost of natural resources (mines, oil wells, etc.) into expense is called *depletion.* [1]

To illustrate the conversion of fixed assets into expense, consider a new plant costing $5,000,000 which is to be depreciated over 20 years, having no value at the end of the 20 years. Hence, the $5,000,000 is deducted from gross profit at a rate of $250,000 per year for 20 years. The $250,000 is a cost incurred for the use of the plant to generate revenue and profits.

In engineering practice, the total depreciation period is usually assumed to be the length of the asset's useful life, and the value at the end of the useful life is assumed to be the probable *scrap* or *salvage value* of the asset.

Salvage value is the amount of money obtainable from the sale of a fixed asset or facility after its useful life, when the fixed asset can give some type of further service and is worth more than scrapping or junking. It should be noted that salvage value does not include the cost of removal or of transportation of the asset to a new owner.

In the event that an asset or facility cannot be disposed of as a useful unit, it can be torn apart and sold as junk to be recycled. The money obtained from such disposal is known as the *scrap value* or *junk value.*

In practice, an engineer or technologist does not wait until the end of the useful life of an asset or a facility to determine the depreciation costs or the salvage value. Depreciation and salvage are usually prorated throughout the useful life, and depreciation cost is included in the calculation of the operating charge incurred each year. Consequently, it is necessary to estimate the useful life of an asset as well as its final value at the end of the useful life.

Consideration of depreciation as a cost allows for profits earned by a firm to be evaluated realistically and thus provides a basis for determination of federal income taxes. Depreciation costs are not subject to taxes, as seen in Equation 1-1. They are set aside each year in order that the capital invested can be fully recovered (excluding salvage or scrap value); then they are used to replace the asset after its useful life, or to buy other equipment or reinvest in other ventures. This depreciation expense, when added to net profit, becomes a cash fund able to flow in or out of a firm to generate additional profits.

---

[1] For further details on amortization and depletion see H. A. Finney and H. E. Miller, *Principles of Accounting,* 6th ed., Prentice-Hall, Englewood Cliffs, N.J., 1965.

The difference between the original value of the asset and all the depreciation charges made to date is known as its *book value*. This value is the worth of the asset as shown on the owner's accounting records.

The price which could be received for an asset if it were placed on sale in the open market is known as its *market value*. The term assumes that the asset is in good condition and that there is always a buyer for it.

The expenditure needed to replace an existing asset at any given time with one capable of rendering the same or better service is known as the asset's *replacement value*.

Predicting *future* or *replacement* values with precision is very difficult because of fluctuations in supply and demand. On the other hand, if the depreciation expense is costed out at a uniform method, it is possible to predict future book values with absolute accuracy. Such methods will be presented in Section 6.3.

Keeping an asset in good shape at all times is known as *maintenance;* replacing or mending any broken parts is known as *repairs.* The extent of maintenance and repairs may alter the depreciation cost, since if property is kept in good condition its useful life is often extended. It should be understood, however, that maintenance and repair costs must be charged against income the same year that the action is taken; therefore, these costs should not be confused with depreciation costs even though they do influence the remaining useful life of the asset.

Example 6-1
    A machine costing $10,000 is to replace a manual operation and hence save $5000 per year in labor costs. The machine will be kept for 10 years, then sold to a buyer for $500. If money for the expenditure comes from internal funds, if it costs $1000 per year to keep the machine in good shape, and if the firm is in the 50% income-tax bracket, determine:
a. Gross profit
b. Salvage value
c. Annual depreciation expense
d. Net profit
e. Cash flow

Solution:
a. Gross profit = savings minus operating expense = 5000 − 1000
    = $4000
b. The salvage value is $500.
c. Annual depreciation expense is total expenditure minus salvage value, divided by useful life $\dfrac{10{,}000 - 500}{10}$ = $950 per year
d. Since there is no interest being paid on the expenditure,

net profit P = gross profit − income tax (gross profit − depreciation)
    or $P = G - t(G - d)$

$$= \$4000 - 0.50(4000 - 950)$$
$$= \$1975 \text{ per year}$$

e. Cash flow = net profit + depreciation expense
$$= \$1975 + 950$$
$$= \$2925$$

6.2   Estimation of Useful Life

The period during which the use of an asset or facility is economically advantageous to the owner is known as its *useful life;* the term is synonymous with *economic life* or *service life.* In estimating the service life of an asset, it is assumed that a reasonable amount of maintenance and repair work will be done at the expense of the owner.

The most widely used source for estimating useful life of assets is the *Depreciation Guidelines,* published by the Internal Revenue Service.[2] Such data are presented in Tables 6-1, 6-2, and 6-3 for general business, nonmanufacturing, and manufacturing activities, respectively. Although

TABLE 6-1   Estimated Life of Assets—General Business

Type of Asset	Life, yr
Office furniture, fixtures, machines, equipment	10
Transportation equipment	
Aircraft	6
Automobiles	3
Buses	9
General purpose trucks	4
Railroad cars	15
Water transportation equipment	18
Land and site improvements	20
Buildings	
Apartments	40
Banks	50
Factories	45
Garages	45
Hotels	40
Office buildings	45
Stores	50
Theaters	40
Warehouses	60

[2] *Depreciation Guidelines and Rules,* IRS publication no. 456.

TABLE 6-2   Estimated Life of Assets—Nonmanufacturing Activities

Type of Asset	Life, yr
Agriculture	
Machinery and equipment	10
Animals	3–10
Farm buildings	25
Contract construction	
General	5
Marine	12
Fishing	*
Mining	10
Recreation and amusement	10
Personal and professional services	10
Wholesale and retail trade	10

*To be determined as situation warrants.

there is no certainty that future conditions will remain constant, it is possible to use these data with confidence.

It should be recognized that the data given in Tables 6-1 through 6-3 are only guidelines; use of the values is not mandatory. If a firm feels that some other estimate is better, it should go ahead and use the better estimate; however, the firm must be prepared to support the claim.

During times of national emergency, Congress may approve rapid depreciation of certain types of assets or facilities to make investment in additional plants and equipment or some other assets more attractive. A 1971 regulation, for example, provided for a 5-year write-off for approved pollution-control facilities.

6.3   Methods of Depreciation

Once the useful life of an asset has been determined, annual depreciation costs can be calculated by a number of different but generally accepted methods, and it is important for an engineer or technologist to understand the basis for each method. The Internal Revenue Service has definite rules and regulations concerning the manner in which depreciation expenses may be determined. Most industries use one of the government-sanctioned methods. These are:

1.   Straight-line method
2.   Declining-balance method
3.   Sum-of-the-years-digits method
4.   Sinking-fund method

TABLE 6-3 Estimated Life of Assets—Manufacturing Activities

Type of Asset	Life, yr
Aerospace industry	8
Apparel and textile products	9
Cement (excluding concrete products)	20
Chemical and allied products	11
Electrical equipment	12
Fabricated metal products	12
Food products (except grains, sugar)	12
Glass products	14
Machinery, except electrical and metalworking	12–16
Paper and allied products	
Petroleum and natural gas	
Drilling, and field service	6
Exploration, drilling and production	14
Petroleum refining	16
Marketing	16
Plastic products	11
Primary metals	
Ferrous metals	18
Nonferrous metals	14
Printing and publishing	11
Scientific instruments	12
Sugar products	18
Textile mill products	14
Tobacco and tobacco products	15
Vegetable oil products	18

The first three methods are arbitrary, giving no consideration to interest costs, while the last one accounts for the time value of money (interest).

STRAIGHT-LINE METHOD

In the straight-line method the cost of the asset less its salvage value is divided equally among the years of its useful life. The yearly depreciation expense can be expressed mathematically as:

$$dI = \frac{(V - V_s)}{n} \qquad \textbf{(6-1)}$$

where dI = annual depreciation expense, in dollars per year
V = original value of the asset at year zero, including delivery and
    installation costs
V_s = salvage value of the asset at the end of useful life
n = useful or service life, in years

In terms of the annual depreciation rate, Equation 6-1 becomes,

$$d = \frac{(V - V_s)}{nI} = \frac{1}{n} \qquad (6\text{-}2)$$

where I = depreciation base $(V - V_s)$

The book value of the asset at any given time can be expressed as

$$V_b = V - a(dI) \qquad (6\text{-}3)$$

where V_b = book value in dollars
    a = number of years in actual use

Because of simplicity, the straight-line method is the one most widely
used for determining annual depreciation costs.

Example 6-2
A new reactor will cost $50,000, and its useful life will be 20
years. It can be installed for $5000 and sold for $2000 at the end of
its useful life. Using the straight-line method determine the following:
a. Annual depreciation cost
b. Annual depreciation rate
c. Book value at the end of 10 years

Solution:

$$V = \$55,000$$
$$V_s = \$2000$$
$$n = 20 \text{ years}$$
$$a = 10 \text{ years}$$

a. By Equation 6-1

$$dI = \frac{(V - V_s)}{n} = \frac{(55,000 - 2000)}{20} = \$2650/\text{yr}$$

b. By Equation 6-2

$$d = \frac{1}{n} = \frac{1}{20} = 0.05 \text{ or } 5\%/\text{yr}$$

   c.   By Equation 6-3

$$V_b = V - a(dI) = 55{,}000 - 10(2650) = \$28{,}500$$

DECLINING-BALANCE METHOD

Because many assets are more valuable in the early years of their useful life than in the later years (their mechanical efficiency tending to decline with age), the declining-balance method expenses a larger fraction of the cost of the asset during the early years of its useful life. The rate of decline in depreciation costs is constant throughout the useful life. The factor f expressing the rate of decline can be determined as follows:

$$f = 1 - \left(\frac{V_s}{V}\right)^{\frac{1}{n}} \tag{6-4}$$

where n = total years of useful life

Hence, the depreciation expense for the asset's first year is

$$dI_1 = Vf \tag{6-5}$$

and at the end of first year the asset's book value is

$$V_b = V(1 - f) \tag{6-6}$$

For the second year the depreciation expense is

$$dI_2 = (V - dI_1)f \tag{6-7}$$

and the book value at the end of the second year is

$$V_b = V(1 - f)^2 \tag{6-8}$$

At the end of a years (the number of years actually used) the book value is

$$V_b = V(1 - f)^a \tag{6-9}$$

while at the end of n years the book value is

$$V_b = V(1 - f)^n = V_s \tag{6-10}$$

which shows that book value equals salvage value at the end of useful life.

Equation 6-4 is seldom used in actual practice since it is in part a function of the salvage value of the asset and is certainly not applicable if the salvage value is zero. To overcome this disadvantage, a fixed-percentage factor is chosen, calculated at twice the corresponding straight-line rate. This procedure is referred to as the *double-declining-balance method*. Hence an asset with a 20-year useful life is depreciated at 10%, or $2/n$, of its undepreciated balance each year. The double-declining depreciation expense can be expressed mathematically as

$$dI_a = V\left[\left(\frac{2}{n}\right)\left(\frac{n-2}{n}\right)^{a-1}\right] \tag{6-11}$$

where a = the number of years actually used.

The accrued depreciation after n years *can never* exceed the depreciable base $(V - V_s)$.

Example 6-3

$$\text{Given } V = 10,000$$
$$V_s = 5000$$
$$n = 5 \text{ years}$$

determine the fixed percentage factor f that can be used in order to accelerate depreciation changes.

Solution:
By Equation 6-4

$$f = 1 - \left(\frac{V_s}{V}\right)^{\frac{1}{n}} = 1 - \left(\frac{5000}{10,000}\right)^{\frac{1}{5}} = 1 - (0.5)^{0.20} = 0.1294, \ 12.94\%$$

Hence, by Equation 6-5, the depreciation cost for the first year is

$$dI_1 = Vf = (10,000)(0.1294) = \$1294$$

which yields a higher depreciation cost than the straight-line method does ($1294 versus $1000). On the other hand, if one desires a much higher expense in the first year of the asset's life, the double-declining-balance method can be used.

By Equation 6-11

$$dI_1 = V\left[\left(\frac{2}{n}\right)\left(\frac{n-2}{n}\right)^{a-1}\right]$$
$$= 10,000\left[\left(\frac{2}{5}\right)\left(\frac{5-2}{5}\right)^{1-1}\right] = 10,000\,[(0.4)(0.6)^0] = \$4000$$

while for the second year

$$dI_2 = 10,000 \ [(0.4)(0.6)^1] = \$2400$$

Example 6-4

An asset has been acquired at a cost of $250,000 and is expected to be used for 5 years then sold for an estimated net of $100,000. Find the annual depreciation cost and the accrued allocation each year.

Solution:

By Equation 6-11, the first year depreciation expense is

$$dI_1 = 250,000 \left[\left(\frac{2}{5}\right)\left(\frac{5-2}{5}\right)^0 \right] = \$100,000$$

the second year expense is

$$dI_2 = 250,000 \ [(0.4)(0.6)^1] = \$60,000$$

The accrued depreciation expense at the end of second year is

$$100,000 + 60,000 = \$160,000$$

This, however, violates the condition that accrued depreciation must never exceed the depreciable base $V - V_s$, which is

$$250,000 - 100,000 = \$150,000$$

Therefore, only $50,000 is permitted for depreciation for year 2, and no amount is permitted for years 3, 4, and 5. Table 6-4 summarizes the depreciation expense and the accrued allocation each year.

TABLE 6-4

Age, yr	Depreciation expense, $	Accrued depreciation at age, $
1	100,000	100,000
2	50,000	150,000
3	0	150,000
4	0	150,000
5	0	150,000

As one can see from both examples just illustrated, the greatest advantage of the declining-balance method over the straight-line method is its ability to repay the investor more rapidly during the early years of service. For firms just starting in business, this method reduces the income tax load at the time when it is most necessary to keep all payout costs (such as federal income tax) at a minimum.

SUM-OF-THE-YEARS-DIGITS METHOD

This method, similar to the declining-balance method, offers accelerated depreciation during the early years of the asset's life. In this method the numbers 1, 2, 3 . . . n are added, where n is the estimated years of useful life. The depreciation expense each year is a fraction in which the denominator is the sum of these digits and the numerator for the first year is n; $n - 1$ for the second year, $n - 2$ for the third year; and so on. Mathematically, the method can be expressed as

$$dI_a = \frac{2(n - a + 1)}{n(n + 1)} (V - V_s) \qquad \textbf{(6-12)}$$

where n = useful life
  a = number of years in actual use

Example 6-5
  Given the data in Example 6-2, determine the depreciation charges for the first two years, using the sum-of-the-years-digits method.

Solution:
  The sum of the digits is $(1 + 2 + 3 + \ldots + 20) = 210$; thus for the first year the depreciation expense is

$$dI_1 = (V - V_s)\frac{n}{210} = (55,000 - 2000)\frac{20}{210} = \$5048$$

or by Equation 6-12

$$dI_1 = \frac{2(n - a + 1)}{n(n + 1)}(V - V_s) = \frac{2(20 - i + 1)}{20(20 + 1)}(55,000 - 2000)$$
$$= \$5048$$

For the second year

$$dI_2 = (55,000 - 2000) \times \frac{19}{20} = \$4795$$

or by Equation 6-12

$$dI_2 = \frac{2(20 - 2 + 1)}{20(20 + 1)} \times 53,000 = \$4795$$

THE SINKING-FUND METHOD

This method takes into consideration the time value of money. It permits a fixed amount to be reinvested at some compound interest rate, to create a sufficient fund to provide the recovery of the original capital invested in the asset; that is, at the end of the useful life, the sum of all the amounts reinvested plus accrued interest will equal the total depreciation expense. The depreciation expense for the first year of the asset's life is

$$dI_1 = (V - V_s)\left[\frac{i}{(1 + i)^n - 1}\right] \qquad (6\text{-}13)$$

where $\dfrac{i}{(1 + i)^n - 1}$ = the sinking-fund factor

For the second year the depreciation expense is

$$dI_2 = dI_1 + (aI_1)\, i \qquad (6\text{-}14)$$

For the third year

$$dI_3 = dI_1 + (dI + dI_2)\, i \qquad (6\text{-}15)$$

For the fourth year

$$dI_4 = dI_1 + (dI_1 + dI_2 + dI_3)\, i \qquad (6\text{-}16)$$

and so forth.

Since the sinking-fund method takes into consideration the time value of money, the annual depreciation expense increases with the use of the equipment, with the smallest and largest expenses being in the first and last years of the useful life, respectively.

Example 6-6

An asset costs $20,000, lasts 10 years, and has a salvage value of $1000 at the end of its useful life. If money is worth 10% per year, determine the depreciation expenses for the first 5 years.

Solution:

By Equation 6-13 and Appendix B

$$dI_1 = (V - V_s)\left[\frac{i}{(1 + i)^n - 1}\right] = 19,000(0.0627) = \$1191$$

By Equations 6-14, 6-15, and 6-16

$$dI_2 = dI_1 + (dI_1)i = 1191 + 1191(0.10) = 1191 + 119 = \$1310$$

$dI_3 = 1191 + (1191 + 1310)0.10 = \$1441$
$dI_4 = 1191 + (1191 + 1310 + 1441)0.10 = \$1585$

Finally,

$$dI_5 = 1191 + (1191 + 1310 + 1441 + 1585)0.10 = \$1744$$

6.4   Evaluation of Depreciation Methods

Although all the depreciation methods presented in this chapter permit full recovery of the cost of the asset less salvage value, the best method for depreciation rests with the timing of current and future cash flows needed by the firm. The following example will illustrate.

Example 6-7

An asset costs $1100, lasts 5 years, and has a salvage value of $100 at the end of the 5 years. If money is worth 10% per year, calculate the annual depreciation expense and the undepreciated balances for each year of depreciable life, using the four methods of depreciation presented in this chapter.

Solution:

Table 6-5 gives the final calculations using Equations 6-1 through 6-15, while Figure 6-1 illustrates graphically the effect of each method on the end-of-year undepreciated balance. As can be seen, the accelerated methods yield higher deductions during the early years of an asset's life and substantially lower deductions during the remaining years of the asset's life. The double-declining-balance method gives the largest deductions for the first 2 years; afterward, if interest is not being considered, the straight-line method appears to be more attractive. If, on the other hand, interest is being considered, after 2 years the sinking-fund method appears to be most attractive.

Of all the depreciation methods, the straight-line is the one most widely used since it is very simple to apply. In general, unless there is a specific reason to do otherwise, most feasibility studies use straight-line depreciation.

It is important to recognize the fundamental nature of depreciation and to understand how it relates to taxes and profitability. Because depreciation is an expense, the manner in which it is allocated over the years has an effect on the bottom line, or profit, for individual years. The following example will illustrate.

Example 6-8

Consider the data and results of Example 6-7. If the gross profit each year for the 5 years is $500, interest is 10%, income tax is 50%, and the firm wishes to show the highest profit at the end of the first year, determine which depreciation method should be used.

TABLE 6-5

Year	Straight-Line Method		Double-Declining-Balance Method		Sum-of-the-Years-Digits Method		Sinking-fund Method (10%)	
	End-of-Year Undepreciated Balance	Annual Depreciation Charge	End-of-Year Undepreciated Balance	Annual Depreciation Charge	End-of-Year Undepreciated Balance	Annual Depreciation Charge	End-of-Year Undepreciated Balance	Annual Depreciation Charge
0	$1000	$ 0	$1000	$ 0	$1000	$ 0	$1000	$ 0
1	800	200	560	440	667	333	836	164
2	600	200	296	264	399	268	656	180
3	400	200	138	158	199	200	458	198
4	200	200	43	95	66	133	240	218
5	0	200	0	43	0	66	0	240

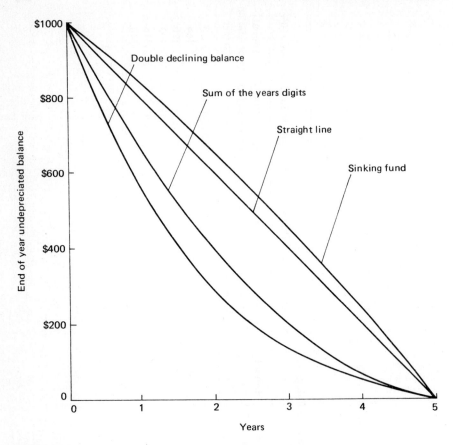

Figure 6-1

Solution:
Using Equation 1-1,

$$P = G - i(I + I_w) - t(G - dI)$$

it is possible to calculate net profit for each year by each method and to display the results as shown in Table 6-6. That is, using straight-line depreciation, at the end of the first year the net profit is

$$P = 500 - 0.10(1000) - 0.50(500 - 200) = \$250$$

As can be seen, the firm should use the double-declining-balance method to expense the depreciation, since it shows the highest net profit at the end of the first operating year. On the other hand, if the

TABLE 6-6   Net Profit Analysis

Year	Straight-Line Method	Double-Declining Balance Method	Sum-of-the-Years Digits Method	Sinking-Fund Method
1	$250	$370	$316	$232
2	250	282	284	240
3	250	229	250	249
4	250	197	218	259
5	250	171	183	270
Average	250	250	250	250

firm wishes to show a steady growth each year, assuming the gross profit remains constant, then the sinking-fund method is clearly the best choice.

Summary

Depreciation, as has been seen, is a significant factor in project evaluation. It allows capital invested in fixed costs to be recovered during the period in which the asset is expected to be useful to the firm. The useful life of an existing asset or of assets similar to those for which historical data have been accumulated, can be determined with little risk. With new ventures, past experience or IRS guidelines (Tables 6-1 through 6-3) are excellent sources of information for estimating useful life. Having the useful life established along with salvage value, the following four methods can be employed for computation of the depreciation:

1.   Straight-line method

$$dI = \frac{(V - V_s)}{n}$$

2.   **a.** Declining-balance method

$$dI = (V - dI_a) f$$

where a = number of years in actual use

f = fixed percentage factor calculated by the equation $f = (V_s/V)\dfrac{1}{n}$

   b.   Double-declining-balance method

$$dI = V \left[\left(\frac{2}{n} \right) \left(\frac{n-2}{n} \right)^{a-1} \right]$$

3. Sum-of-the-years-digits method

$$dI = \frac{2(n - a + 1)}{n(n + 1)}(V - V_s)$$

4. Sinking-fund method

$$dI_1 = (V - V_s)\left(\frac{i}{(1 + i)^n - 1}\right)$$
$$dI_2 = dI_1 + (dI_1)i$$
$$dI_3 = dI_1 + (dI_1 + dI_2)i$$

and so on.

The double-declining-balance method and the sum-of-the-years-dig-its method give accelerated depreciation expenses; that is, depreciation expenses are greater in the early life years. The straight-line method exhibits uniform depreciation while the sinking-fund method, owing to the effect of time on the value of money, exhibits greater depreciation expense in the later life years.

Problems

1. Define the following terms:
   a. Salvage value
   b. Book value
   c. Replacement value
   d. Market value
   e. Maintenance and repair costs
2. A synthetic rubber manufacturer has bought $1,500,000 worth of equipment that has an estimated salvage value of $200,000. Determine
   a. The useful life for tax purposes
   b. The declining-balance factor
3. The initial cost of a completely installed chemical reactor is $70,000, and the salvage value at the end of the useful life is estimated to be $15,000. How many years of useful life should be estimated for the reactor if the straight-line depreciation rate is 12% per year?
4. Two alternative assets A and B show a 15% depreciation of the original value in the fourth year, using sum-of-the-years-digits depreciation. If A has a long life and B has a short one, what was the useful life of each asset, neglecting salvage value?
5. A new piece of equipment lasting 10 years costs $20,000, including installation. Its salvage value is estimated to be $2200 at the end of its useful life. Determine the book value of this equipment after 4 years, 6 years, and 8 years, using

    a. the straight-line method
    b. the declining-balance method
    c. the double-declining-balance method

6. A piece of equipment having an original cost of $60,000 was put into use 12 years ago with an estimated useful life of 20 years. Its scrap value is assumed to be zero at the end of its useful life. Based on this information, a straight-line depreciation fund was set up. This equipment can now be sold for $15,000, and a more advanced model can be installed for $80,000. Assuming that the depreciation fund has not been spent, how much additional capital must be provided to make the purchase?

7. The original cost of a property is $60,000 and is depreciated by the sinking-fund method at $i = 8\%$. What is the annual depreciation charge if the salvage value at the end of its useful life is $5000?

8. The total value of a new waste-treatment plant is $3,000,000. A certificate of necessity has been obtained, permitting a write-off of 75% of the initial value in 5 years. The balance of the plant requires a write-off period of 15 years. Using the straight-line method and assuming negligible salvage and scrap value, determine the total depreciation cost during the first year.

9. Repeat Problem 7 using the double-declining-balance method.

10. An asset has an initial value of $60,000, service life of 25 years, and final salvage value of $5000. Determine the depreciation charge for the sixth year, using
    a. the straight-line method
    b. the declining-balance method
    c. the double-declining-balance method
    d. the sum-of-the-years-digits method
    e. the sinking-fund method, assuming that money is worth 10.75% per year.

11. A firm estimates a sales revenue of $2,000,000 per year, and all expenses except depreciation amount to $1,200,000 per year. At the start of the first year of operation, the total amount of assets subject to depreciation is $840,000. The overall service life is estimated to be 20 years, and the salvage value is estimated to be $40,000. If the firm is in the 50% tax bracket, what would be the reduction in income tax charges for the first year of operation if the sum-of-the-years-digits method were used instead of the straight-line method?

12. In order to make it feasible to purchase a certain new piece of equipment, the annual depreciation charge for the equipment cannot exceed $2000 at any time. The original cost of the equipment is $20,000, and it will have no salvage or scrap value at the end of its useful life. Determine the necessary length of the service life if the equipment is depreciated by
    a. the straight-line method
    b. the double-declining-balance method
    c. the sum-of-the-years-digits method

Taxes

7

Taxes play a significant role in preinvestment analysis. Since taxes influence modern business corporations' net profit considerably (Chapter 1, Equation 1-1), it is essential for the engineer or technologist to have a basic understanding of the fundamental principles of taxation.

7.1 Types of Taxes

Taxes are usually classified into three types: (1) property, (2) excise, and (3) income. They can be levied by federal, state, or local governments, the latter being county, city, or town.

PROPERTY TAXES
Local governments, specifically county, usually have jurisdiction over property taxes. Individual sublocal governments may have special property taxes above and beyond these for industries located within their limits.

Property taxes vary from county to county, with the average being between 1 and 5% of the assessed valuation. Taxes of this type are generally referred to as *direct,* since they must be paid directly by the particular concern and can be passed on to the consumer only indirectly. The way the cost is passed on to the consumer is through the final prices charged for the goods or services.

EXCISE TAXES

Excise taxes are levied by the state and/or the federal government for things like import duties, transfer of stocks and bonds, and sale of such products as gasoline, alcoholic beverages, and cigarettes. Many industries and corporations must also pay excise taxes for the privilege of doing business or manufacturing products in particular localities.

Taxes of this type are usually referred to as *indirect* since they can be passed onto the consumer. They can range from 1 to 15%.

INCOME TAXES

In general, a corporation's income tax is a levy on its net earnings. This revenue is a vital source of capital for both state and federal governments. On the average, state income taxes may range from 0 to 6% of net earnings. Federal income tax ranges are described below.

7.2   Federal Income Taxes

Business corporations are subject to extremely complex systems of federal income tax. The systems are designed by the legislative body of the government. Tax laws change nearly each year, and it would be impossible to present all the current rules and regulations. Accordingly, this section will present only the basic federal income tax regulations and the basic methods for determining the amount of the tax. It cannot be overemphasized that the final computation of a firm's income tax should be made with the aid of expert accountants.

Table 7-1 exhibits corporate income tax rates in the United States from 1929 through 1977. As can be seen, the rates have varied widely. From 1913 to 1941 the tax rate based on gross earnings increased from 1 to 31%. The Second World War increased the tax rate to 40% plus an excess-profits tax. During the post-War years the regular rate was reduced to 38%, but in 1950 it was increased to 42% plus an excess-profits tax. Excess-profits taxes were also levied during the Korean and Vietnam Wars. From 1971 to 1977, the tax rate remained 48% with no excess-profits tax.

The present 48% income tax rate is applicable to corporations whose taxable income is $50,000 or above. Those with taxable income up to $25,000 are subject to a tax of 20%. Corporations with taxable income between $25,000 and $50,000 must pay a tax of 22%.

Example 7-1

If the gross profit of a corporation is $250,000 for the year, determine the income tax it will be paying to the federal government. Assume no other deductions.

TABLE 7-1   Income Tax Rates in the United States on Corporation Profits

Year	Regular Tax Rate, % of Gross Income	Excess-Profits Tax, % of Gross Income
1929	11	
1930–1931	12	
1932–1935	13.75	
1936–1937	15	
1938–1939	19	
1940	24	
1941	31	
1942–1943	40	40
1944–1945	40	32
1946–1949	38	
1950	42	10
1951	50.75	17.25
1952–1953	52	18
1954–1963	52	
1964	50	
1965–1967	48	
1968–1969	48	4.8*
1970	48	1.2**
1971–1977	48	

*Effective surcharge rate: 10% on 48% rate.
**Effective surcharge rate: 2.5% on 48% rate.

Solution:
Since there are no other deductions, gross profit G equals taxable income, or \$250,000. Hence,

$$t = \$25,000(0.20) + (\$50,000 - \$25,000)0.22 + (\$250,000 - \$50,000)(0.48)$$
$$= \$5,000 + \$5,500 + \$96,000$$
$$= \$106,500$$

where t = income tax

Example 7-2
A corporation realized an operating revenue of \$700,000 for the year while incurring operating costs of \$660,000. Assuming no other deductions, determine its taxable income and total income tax for the year.

Solution:
Since there are no deductions other than the above costs, taxable income = $G = R - C = 700,000 - 660,000 = \$40,000$. Then,

$$t = (\$25,000)\ 0.20 + (\$40,000 - 25,000)\ (0.22)$$
$$= \$8,300$$

COMBINING FEDERAL, STATE, AND MUNICIPAL INCOME TAXES INTO A SINGLE EFFECTIVE TAX RATE

Most states and a few municipalities levy a tax on corporate income. These taxes tend to be much lower than federal taxes yet must not be neglected when performing engineering-economic studies.

It is usually convenient to work with a single composite rate which effectively combines federal, state, and municipal rates. This composite rate is determined most often by simply taking the previous year's total tax bill and dividing it by total net profits. For very small corporations, this rate may approach the lower limit of 20%, while most corporations have a rate that may be nearly 50%. The common rule of thumb in large corporations is that a particular project's tax bill will be 50% of the net profit.

INVESTMENT CREDIT

The investment credit system for reducing taxes was devised in order to encourage companies to expand.[1] This credit applies to most machinery and equipment and does not apply to buildings and land.[2] Certain building equipment items such as elevators, escalators, and air conditioners are included. An appropriate rate depends upon the life of the qualifying property. Table 7-2 exhibits this schedule based on 1977 tax laws, where n equals the life of the project.

TABLE 7-2   Investment Credit Schedule

	$n < 3$	$3 \leqq n < 5$	$5 \leqq n < 7$	$7 \leqq n$
Industrials	0.00%	3.33%	6.67%	10.00%
Utilities	0.00	3.33	6.67	10.00

Furthermore, effective 1977, industrials can get an additional 1% investment credit if this is used to purchase the firm's stock for distribution to employees. The 1% must be paid to a trust, which then purchases the stock for the employees.

The amount of reduction may not exceed the calculated tax shown before this credit is taken. It also may not exceed $25,000 plus 50% of the tax liability in excess of $25,000. In analyzing the profitability of a plant, this tax relief is generally ignored.

---

[1] With some exceptions, benefits of the Investment Credit Act were suspended from September 1966 to March 1967 and from April 1969 to April 1971.
[2] For details consult an up-to-date accounting manual.

Example 7-3
A firm is to pay $800,000 for new equipment. If the firm's income tax is figured to be $44,000, what tax is actually to be paid? Assume the useful life of the equipment is 10 years. Neglect 1% additional credit for distribution of stock to employees.

Solution:

Maximum investment credit = $800,000 × 0.10 = $80,000
Limit on investment credit = $25,000 + 0.5 ($44,000 − $25,000)
                                                = $34,500
Then income tax   = $44,000 − $34,500 = $9500

Under certain circumstances the remaining $45,000 ($80,000 − $34,500) investment credit can be carried back or carried foward in the following year.

THE EFFECT OF INTEREST ON INCOME TAXES
Interest paid for borrowed funds by an individual or a corporation to carry on a profession, trade, or business is deductible from income as an expense of carrying on that activity. Therefore, the amount of funds borrowed has an effect on the amount of income tax that must be paid.

Example 7-4
Firm A has borrowed $100,000 at an annual interest rate of 9%. If the taxable income of the firm before interest payments will be $40,000, determine the firm's actual taxable income.

Solution:

$$40,000 - (0.09)(100,000) = 40,000 - 9,000 = \$31,000$$

Example 7-5
Consider another firm, B, which has a taxable income of $40,000; however, it has not borrowed any funds in order to operate. What is its actual taxable income?

Solution:
For firm B, actual taxable income remains as before, $40,000. The income tax for firm A will be

$$(0.20)(25,000) + (0.22)(31,000 - 25,000) = \$6320$$

and for firm B

$$(25,000)(0.20) + (40,000 - 25,000)(0.22) = \$8300$$

$$\text{Difference} = 8300 - 6320 = 1980$$

Thus the net cost to firm A for borrowing the money is

$$\frac{9000 - 1980}{100,000} = 0.0702, \text{ or } 7.02\%$$

TAXES ON CAPITAL GAINS AND LOSSES

A capital-gains tax is levied on profits made from the sale of capital assets (or certain noncapital assets such as land, buildings, or equipment, which are treated as if they were capital assets). If held for 1 year or less (effective 1978, based on 1977 tax law), the profit is known as a *short-term capital gain*. When sold after being held in possession for more than 1 year, the profit is known as a *long-term capital gain*. In order to provide incentive to convert unneeded property to cash, the tax rate employed on long-term capital gains is 30%.

If the aggregate of short-term and long-term activities results in a net gain, it is added in full as an item of income. It is then subjected to the normal tax rate and the surtax rate.

The tax rate on long-term capital losses, however, is not 30% but 50%. If the aggregate of short-term and long-term activities results in a net loss for a year, a firm may not deduct such a loss from current income. But the loss may be carried back 3 years and then carried forward for five subsequent years, being considered as a short-term capital loss, and offset against capital gains during that period.

Example 7-6

Ten years ago, a machine costing $100,000 and having an original salvage value of $5000 replaced a manual operation and hence saved $50,000 each year in labor costs. This machine has just been sold for $10,000. If the straight-line method was used to depreciate this machine, determine the net profit after taxes that will be realized at the end of this year. Assume an income tax rate of 50%.

Solution

Annual depreciation expense is total expenditure minus salvage value divided by useful life.

$$\frac{100,000 - 5000}{10} = \$9500 \text{ yr}$$

Hence for the last 5 years and disregarding the time value of money the net profit has been:

$$P = 50,000 - 0.50(50,000 - 9500) = \$29,750$$

At the end of this year, however, the net profit will be

$$P = 29,750 + 10,000 - 0.25(10,000 - 5000)$$
$$= 29,750 + 10,000 - 1500 = \$38,250$$

where 29,750 = normal net profit
      10,000 = actual salvage
10,000 − 5000 = capital gain
        0.25 = capital gains tax rate

On the other hand, if the firm had to pay $5000 to have the machine removed, the net profit would be as follows:

$$P = 29{,}750 - 5000 + (0.50)(9500 + 5000)$$
$$= 29{,}750 - 5000 + 7250 = \$32{,}000$$

where $7250 is the tax credit received.

7.3   Depreciation and Income Taxes

Because federal income taxes are based on gross earnings, or gross profit G, which means that most[3] costs have been deducted, the Internal Revenue Service has devoted considerable effort to controlling one of the major costs in industrial operations, that is, the cost for depreciation. The subject of depreciation costs has been covered in Chapter 6, where some of the tax regulations by the IRS have been presented.

In determining the influence of depreciation costs on income taxes, it should be clear from Equation 1-1 that depreciation costs represent a deduction from taxable gross income or gross earnings. Thus if d is the depreciation rate for the year, I is the fixed capital investment, and t is the fractional tax rate, then

$$\text{Tax credit for depreciation} = tdI \qquad \text{(7-1)}$$

As stated in Chapter 6, funds set aside for depreciation, although they represent a cost, normally go directly into the corporation treasury. Therefore, the net annual cash flow to the company after taxes, or the after-tax cash flow (ATCF), can be expressed as follows:

$$\text{ATCF} = (R - C - dI)(1 - t) + dI = (R - C)(1 - t) + tdI \qquad \text{(7-2)}$$

Since $G = R - C$ and $P = G(1 - t)$ then, by substitution

$$\text{ATCF} = G(1 - t) + tdI = P + tdI \qquad \text{(7-3)}$$

Example 7-8
An asset costs $1,100,000, lasts 5 years, and has a salvage value of $100,000 at the end of the 5 years. If this investment will realize

---

[3] Excluded are interest and depreciation, which are tax-deductible.

a yearly gross profit for the next 5 years of $500,000 and tax rate is 50%, determine via the double-declining-balance method:

a. The tax credit for depreciation for the 5 years
b. The net annual cash flow for the 5 years

Solution:
By Equation 6-11, for the first year

$$dI_1 = V\left[\frac{2}{n}\left(\frac{n-2}{n}\right)\right]^{a-1}$$

$$= 1,100,000\left[\frac{2}{5}\left(\frac{5-2}{5}\right)^0\right]$$

$$= 1,100,000\,(0.4)(0.6)^0$$

$$= \$440,000$$

Hence by Equation 7-1 the tax credit for depreciation for year 1 is

$$tdI_1 = (0.50)(440,000) = \$220,000$$

Then by Equation 7-3

$$ATCF_1 = P(1-t) + tdI = 500,000(0.50) + 220,000 = \$470,000$$
$$dI_2 = 1,100,000\,[(0.4)(0.6)^1] = \$264,000$$
$$tdI_2 = 050(264,000) = \$132,000$$
$$ATCF_2 = 500,000(0.50) + 132,000 = \$382,000$$

Finally, the remaining years are shown below:

Year	dI	tdI	$ATCF$
1	$440,000	$220,000	$470,000
2	264,000	132,000	382,000
3	158,400	79,200	329,200
4	95,040	47,520	297,520
5	57,024	28,512	278,512

Example 7-9
Consider a comparison between two alternatives, identical except for useful life. The following estimates have been made:

	Alternative A	Alternative B
Capital investment	$120,000	Same as A
Salvage value	0	Same as A
Useful life, years	30	40
Income tax rate	50%	Same as A

	Alternative A	Alternative B
· Gross profit per year	$22,000	Same as A
· Depreciation method	Straight-line	Same as A

Which alternative is more attractive?

Solution:

    In tabular form the analysis is as follows:

	Alternative A	Alternative B
· Gross profit/yr	$ 22,000	$ 22,000
Less depreciation expense	4,000	3,000
· Equals taxable income	$ 18,000	$ 19,000
Less income tax @ 50%	9,000	9,500
· Equals net profit	$ 9,000	$ 9,500

    At first inspection one would be tempted to choose the alternative with greater "reported" net profit. Resisting this temptation, we might add depreciation expense and net profit to find the after-tax cash flow, which is $13,000 ($4000 + $9000) for alternative A and $12,500 ($3000 + $9500) for alternative B. This result is something of a surprise in the light of the above analysis. The tricky result is due to depreciation and income taxes.

    One may argue, however, that B has the advantage of longer life which could be expressed as an annual equivalent of savings due to longer life, using the capital-recovery factor (Equation 5-8):

$$B\text{'s advantage} = \$120,000 \left[\frac{i(1 + i)^{n_A}}{(1 + i)^{n_A} - 1} - \frac{i(1 + i)^{n_B}}{(1 + i)^{n_B} - 1} \right]$$

$$= \$120,000 \left[\frac{0.10(1 + 0.10)^{30}}{(1 + 0.10)^{20} - 1} - \frac{0.10(1 + 0.10)^{40}}{(1 + 0.10)^{30} - 1} \right]$$

$$= \$120,000 \, [0.10608 - 0.10226]$$

$$= \$458/\text{yr in savings}$$

For alternative A, however, there is an advantage of lower income tax because of greater depreciation.

$$A\text{'s advantage} = \$120,000 \left[\frac{1}{30} - \frac{1}{40} \right] (t)$$

$$= \$120,000 \left[\frac{1}{30} - \frac{1}{40} \right] (0.50) \quad (50\% \text{ tax rate})$$

$$= \$500/\text{yr in savings}$$

Summary

The specific income tax regulations of the government occupy many times the volume of this entire book. Thorough treatment involving examples and interpretations would require still more space. The detail provided here is obviously not intended for actual tax liability; however, it satisfies the needs of the feasibility study by permitting computation of estimated income tax liability.

The types of taxes usually encountered are property, excise, and income. The property taxes are usually levied by local governments and range between 1 to 5% of assessed valuation. Excise taxes are levied by state and federal governments (on gasoline, alcoholic beverages, cigarettes) and usually are referred to as indirect taxes since they are passed on to the consumer. Income taxes are a levy on the firm's net earning; they tax the difference between the income derived from and expense incurred in business activity. On the average, state income taxes may range from 0 to 5% of net earnings while the federal income tax breaks down as follows:

	Taxable income	*Percent*
·	Up to $25,000	20.0
·	$25,000 to $50,000	22.0
·	$50,000 and above	48.0

Investment credit encourages companies to expand. This credit applies to machinery and equipment and does not apply to buildings and land. For new or used assets that are acquired and will last at least 7 years, a company's tax liability may be reduced by up to 10% of the investment. For less than 7 years, Table 7-2 can be consulted.

A capital-gains tax is levied on profits made from the sale of capital assets or property, such as land, buildings, or equipment. When they are sold after being held in possession for more than 1 year, the profit is known as a long-term capital gain. The tax rate on long-term capital gains is 30%. On long-term capital losses, however, it is not 30% but 50%. Capital losses must be offset against capital gains either in the current period or in the carry-over period.

Depreciation costs represent a deduction from taxable gross income. They go directly into the corporation's treasury, and are known as a tax credit which can be expressed as

$$\text{Tax credit for depreciation} = tdI$$

where I = capital investment
  t = fractional tax rate
  d = depreciation rate for the year

The net cash flow after taxes, which is tax credit plus net profit, can be expressed as

$$ATCF = (R - C - dI)(1 = t) + dI = (R - C)(1 - t) + (tdI)$$
$$= G(1 - t) + tdI = P + tdI$$

where R = revenue from sales or operation
  C = cost of sales or operation
  G = gross income
  P = net income

As can be seen, income taxes exert a major influence on a decision regarding whether or not a project will even be considered.

Problems

1. A corporation's taxable income for next year is estimated at $500,000. It is considering an activity for next year which it is estimated will result in an additional taxable income of $50,000. Calculate the amount of income tax it will be paying next year.
2. The corporation described in problem 1 has undertaken a new activity, but instead of resulting in an increase of $50,000 in taxable income as estimated, the activity has resulted in a decrease in taxable income of $40,000. Calculate the amount of income tax the corporation will be paying.
3. Suppose an asset purchased for $7000 has a life of 3 years and a salvage value of $1000 at the end of the 3 years. If it produces revenue of $4000 per year and is depreciated by the straight-line method, determine the net profit to the corporation each year for the next 3 years.
4. Repeat Problem 3, this time assuming that $1500 is received from the disposal of the asset at the end of the third year.
5. An outlay of $50,000 for materials-handling equipment is proposed. It is estimated that this equipment will make this operation more efficient and hence save $14,000 a year for the next 10 years. However, it will cost $5000 per year to maintain and insure this equipment. The firm elects to use the straight-line method in its depreciation accounting. Given that internal funds will be used to purchase the equipment, the salvage value is zero, and the minimum rate of return is 20%, determine whether this expenditure should be undertaken. Use a tax rate of 48%.
6. Repeat Problem 5, given that a state tax of 5% is also being levied on the gross income.
7. Let the incremental federal tax rate = 48%, and the incremental state tax rate = 5%. Calculate a single effective tax rate, given that:
   a. Federal income tax is *not* deductible in computing state income tax.
   b. Federal income tax *is* deductible.
8. A company's methods engineering department has devised an improved plant layout for existing production equipment in an existing

TAXES 157

building. An immediate outlay of $50,000 will be required to rear-range the machinery. It is estimated that the new layout will realize an additional $10,000 a year in profits for the next 10 years. Because the $50,000 outlay is not a capital expenditure, the entire amount will be treated as a current expense for accounting and income tax purposes in the year in which it is made. Given that the income tax rate is 50% and the minimum rate of return is 15%, should this expense be undertaken?

9. A corporation is considering a study to develop a new process to replace the present method of manufacturing synthetic rubber. If successful, this method is estimated to result in a savings of $300,000 during the current tax year. The study is estimated to cost $35,000 during the same tax year. If the new process is not successful, the taxable income will be $5,000,000.
   a. If the study is successful, what will be the increase in income after taxes?
   b. If the study is unsuccessful, what will be the decrease in income after taxes?

10. A corporation has a taxable income of $21,000 during a year. It is considering a product line expansion that will result in an additional income of $11,000 during next year.
   a. What is the effective income tax rate if earnings remain at $21,000?
   b. What is the effective income tax rate if the new venture is undertaken and turns out as estimated?

11. To develop a new product a corporation is considering an invest-ment of $15,000 in research and development. It is estimated that the increase in taxable income from marketing the new product in the coming year will be $60,000. Currently, the firm's taxable in-come is $30,000 per year.
   a. What will be the increase in the net income after taxes if the research and marketing program is successful?
   b. What will be the decrease if it is not successful?

12. An asset with an estimated life of 10 years and a salvage value of $5000 is purchased for $60,000. The firm's effective tax rate is 50% and the minimum rate of return is 10%. The gross profit from the asset before depreciation and taxes and will be $8500 per year. Calculate the net profit using the straight-line and the sum-of-the-years-digits methods of depreciation. Should this asset be pur-chased?

13. A proposed capital investment for an existing chemical plant is $15,000,000. Annual property taxes amount to 1% of the fixed cap-ital investment, and state income taxes are 5% of gross income. The net income per year after all taxes is $1,500,000, and the federal income tax rate is 48% of gross income. If the same plant had been constructed at a location where property taxes were 3% and state income taxes were 3.2%, what would be the yearly income after taxes, assuming all other cost factors are unchanged?

14. An asset is being considered whose cost, useful life, salvage value, and annual operating expense, respectively, are estimated at $15,000, 10 years, zero, and $1000. The asset will be depreciated by the straight-line method. The effective income tax rate is 48%. Determine the after-tax cash flow if:
     a. The investment is made from internal funds.
     b. The investment is borrowed at 8% with repayment of principal and interest in 10 equal annual amounts.
     c. Same as b, except repayment of interest is made at the end of each period and the loan principal repaid at the end of 10 years.
15. A firm has $30,000 available for investment. Three possible alternatives have been suggested, and they are considered to be mutually exclusive (one of the three or none). Alternative *A* and alternative *B* differ only in the method of depreciation used in the calculation of their after-tax cash flows. Alternative *A* requires the double-declining-balance method while alternative *B* requires the straight-line method. Alternative *C* is somewhat different from *A* and *B* in that it requires an investment of $50,000. Since the firm has only $30,000 available it must borrow the additional $20,000 required at an annual interest rate of 8%. This alternative has a useful life of 5 years, similar to *A* and *B*, but the estimated salvage value at the end of its useful life is expected to be $25,000 (zero for *A* and *B*). The net before-tax cash flows for all three alternatives are presented in Table 7-3. If the effective tax rate is 48% and the minimum rate of return is 10%, which alternative should be chosen? Use DCF method.

TABLE 7-3   Before-Tax Cash Flow

End of Year	Alternative *A*	Alternative *B*	Alternative *C*
1	$10,000	$10,000	$12,000
2	10,000	10,000	12,000
3	10,000	10,000	12,000
4	10,000	10,000	12,000
5	10,000	10,000	12,000

16. An investment proposal is described by Table 7-4.

TABLE 7-4

	Year						
	1	2	3	4	5	6	7
Gross income	$ 8000	16,000	20,000	20,000	20,000	20,000	20,000
Investment	14,000	10,000	0	0	0	0	0
Operating cost	2000	3000	4000	5000	6000	7000	8000
Depreciation charge	8000	8000	8000	8000	8000	8000	8000

    a. Find the ROI before and after taxes if *t* is 48%.
    b. Find the before- and after-tax DCF.

17. In Table 7-5, assume investment credit is in effect and show the investment credit rate, if any, which applies.

TABLE 7-5

Company	Item Purchased	Useful Life, yr
a. New Jersey Bell	heavy duty vehicles	7
b. Sears, Roebuck	land for future use	
c. Mobil Oil	computer equipment	5
d. General Motors	fabricating equipment	3
e. American Airlines	office building	40
f. Allied Chemical	plant equipment	20
g. Consolidated Edison	generating facilities	30

18. Two proposals for additional machinery for a certain manufacturing operation are under consideration. Alternative *A* is to do nothing and continue operating as is; alternatives *B* and *C* are the two possible plans for change. The information in Table 7-6 is given. Which alternative should be chosen if the minimum rate of return is 10% after income taxes? Assume straight-line depreciation for tax purposes. Would your answer change if any one of the other methods of depreciation were employed?

TABLE 7-6

	Alternative *A*	Alternative *B*	Alternative *C*
Fixed investment	none	$20,000	$60,000
Useful life, yr	———	10	20
Annual cost for labor and extras	$40,000	$33,000	$25,000
Annual property taxes, insurance and maintenance costs	$ 4,000	$ 6,000	$10,000

19. An investment of $150,000 in a certain income property is under consideration: $90,000 is for land and $60,000 for a building which has an estimated remaining life of 15 years. It is estimated that the building can be rented for $20,000 per year. Although the building will be worthless at the end of the 15 years, it is estimated that the land can be sold for $170,000. Compute the prospective return on investment after taxes for the first and fifteenth year assuming the straight-line method of depreciation is employed. Use a 48% tax rate.

Project Planning and Cost Control

8

A project does not usually end with a feasibility analysis, that is, with the prediction of investment and working-capital costs and the measuring of these against profits realized. Projects that have been evaluated and found economically sound must then be carried out. Plants, offices, schools, amusement parks, ships, airports, bridges, etc., must be built. Planning and scheduling their erection and controlling the costs are very essential. Many excellent, economically attractive projects have been ruined by unsound planning and inadequate control of costs.

In this chapter the term *project* is used to signify the accomplishment of a number of events and activities in order to reach an objective. For example, a project might be getting a college degree, which requires choosing a college, taking a series of pertinent courses, passing a series of examinations, and so on, in order to be graduated. Another example of a project might be the introduction of a new product to the market, which requires advertising, a sales force, packaging experts, and so on.

8.1 Project Planning and Scheduling

The central focus of a project as a whole is planning the important activities and giving close attention to how the workings of a project mesh together to achieve the total end result. Which activities are dependent

160

on the execution and completion of other activities? Which activities can proceed independently or simultaneously with other activities? The very nature of one-time projects requires that the planning of events and the scheduling of performance must be done together; they are interdependent.

The most widely used technique for project planning and scheduling is the *bar chart*. This chart consists of a scale divided into units of time (days, weeks, months) across the top or bottom and a listing of the project elements down the left hand side. Open bars or double lines are used to indicate the schedule and status of each element in relation to a time scale. The bar chart shows a sequence of steps necessary to complete a given project, together with the time available for completion, and provides a summary reporting technique in terms of the total job. Figure 8-1 represents a typical bar chart with the elements of a project (activities A to J in this case) listed on the left-hand side, and the units of time (workweeks) as shown at the top. Work accomplished is indicated by filling in the bar or the double lines, as shown in Figure 8-2. The weeks are usually subdivided into 5 or 7 days, whereas months are usually subdivided into weeks.

A project-planning chart is usually prepared as follows:

1. The project is broken down into elements or activities to be scheduled.
2. These are then sequenced.
3. Duration times for each element or activity are estimated.
4. Elements of activities are listed down the left-hand side in sequence of time, considering those which are to be performed sequentially as well as those which can be performed simultaneously. If project com-

Figure 8-1

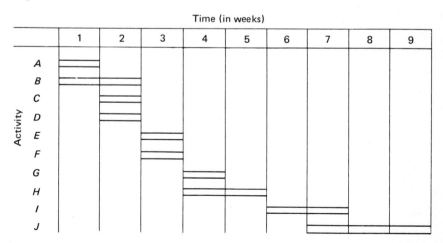

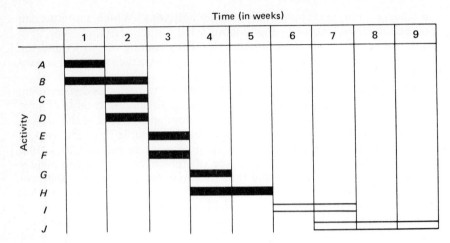

Figure 8-2

pletion date is available, the elements or activities can be sequenced by working backward from the completion date.

The following example will illustrate the construction of a bar chart.

Example 8-1
Consider building a livable house as a project. Given this limited information, prepare a bar chart.

Solution:
The project can be broken down into 14 activities, as shown below. The order or sequence of activities is not essential at this time.

- Excavation
- Foundation
- Roof
- Exterior plumbing
- Interior plumbing
- Flooring
- Wallboard
- Exterior painting
- Interior painting
- Exterior siding
- Electrical work
- Exterior fixtures
- Interior fixtures
- Rough wall

Next, the list is arranged in an activity sequence, along with an estimated duration for each activity.

· Excavation	2 weeks
· Foundation	4
· Rough wall	8
· Roof	6
· Exterior plumbing	4
· Interior plumbing	5
· Electrical work	7
· Wallboard	8
· Flooring	4
· Interior painting	5
· Interior fixtures	6
· Exterior siding	7
· Exterior painting	9
· Exterior fixtures	2

With the above information on hand a bar chart can be constructed, as shown in Figure 8-3. Notice the activities that must be performed sequentially and those that can be performed simultaneously. As can be seen, the project can be completed in 42 weeks.

The primary advantage of the bar chart is that the plan, schedule, and progress of the project can all be portrayed graphically together. The progress of the project can be monitored by filling in the bars of the chart, as was shown in Figure 8-2. It is particularly effective in showing the status of the project activities and identifying the activities that are behind or ahead of schedule.

The bar chart, however, provides no means of assessing the impact of an activity when it is behind or ahead of schedule. The interrelationships between the activities are not always clear because the chart cannot easily portray them. It shows the earliest time that each activity can begin and end, but it does not show the latest time that each activity can begin in order that its completion time does not interfere with the start of succeeding activities. Basically, it does not show the crucial information about precedence requirements. For that, network diagrams are more useful.

8.2   Network Diagrams and Their Advantage

Network diagrams represent projects in terms of the interrelationships among critical project elements. These pictorial displays are composed of connected arrows that describe relationships between activities. Activities, as previously defined, are jobs and tasks, including administrative tasks, that must be performed to accomplish the project's objectives. The

Figure 8-3

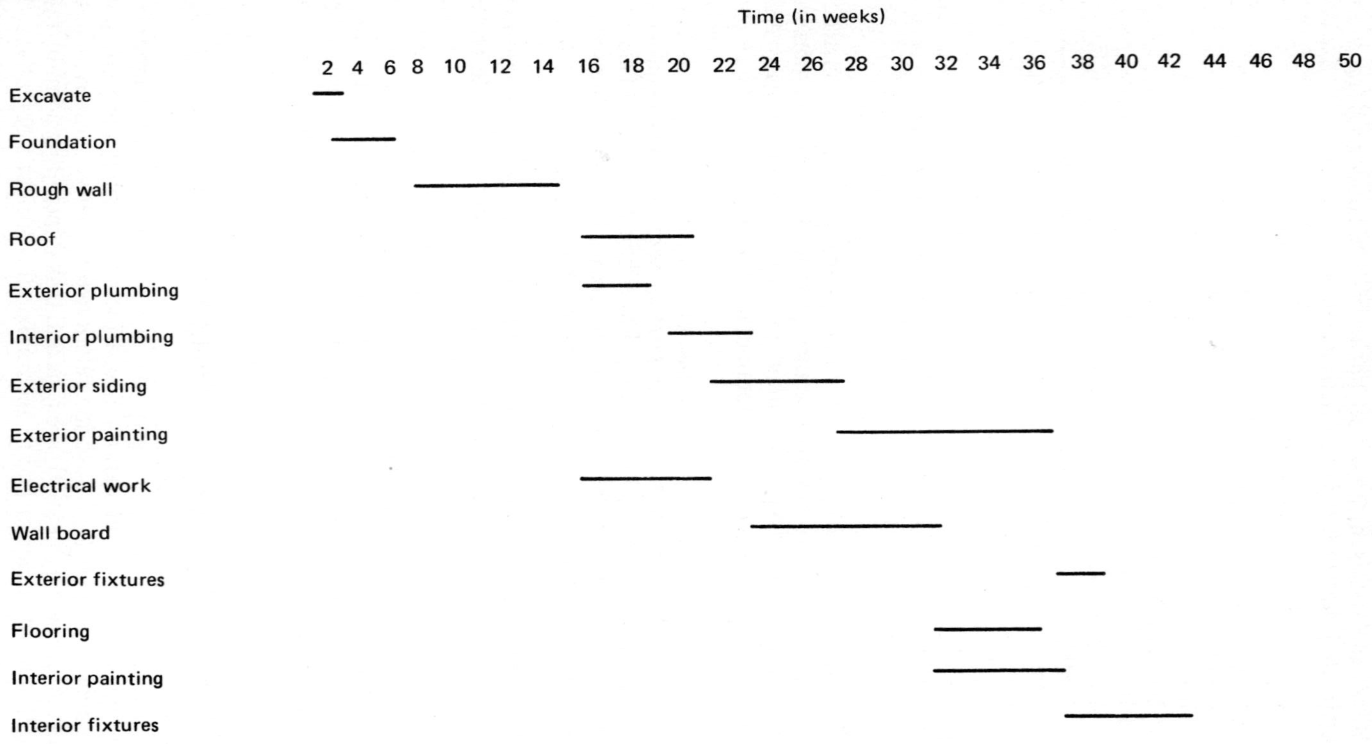
Time (in weeks)
2 4 6 8 10 12 14 16 18 20 22 24 26 28 30 32 34 36 38 40 42 44 46 48 50
Excavate
Foundation
Rough wall
Roof
Exterior plumbing
Interior plumbing
Exterior siding
Exterior painting
Electrical work
Wall board
Exterior fixtures
Flooring
Interior painting
Interior fixtures

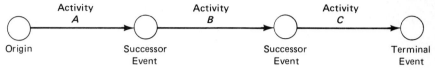

Figure 8-4

beginning and ending of an activity are indicated by numbers inside circles or squares. These circled or squared numbers are called *events,* which represent particular points or instances in time. Events do not consume resources; only the activities leading up to events do so.

The network diagram is constructed by drawing direct lines and circles in the sequence in which the activities and events are to be accomplished. The network begins at an *origin,* which represents the start of a project and from which lines are drawn to represent activities. These lines terminate with an arrow and a circle or square representing an event, which may represent completion of a project element or activity. All succeeding activities, that is, activities to be performed next, are then added by drawing a direct line from the previous event. Figure 8-4 represents a simple network diagram having three activities, *A, B,* and *C.* A *sink* or *terminal* event is the event which corresponds to the completion of the planned project and to which all the activities lead. A network diagram may terminate with one or more events, such as shown in Figure 8-5.

The progress from one event to the next requires that an activity be performed. Each activity begins and ends with an event starting from the *predecessor event* (at the tail of the arrow) to the *successor event* (at the head of the arrow). Activities normally flow from left to right throughout the network.

Two activities with a predecessor-successor relationship are called *sequential activities.* The start of the successor activity depends upon the

Figure 8-5

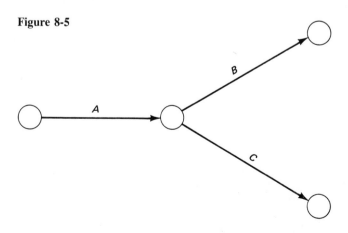

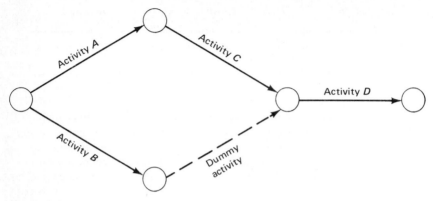

Figure 8-6

completion of the predecessor activity. Activities performed concurrently must be independent of one another. Often, however, activities independent of one another cannot be performed concurrently and must be performed in sequence—for instance, taking a prerequisite course before some other course can be taken (both of which are part of getting a college degree). In such cases, they are joined by an activity called a *dummy activity* (represented by a dashed line). Dummy activities show precedence relationships only; they do not represent real activities. Independent activities may have a common predecessor event or a common successor event, but not both. Figure 8-6 illustrates this concept.

To illustrate the development of a network diagram, let us consider a project made up of three tasks, designated *A, B,* and *C*. Task *B* must be completed before *C* can start. Task *A* is not dependent upon *B* and *C* but both *A* and *C* must be completed before the project is considered finished. This arrangement with lines indicating the tasks (activities) is shown in Figure 8-7. Events 1 and 3 are origin and terminal events, respectively, representing the start and completion of the project.

Figure 8-7

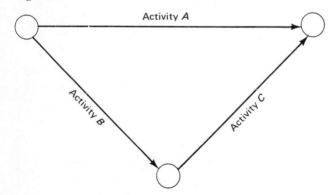

Only a few practical guidelines can be given for general use in preparing network diagrams. Obviously, if the network is to serve as an adequate plan, it must contain sufficient detail for scheduling the project and measuring progress versus the plan. But what is sufficient detail? Planners often become obsessed with incorporating the smallest details in order that nothing is left out, generating a network diagram resembling a map of the United States. The correct procedure is to consider carefully which activities are required, which ones are not clearly defined, which ones are not essential, and how the activities interrelate. Activities should represent efforts requiring 4 to 6 weeks to complete.

Example 8-2

Consider building the house in Example 8-1. The breakdown and sequence of activities that has been developed can now be transformed into a network diagram, as shown in Figure 8-8. The constraint between events 5 and 8, denoted as dummy activity 5-8, is shown so that the activities "exterior plumbing" and "exterior siding" will not have common predecessor and successor events. Dummy activity 11-12 is used for the same reason. The dummy activities clearly indicate that the exterior plumbing must be completed before exterior painting can begin and the flooring must obviously be completed before the fixtures are installed.

Example 8-3

Consider a project involving the replacement of a motor on an existing pump. The activities involved are the following:
A. Obtain a new motor.
B. Dismantle the pump.
C. Replace worn wiring.
D. Install the replacement motor.
E. Test the pump.

These activities might be presented by the network diagram shown in Figure 8-9. However, in carrying out this job, it is possible to replace worn wiring as soon as the pump is dismantled, and this activity does not have to wait for the replacement motor to arrive. But the network shown in Figure 8-9 restricts the start of activity C (replace worn wiring) until both activity A (obtain replacement motor) and activity B (dismantle the pump) have been completed. To overcome this difficulty a dummy activity is added, as shown in Figure 8-10.

Example 8-4

Consider a project involving activities A, B, C, and D. Suppose D is dependent on the completion of B and C and on the completion of the *first half* of A. Completing the second half of A is independent of B, C, and D. Diagram this situation.

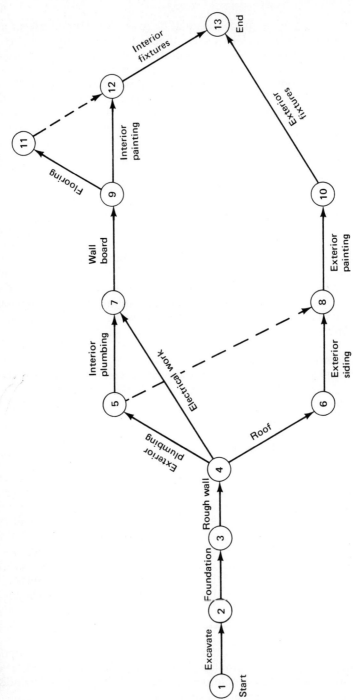

Figure 8-8

168

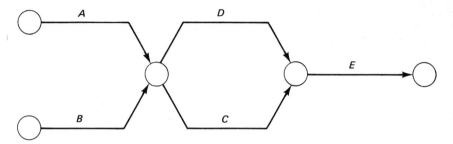

Figure 8-9

Solution:
　　One might diagram the above situation as shown in Figure 8-11. However, Figure 8-12 represents a correct network diagram incorporating a dummy activity.

Example 8-5
　　Consider a project involving a study to determine sex differences in job satisfaction among office managers. The following activities are specified:
A. Plan survey.
B. Hire researchers.
C. Design questionnaire to be used.
D. Select managers to be sampled.
E. Print questionnaire.
F. Train researchers.
G. Administer questionnaires to subjects.
H. Analyze results.
I. Publish findings.

Prepare a network diagram that will depict the above flow of work.

Figure 8-10

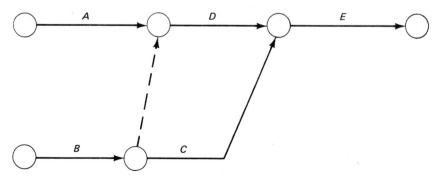

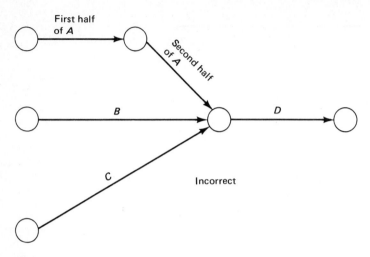

Figure 8-11

Solution:
       This project is networked as shown in Figure 8-13 with the necessary dummy activities.

8.3   Analysis of Network Diagrams

The project network diagram displays the activities, events, and constraints, as well as specifying the objective of a project. However, for a

Figure 8-12

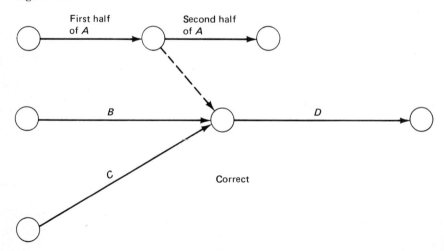

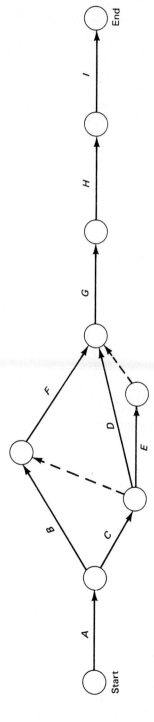

Figure 8-13

network diagram to be useful for planning and controlling the project, time estimates must be provided for the various activities involved so that a project may meet a deadline.

Hence, the next step is to estimate the time required for each of the activities. These times are used to calculate two basic quantities for each event, namely, its *earliest time* and its *latest time*. The earliest time for an event is the length of the longest path from the origin to the event, that is, the earliest time at which the end event can occur. (The earliest time is also the shortest time required to complete the entire project.) Using this definition, the earliest times are obtained successively for the events by making a forward pass through the network, starting with the origin event and proceeding to its successor event, then to another successor event, etc., until the final or terminal event is reached. The length of a network path is the sum of the durations for all those activities on the path. In calculating earliest event times the initiation of a project is considered as time equal to zero. If an event has more than one predecessor event, the calculation is made for each of them, and the largest sum is selected as the earliest time for the event.

The latest time for an event is the latest time at which the event can occur relative to the timing of the terminal event without delaying the completion of the project beyond its earliest time. Latest times are obtained successively for the events by working backward through the network starting from the final events and going toward the initial event. Then, for each event, the time for its successor activity is subtracted from the latest time for its successor event. If an event has more than one successor event, the calculation is made for each, and the smallest result is used as the latest time for the event.

The *slack time* for an event is the *difference* between its latest and its earliest time. Thus, a slack time indicates how much delay in reaching the event can be tolerated without delaying the project completion.

Example 8-6

The network diagram presented in Figure 8-13 (Example 8-5) is shown again in Figure 8-14 with estimated duration times, in months. Determine the earliest and latest time for completion of the project as well as slack time.

Solution:

As stated above, event 1 is assumed to occur at time 0. Therefore, event 2 can occur after 2 months (which is the sum of the earliest start of activity 1–2 added to the duration of the activity). Similarly, the earliest that event 3 can occur (1–2–3) is $2 + 2 = 4$ months after the start of the project. Event 4 is constrained by two activities (1–2–4 and 1–2–3–4), and the earliest at which it can occur is the latest of the three times determined by these activities. 1–2–4 can be completed in 5 months, while 1–2–3–4 can be completed in 4 months. It should be recognized that dummy activities have zero

TABLE 8-1 Calculation of Earliest Times for Example 8-6

Event	Immediately Preceding Event	Earliest Time	+	Activity Time	= Maximum Earliest Time
1	———	0		———	0
2	1	0	+	2	2
3	1–2	2	+	2	4
4	1–2	2	+	3	5
	1–2–3	2+2	+	0	4
5	1–2–3	4	+	1	5
6	1–2–4	5	+	1	6
	1–2–3	4	+	3	7
	1–2–3–4	4	+	1	5
	1–2–3–5	5	+	0	5
7	1–2–4–6	6	+	1	7.
	1–2–3–6	7	+	1	8
	1–2–3–4–6	5	+	1	6
	1–2–3–5–6	5	+	1	6
8	1–2–4–6–7	7	+	3	10
	1–2–3–6–7	8	+	3	11
	1–2–3–4–6–7	6	+	3	9
	1–2–3–5–6–7	6	+	3	9
9	1–2–4–6–7–8	10	+	3	13
	1–2–3–6–7–8	11	+	3	⎴14⎵
	1–2–3–4–6–7–8	9	+	3	12
	1–2–3–5–6–7–8	9	+	3	12

duration time. Hence, the earliest time that event 4 can be completed is 5 months, since it is the latest of the two duration times for this event. Event 5 (1–2–3–5) occurs after 5 months while event 6 is constrained by 4 activities, 1–2–4–6, 1–2–3–6, 1–2–3–4–6, and 1–2–3–5–6 occurring after 6 months, 7 months, 5 months, and 5 months, respectively. Hence the earliest time for event 6 is 7 months. This process can be continued, as shown in Table 8-1, to yield the earliest project completion time of 14 months.

The latest time for the events is computed by making a backward pass through the events starting from the time of completion of the project, or 14 months. If several activities are starting from the event, the least of the latest starting times of these determines the latest time at which the event must occur.

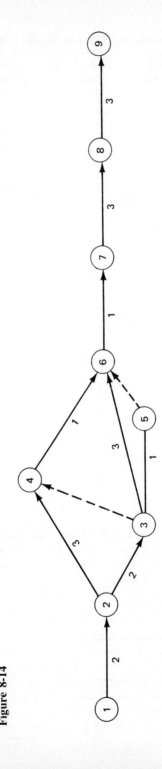

Figure 8-14

TABLE 8-2   Calculation of Latest Times for Example 8-6

Event	Immediately Following Event	Latest Time	_	Activity Time	= Minimum Latest Time
9	———		–		14
8	9	14	–	3	11
7	9–8	11	–	3	8
6	9–8–7	8	–	1	7
5	9–8–7–6	7	–	0	7
4	9–8–7–6	7	–	1	6
3	9–8–7–6	7	–	3	4
	9–8–7–6–5	7	–	1	6
	9–8–7–6–4	6	–	0	6
2	9–8–7–6–4	6	–	3	3
	9–8–7–6–3	4	–	2	2
	9–8–7–6–4–3	6	–	2	4
	9–8–7–6–5–3	6	–	2	4
1	9–8–7–6–4–2	3	–	2	1
	9–8–7–6–3–2	2	–	2	0
	9–8–7–6–4–3–2	4	–	2	2
	9–8–7–6–5–3–2	4	–	2	2

Hence, referring to Figure 8-14, the latest time for event 8 is 14 − 3 = 11 months (which is the latest time of the end event less the activity duration). The latest times for events 7 and 6 must therefore be 11 − 3 = 8 months and 8 − 1 = 7 months, respectively. This process is continued as shown in Table 8-2.

Figure 8-15 shows the final network diagram with all the important results from both tables entered. In practice, the results are normally entered on the diagram as they are calculated.

Slack times for events 1 through 9 are 0, 0, 0, 2, 2, 0, 0, 0, and 0, respectively. The events having identical earliest and latest times, that is, those having slack time equal to zero, are called *critical,* in the sense that there is no flexibility in the time at which they occur. In Figure 8-15, events 1, 2, 3, 6, 7, and 8 are critical; they must be completed independently at the shown times (0, 2, 4, 7, 8, and 11 months, respectively) or the overall project completion will be delayed. On the other hand, where the earliest and latest event times are not equal (events 4 and 5), there is some flexibility between the possible earliest time and the necessary

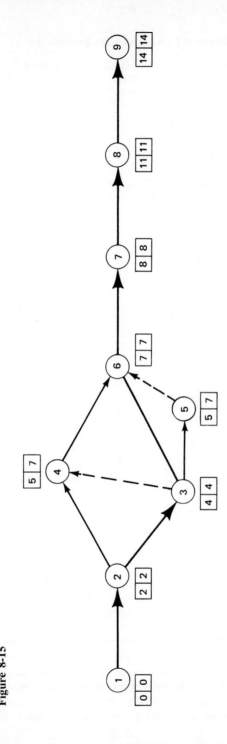

Figure 8-15

latest time of the event. Event 4, for example, is not critical; it is possible to delay completion from 5 months to 7 months (but not beyond).

The seven critical events form a *critical path,* which can be defined as the longest network path on which events have zero slack time. The critical path is shown in Figure 8-15 by the heavier line (1-2-3-6-7-8-9). The method just illustrated for analyzing network diagrams is known as the critical path method (CPM).

The critical path method, in use since 1958, is a very powerful tool for project planning and scheduling. It identifies the critical and noncritical events of the project so that resources (labor and funds) from the former may be reallocated to the latter, hence permitting faster accomplishment of the project or at least preventing the project from falling behind schedule. In the real world, this is seldom possible, but the direction in which resource shifts should be made to advance the completion date can be indicated via CPM. It can reveal all the information needed to keep a project going smoothly with respect to time and expenditure. It cannot correct deficiencies in time estimates, but it can reduce their frequency by indicating a need for reassessment.

Example 8-7

Determine the critical path for the network diagram shown in Figure 8-16. The duration of activities is given in weeks.

Solution:

Calculation of earliest times is shown in Table 8-3. As can be seen, the earliest project completion time is 26 weeks.

Calculation of latest times is shown in Table 8-4.

Figure 8-17 shows in the boxes the earliest and latest times, respectively, for each event. The critical path is shown by the heavy line (1-3-6-7).

Figure 8-16

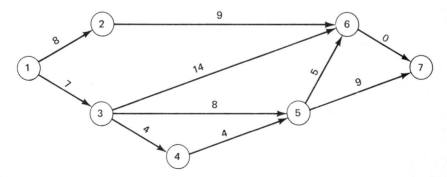

TABLE 8-3 Calculation of Earliest Times for Example 8-7

Event	Immediately Preceding Event	Earliest Time	+	Activity Time	= Maximum Earliest Time
1	——	——		——	0
2	1	0	+	8	8
3	1	0	+	7	7
4	1–3	7	+	4	11
5	1–3	7	+	8	15
	1–3–4	11	+	4	15
6	1–2	8	+	9	17
	1–3	7	+	14	21
	1–2–5	15	+	5	20
	1–3–4–5	15	+	5	20
7	1–2–6	17	+	5	22
	1–3–6	21	+	5	26
	1–3–5–6	20	+	5	25
	1–3–4–5–6	20	+	5	25
	1–3–5	15	+	9	24
	1–3–4–5	15	+	9	24

Figure 8-17

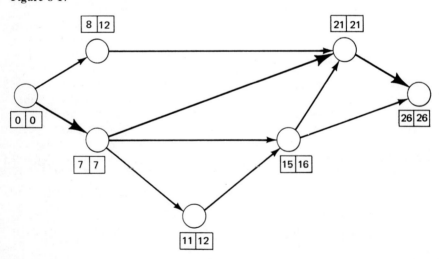

TABLE 8-4 Calculation of Latest Times for Example 8-7

Event	Immediately Following Event	Latest Time	–	Activity Time	= Minimum Latest Time
7	————		–		26
6	7	26	–	5	21
5	7–6	21	–	5	16
	7	26	–	9	17
4	7–6–5	16	–	4	12
	7–5	17	–	4	13
3	7–6	21	–	14	7
	7–6–5	16	–	8	8
	7–6–5–4	12	–	4	8
	7–5	17	–	8	9
	7–5–4	13	–	4	9
2	7–6	21	–	9	12
1	7–6–2	12	–	8	4
	7–6–3	7	–	7	0
	7–6–5–3	8	–	7	1
	7–6–5–4–3	8	–	7	1
	7–5–3	9	–	7	2
	7–5–4–3	9	–	7	2

The critical path method is very adaptable to computer programming, and the critical path can be reevaluated along the way to keep it up to date. CPM can also be done by a manual technique, as shown in Examples 8-7 and 8-8, with the break-even point at about 200 activities. For large projects involving thousands of activities, CPM can be justified only on a computer. Computer programming for network analysis is a topic too complex to be covered here, but discussions can be found in a number of intermediate texts. Several of the texts are suggested in Appendix D. It should be mentioned, however, that all major computer manufacturers provide computer programs for use on their machines. One needs to know only the duration of the activities and the sequence of events, and the computer generates the critical path. Critical activities are generally represented distinctively, and in some systems, graphic output is provided as well. If one does get involved with a large project, a hand computation on a simplified basis is recommended for a first trial in order to become completely familiar with the project and to be able to modify it to get the best network.

8.4   Project Control

Once a project has been planned, it must be controlled so that allocated resources budgeted (people and funds) are not exceeded, all activities and events tie in with each other as planned, and the project is completed as soon as possible.

Almost invariably, the use of network analysis as illustrated helps to provide information on the action necessary to achieve the project's objective. As the network diagram is being developed, decisions on changes in the logic or in the time requirements of the individual tasks will have to be made to bring the planned results in line with the objectives. Once the plan goes into action or the project has been started, a constant monitoring of results and updating of the plans must be carried out. These objectives often fail, however, because of a lack of feedback, updating, and sound project performance appraisal. Accordingly, control must be carefully planned out and introduced to ensure that the plan is adhered to or at least that deviations from the plan do not get out of hand with regard to cost and time of completion. Project control begins when the first germ of an idea for a project appears, and continues throughout the life cycle of the project.

During the execution of the project, actual performance can be monitored with the aid of network diagrams, which will provide up-to-the-minute assessments of the effect of differences between actual and expected performance. Each time the network diagram is reanalyzed, new plans and schedules may be produced which will secure achievement of the objectives or at least minimize deviation from the objectives.

As can be seen, network analysis is a powerful tool, providing information necessary for decision making through all the stages of the project up to completion. In developing a network diagram for control purposes, it is essential to include all the conditions relating to each activity so that if modification in an activity is warranted, all the related conditions can be taken into account and modified accordingly.

The construction of bar charts and related network diagrams is a function of line management; that is, only persons directly concerned with the management of a project have sufficient knowledge of the relationships and interrelationships of the various events and activities to construct a model that properly represents the project. Often, a person is more reluctant to modify a network diagram devised by others than a diagram of his or her own. Activities described as dependent often turn out to be independent in practice and can hence be undertaken simultaneously. The project leader or project manager is more likely to screen out such situations than someone not directly associated with the project. A special operations research group can, however, be assigned to take on the responsibility of routine updating of the network diagrams, using the feedback provided by the project leader or project manager.

The proper person to estimate activity durations is the person who directly supervises that activity. The project leader or project manager should review these estimates, however, since there is a tendency to be conservative and insert liberal fudge factors. A supervisor can easily become a hero or heroine by giving liberal estimates of activity durations then finishing ahead of schedule. Such practice is a poor form of project planning or estimating. Overplanning is just as bad as underplanning since the extra resources that had to be allocated to the project could have been used on another project, which may have had to be cancelled because of a lack of funds.

Once the draft of the network has been prepared and the schedule of activities defined, overall review by the project team, project leader, or project manager is a must. Logical relationships should be checked, to ensure that they are correct and that they have been correctly represented in the network diagram.

The level and sophistication of the control is dependent on the complexity of the project. A simple project may require only a few indicators to determine its progress and performance as related to plan and allocated budget. On the other hand, a major project may require a massive control system that will identify and report many conditions that reflect its progress. Regardless of the level of sophistication, a project control system must possess the following properties:

1. It must be understood by those who use it and obtain feedback from it.
2. It must anticipate and respond to any deviations so that corrective action can be taken before major deviation actually occurs.
3. It must be flexible enough to adjust rapidly to any changes in organizational environment.
4. It should be expressed in words, pictures, graphs, or tables which permit a visual display that is easy to read and understand.
5. It must be economical; the benefit that will be realized from it must exceed the cost of implementation plus its maintenance expense.

In addition to the above five properties, it is important to determine who provides the information that is used for the control. Basically, it should be the personnel in charge of the actual execution of the activities involved. Thus, the project engineer or technologist will report quantitative and qualitative information back to the project leader, who in turn may report to a project manager. The project manager, however, would require greater details of what action is to be taken to keep any deviations of event completion times in line with the schedule. Often a project manager may suggest to senior management the need to alter objectives (events completion times) or may even demand additional funds to carry out the objectives in the specified time period.

Another requirement of a control system is to define the frequency of progress reports. For long-term projects, monthly reporting is usually adequate, though more frequent special reports on critical and noncritical paths may be needed. For short-term projects, on the other hand, those lasting several weeks or days, daily or hourly feedback is usually required. The frequency of reporting largely depends on the judgment of the project manager and of the senior managers involved in the implementation.

PROJECT EVALUATION AND STATUS REPORTS

As has been shown in the preceding sections, the bar chart and the network diagram along with its critical path are powerful tools for guiding and controlling the tempo and direction of a project, especially the latter. These are excellent for setting target dates and for calling attention to areas threatening timely job completion. As the project progresses, if there is little or no difference between the planned and actual results, the bar chart or the network diagram are merely marked with the results to date. Marking is usually done on the chart or network itself, where, in the case of the chart, the bars are filled in as shown in Figure 8-2, or, in the case of the network diagram, dashed lines as shown in Figure 8-18, or with check-off marks as shown in Figure 8-19. Regardless of the method employed, the chart or network should always be time-scaled, preferably calendar scale, as shown in Figure 8-18 and 8-19. Presentations are very effective, and they make it very easy to spot deviations from plan.

One major problem with using the above concept as the only method for control is the inability to effectively monitor project performance as a function of expenditure or the costs incurred, since both bar charts and network diagrams consider only time, not cost, as a basis. Although individual activities are usually budgeted along with the project as a total, relating costs to progress as a percentage of completion while carrying out the activities is very difficult. Computers can help in monitoring but cannot eliminate the problem of excessive paperwork.

In response to this need, the author developed the project perform-

Figure 8-18

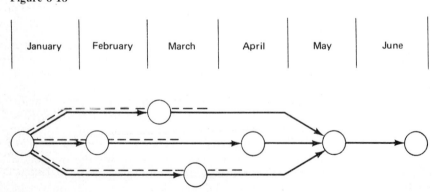

| January | February | March | April | May | June |

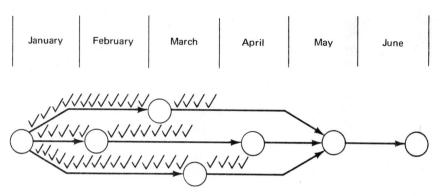

Figure 8-19

ance valuation technique (PPET),[1] which provides integrated evaluations of progress of any project to date, and the progress outlook. PPET employs the concept of benefit over cost as a means of evaluating project performance. Its utility, however, is limited to control. Bar charts and CPM should be used for planning and scheduling.

The concept considers *cost* as money allocated to a given project, that is, funds budgeted to carry out a specific program, for instance, cost budgeted for development of a new product, or money granted by a foundation to study sex differences in job satisfaction among office managers.

The *benefit*, on the other hand, is not the cash flow that will be generated upon completion of a given project, but completion of the project itself. Development of a new product so it can generate revenues upon acceptance by customers is the benefit; or completion of the above mentioned study in sex differences is the benefit so that all employees in an organization may work to their fullest capacity.

The above definitions of cost-benefit permit measurable costs to be weighed against measurable benefits, or vice versa. But how can benefit be measured objectively or quantitatively as costs accrue for a given project? Without much difficulty, as will be seen shortly.

Consider project flow as illustrated in Figure 8-20, which is a reproduction of Figure 8-8 (building a livable house). If one lets the beginning and the end of the project equal 0% to 100%, then as work on the project progresses per unit of time (week, month, quarter) towards completion, incremental benefits and incremental costs are being realized as well. Hence as the project approaches 20% completion, the money to reach this point expressed as percent of total budget allocated to the project

---

[1] Kasner, E. "Project Performance Evaluation Technique (PPET)," unpublished reports, April 1976 and December 30, 1976.

Figure 8-20

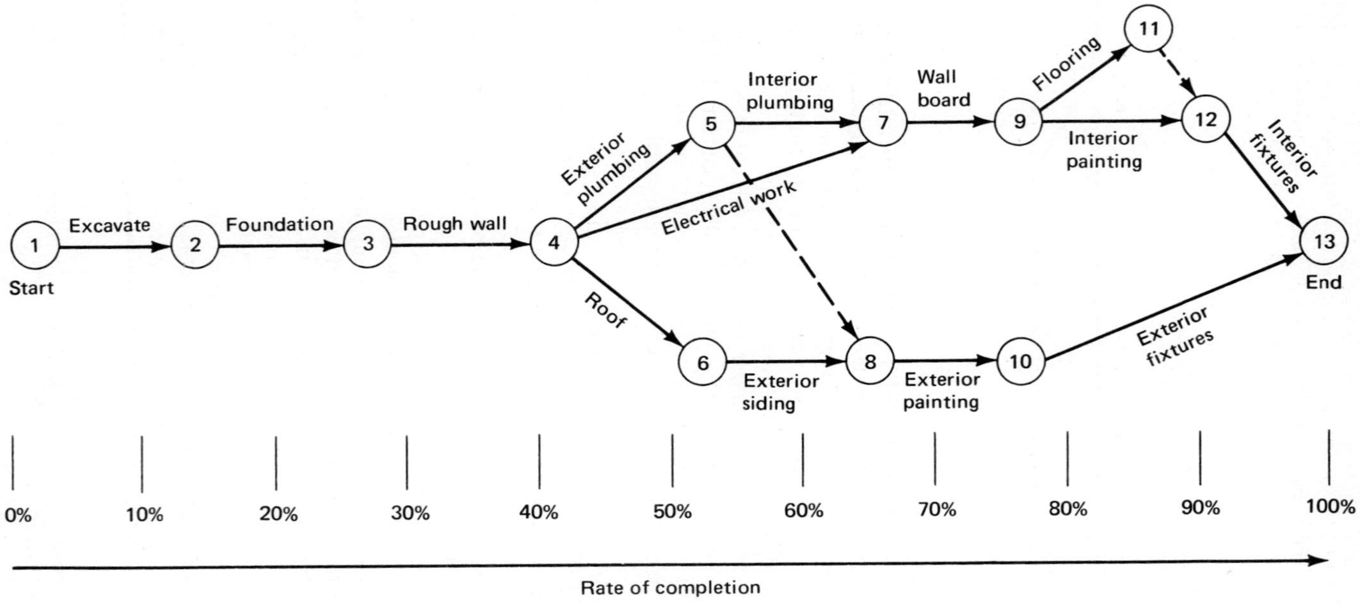
Excavate
Foundation
Rough wall
Start
1
2
3
4
Exterior plumbing
Electrical work
Roof
5
6
Interior plumbing
Exterior siding
7
8
Wall board
Exterior painting
9
10
Flooring
Interior painting
11
12
Interior fixtures
Exterior fixtures
13
End
0%
10%
20%
30%
40%
50%
60%
70%
80%
90%
100%
Rate of completion

should also be equal to 20%. At 30% completion, 30% of the money budgeted should have been spent, and so on. With this in mind, it is possible to express the benefit/cost ratio mathematically as

$$\text{benefit/cost} = \frac{\text{percent completed}}{(\text{cost to date/total budget}) \times 100} \qquad (8\text{-}1)$$

Careful inspection of the above ratio indicates that at a ratio of 1.00, the project is performing as expected; that is, the sum of the incremental benefits is equal to the sum of the incremental costs. On the other hand, below 1.00, performance is poor, or not enough money has been budgeted to the project. Similarly, above 1.00, performance is good, but too much money has been allocated to the project. Whenever the ratio is below or above 1.00, careful assessment of the project is warranted since deviation from plan is obvious.

As can be seen, the above concept considers the total budget only. Accordingly, the budgets for individual activities are needed only initially, to determine the total budget for the project, and not during the actual progress of the project. This should alleviate the problem of excessive paperwork.

It should be recognized immediately, however, that for some projects, costs and/or benefits do not accrue linearly. Hence the benefit/cost ratio may deviate considerably from 1.00 month to month. How much deviation from 1.00 may be permissible on a given project before the red flag is waved is up to the individual organization. Experience indicates that above 50% project completion a ratio of 1.00 ± 0.2 is considered par performance, and below 50% completion, a ratio of 1.00 ± 0.35. The following examples will illustrate the technique.

Example 8-8

A foundation has granted $200,000 for the study given in Example 8-5. The activities of the project are exhibited in Figure 8-21. Assess the performance of this project to date, given that the questionnaire has been administered to the subject but not analyzed, at a total cost to date of $140,000.

Solution:

We see from Figure 8-21 that the project has been 72.5% completed; hence using Equation 8-1, the benefit/cost ratio is

$$\text{benefit/cost} = \frac{72.5}{(140,000/200,000) \times 100} = 1.036$$

Hence the project is performing as expected.

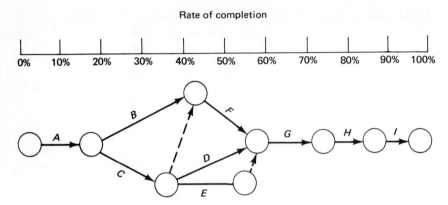

Figure 8-21

Example 8-9

Consider as a project the development of a process for a new chemical product. The research department has developed the product, which has been transferred along with the crude process to the development department. The development department's responsibility is to develop an optimum process, then introduce the process to an operating or a newly built plant such that favorable research results become profitable commercial ventures. There is a $75,000 budget for the project.

Figure 8-22 presents a crude bar chart of the flow of work. Assuming that the process has just been successfully optimized at the laboratory level and the cost of development work to date is $30,000, how is the project performing?

Solution:

We see from Figure 8-22 that 25% of the project has been completed. Hence using Equation 8-1 the benefit/cost ratio is

$$\text{benefit/cost} = \frac{25}{(30,000/75,000) \times 100} = 0.625$$

Based on our rule of thumb, the above ratio indicates poor performance. Careful performance evaluation by the project leader or project manager is warranted.

As can be seen, the PPET concept is applicable to any type of project, small or large, especially government-sponsored programs where cost-benefit analysis is essential.

For reporting project status, Tables 8-5 and 8-6 are suggested as the best formats. Both tables provide key project information, such as project

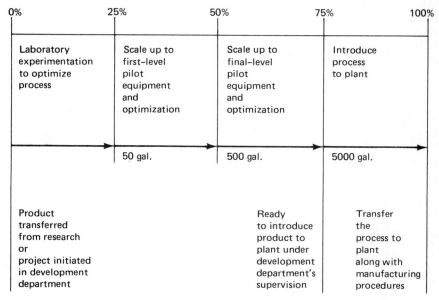

Figure 8-22

number, project name, total budget, project start date, deadline, expenditure to date, percent completion to date, benefit/cost ratio, and the name of project leader. Table 8-5 lends itself to multiproject status reporting, which can be done on one status report as shown. Table 8-6, on the other hand, illustrates single-project cumulative information (weekly, monthly, or quarterly), giving additional details. It should be noted in Table 8-6 that the completion date was extended from 12/31/1977 to 12/31/1978 and the project leader was changed as well.

This format has been used extensively by the author when employed as a project manager. It was found to be quite effective in providing the basic and essential project information.

Summary

A viable project never ends with just a feasibility analysis and a cost estimation. It is continuous with the carry-out, construction, and completion. Accordingly, sound planning, scheduling, and control of all the activities associated with carrying it out are equally essential to successful completion.

The most widely used techniques for project planning and scheduling are the bar chart and the network diagram. The network diagram can be

TABLE 8-5 Cumulative Project Status to Date

Project Number	Project Name	Total Budget	Start Date	Deadline	Expenditure to Date	% Completion to Date	Benefit/ Cost	Project Leader
001-RD-6	Installation of new power house	$135,000	1/1/75	12/31/77	$89,500	65.00	0.98	Doe
026-PM-12	High purity paint pigment	45,000	1/5/77	12/31/77	13,000	30.00	1.04	Smith
057-CR-18	Ion exchange effluent recovery	10,000	1/1/76	1/31/77	3,000	20.00	0.67	Rose

TABLE 8-6 Cumulative Project Status to Date
Project Number: 001-RD-6. Project Start Date: 1/5/77

Reporting Period	Project Name	Total Budget	Expenditure for the Period	Deadline	Expenditure to Date	% Completion to Date	Benefit/ Cost	Project Leader
1/1/77	Installation of new power house	$135,000	$0	12/31/77	$0	0	0	Smith
2/1/77	Installation of new power house	135,000	5,000	12/31/77	5,000	5.00	1.35	Smith
3/1/77	Installation of new power house	135,000	21,000	2/15/78	26,000	15.00	0.78	Smith
4/1/77	Installation of new power house	135,000	10,000	2/15/78	36,000	35.00	1.31	Rose

further analyzed using the critical path method (CPM). The bar chart shows a sequence of steps necessary to complete a given project. It does not however show the interrelationship among the activities as would a network diagram.

With regard to project evaluation and control, the above two techniques are ineffective tools. This is due to the fact that these techniques are unable to effectively monitor project performance as a function of progress and costs incurred.

In response to this need, project performance evaluation technique (PPET) was developed. It employs the concept of benefit to cost ratio. At a ratio of 1.0 (benefits realized are equal to the costs incurred) the project is performing at par. Whenever the ratio is above or below 1.0, careful assessment of the project is warranted, since deviation from plan exists.

Problems

1. A project is composed of five activities, *A, B, C, D,* and *E*. Task *A* must be done before either *C* or *D* can start; both *B* and *C* must be done before *E* can start; and both *D* and *E* must be accomplished before the project is considered finished.

    The times required (in weeks) for each of these activities are as follows:

Activity	Time required
A	5
B	9
C	2
D	6
E	4

    a. Construct a bar chart for the project.
    b. Construct a network diagram.
    c. Using the given times, determine the critical path for the project.
    d. Estimate project completion time.
2. Consider as a project the servicing of a car at a filling station. Services provided by the station include cleaning the windshield and checking the tires, battery, oil, and radiator. Sufficient personnel are available to perform all services simultaneously. List the activities in sequential order, then draw a network diagram of the project. The windshield cannot be cleaned while the hood is raised. Hint: At least 3 dummy activities are needed.
3. Given the activities and relationships listed on page 190, draw an accurate network diagram.

· Activity	Depends on activity
· A	none
· B	none
· C	A
· D	A
· E	B and C
· F	D and E

4. Given the activities and relationships listed below, draw an accurate network diagram.

· Activity	Depends on activity
· A	none
· B	A
· C	B
· D	C
· E	C
· F	D
· G	E
· H	C
· I	F and G
· J	H and I
· K	C
· L	K
· M	L
· N	C
· O	N
· P	O
· Q	M and P

5. Determine the critical path for the network diagram shown below, which depicts the flow of work to construct a simple secondary effluent-treatment plant. The activity times shown are in weeks.

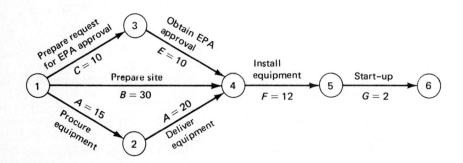

6. Consider the following project network diagram. Find the earliest time, latest time, and slack time. Identify the critical path as well.

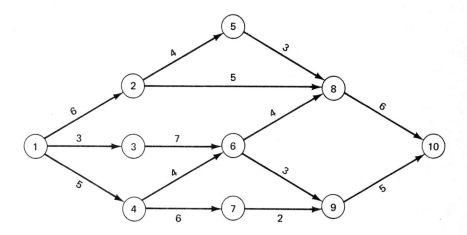

7. Convert the network diagram given in problem 6 to a bar chart.

8. A common error in the preparation of a network diagram is to place the activities in the network according to the order in which one plans to carry them out, rather than as dictated by technological predecessor-successor relationships. Consider the network diagram shown below. If the true technological requirements on activity D are that only A must precede D, and no other activity depends on activity D, how should this network diagram be drawn?

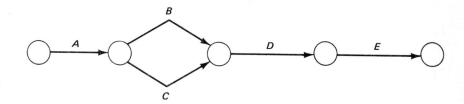

9. Consider a project to develop a new chemical and the process for it then introduce the process and product to a manufacturing facility. The precedents for each activity have been determined using historical information. The duration times are in months. (See Table 8-7.)

TABLE 8-7

Symbol	Activity	Duration	Depends on Activity
A	Product development	6	—
B	Market evaluation (samples)	5	A
C	Preliminary feasibility study	2	A
D	Transfer of product from research to process development	1	B and C
E	Securing of equipment for process development	4	B
F	Process development	6	D and E
G	Market evaluation (samples)	2	F
H	Production trial runs and adjustment to process	3	F
I	Process economics	1	G
J	Manufacturing cost estimate	1	H
K	Transfer of product and process to manufacturing	1	I and J

    a. Develop a network diagram for this project. Hint: At least three dummy activities are required.

    b. Determine the critical path and its length.

    c. What is the estimated project completion time?

10. Express the network diagram given in problem 5 in terms of incremental percent completion.

11. Express the network diagram prepared for problem 9 in terms of increment percent completion.

12. The project described in problem 9 has been given a budget of $250,000. Process development is being initiated at a cost to date of $150,000. Evaluate the performance of the project to date.

13. For the project described in problems 9 and 12, $200,000 has been spent to date, with production trials completed without any delays. Evaluate the performance of the project to date.

14. The project described in problems 9 and 12 has been completed at a cost of $325,000, or $75,000 in excess of the budget. Determine the benefit/cost ratio.

Results
Reporting

9

When sound conclusions regarding engineering feasibility have been reached through extensive effort and accurate calculations, most engineers and technologists tend to feel that their conclusions are self-evident truths. In the real world, however, this is far from fact. Conclusions must be passed on to others; the project must be approved by higher management. The presentation of the results is as essential as the conclusions themselves. The value of a feasibility or engineering study is measured to a large extent by the results provided in the written reports and the manner in which these are presented.

Engineers and technologists have the reputation of being poor writers and poor communicators. This, however, need not be the case if one recognizes that a good presentation is intended for others. The abilities, the functions, and the needs of the reader are prerequisite considerations in preparing any type of report. What the reader obtains from the report determines its usefulness. The reader must not be bored, or must it be assumed that he has the time to read a lengthy report. The reader does not want to search through unessential details to get to the crux of the report. Many presentations lose effectiveness because extensive border-line material is presented in the body of the report rather than relegated to an appendix. It is essential that the writer keep in mind the following information before writing, during writing, and upon completing a report:

· The purpose of the report
· Who the reader is
· The reader's need
· The reader's responsibility and function
· The reader's level of technical understanding
· The reader's familiarity with background information

Armed with this information, the writer is provided with cues as to what should be presented, the amount of detail required, and the method of presentation.

9.1 Types of Reports

The two types of reports used in nearly all industries can be designated as *conventional* and *unconventional*. Conventional, or formal, reports are encountered usually in research and development, engineering design, or feasibility studies among alternatives. These require considerable detail and often offer the writer much leeway in choosing the type of presentation. Unconventional, or informal, reports are usually short and straightforward, taking the form of memorandums, letters, progress updates, or survey results where only results are given without including detailed information. Figures 9-1 through 9-4 show typical forms that are and can be used for presenting summarized results of economic evaluations. Figure 9-5 presents a project summary sheet, and Figure 9-6 shows a typical progress report form for indicating the status of an ongoing project.

9.2 Organization of Reports

Although many general rules can be applied to the preparation of reports, it should be recognized that every firm, and often each department within a firm, has its own specifications and regulations. Many companies have a standard report format that must be followed for conventional reports. Figure 9-7 shows an example of a format designed by the author for the Development Department, Industrial Chemicals Division, of NL Industries, Incorporated.

As can be seen from Figure 9-7, a conventional report consists of several essentially independent parts, with each succeeding part giving greater detail on the subject in question. Most reports are accompanied by a covering letter, the purpose of which is to refer to the original instructions or developments that have made the report necessary. Such letters are usually brief but can call the reader's attention to certain important results. The writer or the writer's supervisor can also express any personal opinions in the covering letter rather than in the report

```
┌──────────────────────────────────────────────────────────────┐
│                                                                │
│                  MANUFACTURING COST ESTIMATE                   │
│                                                                │
│                                                                │
│    Estimator_____   Date_____    │
│                                                                │
│    Product _____   Capacity_____    │
│                                                                │
│    Plant Location_____   Production Rate_____  │
│                                                                │
│    Marshall & Stevens Index_____   Labor Rate_____   │
│                                                                │
│                                                                │
│                                                                │
│    Raw Materials Less Salvage Value     _____           │
│                                                                │
│    Operating Labor                      _____           │
│                                                                │
│    Utilities                            _____           │
│                                                                │
│    Operating Supervision                _____           │
│                                                                │
│    Maintenance and Repairs              _____           │
│                                                                │
│    Operating Supplies                   _____           │
│                                                                │
│    Miscellaneous                        _____           │
│                                                                │
│                                                                │
│        Direct Operating Cost                        _____ │
│                                                                │
│                                                                │
│    Depreciation                         _____           │
│                                                                │
│    Rent                                 _____           │
│                                                                │
│    Property Taxes                       _____           │
│                                                                │
│    Insurance                            _____           │
│                                                                │
│    Interest                             _____           │
│                                                                │
│        Indirect Operating Cost                      _____ │
│                                                                │
│    Overhead Cost                                    _____ │
│                                                                │
│    Administrative Cost                              _____ │
│                                                                │
│    Distribution and Marketing Cost                  _____ │
│                                                                │
│        TOTAL MANUFACTURING (OPERATING) COST         _____ │
│                                                                │
└──────────────────────────────────────────────────────────────┘
```

Figure 9-1

CAPITAL INVESTMENT ESTIMATE

Estimator_____   Date_____

Product_____   Capacity_____

Plant Location_____   M & S Index_____

Purchased Equipment (Delivered)   _____

Equipment Installation   _____

Piping, Installed   _____

Electrical, Installed   _____

Instrumentation, Installed   _____

Buildings   _____

Utilities, Installed   _____

Land   _____

Engineering, Overhead, etc.   _____

Contractor's Fee   _____

Contingency   _____

   Fixed Capital Investment   _____

Raw Materials Inventory   _____

Intermediate & Finished Product
            Inventory   _____

Accounts Receivable   _____

Cash   _____

Accounts Payable   _____

Taxes Payable   _____

   Work Capital   _____

   TOTAL CAPITAL INVESTMENT   _____

Figure 9-2

itself. Personal pronouns and an informal business style of writing may be used.

It should be mentioned that the summary is probably the most important part of a report, since it is often the only part of the report that is read. Its purpose is to give the reader the entire contents of the report, along with conclusions and recommendations, in one or two pages.

9.3 Preparation of the Report

The process of preparing a report can be divided into the following steps:

1. *Definition of subject matter, scope, and intended audience.* This part has been covered already in the introductory section of this chapter. One point should be stressed however which deals with the intended audience. One should prepare a circulation list and consider the backgrounds and interest of the people on it. This should be assessed before writing begins rather than upon completion, to avoid facing the question: "Whom should I send this to?" If the circulation list contains a nonuniform readership, from a highly technical research scientist to a sales manager (who may be ignorant of technical details), then the report must be adapted to the average technical level of the readers. The technical complexity of the report should increase from start to finish, and so satisfy the wide range of readers. The initial sections (summary, conclusions, and recommendations) should be comprehensible to all, the middle section (discussion) digestible by most, and the most technical sections placed in an appendix.

2. *Outline preparation.* The aim is to create a logic from which one can begin to write, and prepare the principal tables, graphs, and exhibits as they will actually appear in the report.

3. *First draft.* Scribbled notes and semilegible pages are converted to a neat and readable handwritten report to be typed. It is highly recommended that the typed draft be double-spaced to allow for any correction.

4. *Improvement of the first draft and final form preparation.* Upon return of the typed draft, it is highly advantageous to let it rest for a couple of days before rereading it and making any corrections. The elapsed time will generally open a fresh eye to improvements. Since making improvements can go on indefinitely, an arbitrary limit should be set on time devoted to corrections. Major changes can still be made in that time span. Quick additions, deletions, and reassembling of sections can be made quite effectively using scissors and a stapler. It should take no more than 2 to 3 days to make the necessary corrections since absolute brilliance is almost an impossibility; besides, beyond that time one begins to be tired of the whole subject and a diminishing return is realized.

ECONOMIC JUSTIFICATION PART A

Estimator _____   Date _____

Project Title _____   M & S Index _____

Project No. _____   Location _____

NET SALES:	CURRENT YEAR	2 19	3 19	4 19	5 19	5 YEAR TOTAL
		19				
1. Volume: Units _____						
2. Avg. Realized Price $						
3. NET SALES						

COSTS, EXPENSES & INCOME:

4. Direct Material						
5. Direct Labor						
6. Indirect Labor						
7. Supervision						
8. Fringe Benefits						
9. Utilities						
10. Maintenance						
11.						
12.						
13. **Gross Profit Contribution**						
14.						
15. Book Depreciation						
16. Cost Depletion						
17. **Gross Trading Margin**						
18. Distribution Expense						
19. **Net Trading Margin**						
20. Sales & Marketing Expense						
21. Research & Development						
22. Administration Expense						
23.						
24.						
25. **Operating Profit**						
26. Property Expense						
27. Start-up Costs						
28. (Gain) Loss on Disposals						
29.						
30. **BOOK PRE-TAX PROFIT**						
31. State Tax @_____%						
32. **Sub-Total** (30–31)						
33. Federal Tax @___%						
34. Tax Credits						
35. **NET INCOME** (32–33+34)						

Figure 9-3a

ECONOMIC JUSTIFICATION PART B

Estimator_____   Date_____

Project Title_____   M & S Index_____

Project No. _____   Location_____

CASH GENERATION:	CURRENT YEAR	2 19	3 19	4 19	5 19	5 YEAR TOTAL
36. **BOOK PRE-TAX PROFIT** (30)						
37. Add Back Lines (15 + 16 + 28)						
38. Accelerated Depreciation						
39. Percentage Depletion						
40. **Sub-Total** (36 + 37 − 38 − 39)						
41. State Tax @___%						
42. **Sub-Total** (40 − 41)						
43. Federal Tax @____ %						
44. Tax Credits						
45. **Sub-Total** (42 − 43 + 44)						
46. Accelerated Depreciation						
47. Percentage Depletion						
48. Disposal of Obsolete Assets						
49. Project Terminal Value						
50. **CASH GENERATION** {(45 + 46 + 47 + 48 + 49)						
51. Cum. Cash Generation						
ANNUAL INVESTMENT REQUIREMENTS:						
52. Land						
53. Buildings						
54. Machinery & Equipment						
55. Other Fixed Capital						
56. **Total Fixed Capital**						
57.						
58. Accounts Receivable						
59. Inventories						
60. Other Assets						
61. **ANNUAL INVESTMENT** {(56 + 57 + 58 + 59 + 60)						
62. Cumulative Gross Investment						
RETURN ON INVESTMENT:						
63. Cum. Book Value of Disposals						
64. Cum. Book Depreciation						
65. Net Assets (62 − 63 − 64)						
66. **RETURN ON INVESTMENT**						
67. **NET CASH FLOW** (50 − 61)						
68. **CASH PAYBACK**						

Figure 9-3b

ESTIMATED INCOME AND RETURN STATEMENT

Estimator _____   Date _____

Project Title _____   M & S Index _____

Project No. _____   Location _____

	FORECAST					ANNUAL % GROWTH
WITH APPROPRIATION REQUEST	19	19	19	19	19	
Volume: Units_____ 1						
Net Sales 3						
Manufacturing Cost (3–17)						
SG & A Expense (19–25)						
Net Income 35						
Return on Net Assets 66						

INCREMENTAL

Volume: Units_____ 1						
Net Sales 3						
Manufacturing Cost (3–17)						
SG & A Expense (19–25)						
Net Income 35						
Return on Investment 66						

PROJECT CASH FLOW

Cash Generation 50						
Depreciation 38						
Capital Expenditures 56						
Net Cash Flow 67						

PER UNIT

Price per Unit 2						
Cost per Unit (3–17)/1						
Gross Trading Margin/Unit 17/1						
% Return on Sales 35/3						

MAJOR RAW MATERIALS

A._____ Volume_____						
Unit Price						
B._____ Volume_____						
Unit Price						

Figure 9-4

Engineering Department
PROJECT SUMMARY SHEET

Project No. _____

Project Eng'r. _____

Title _____

_____

_____

_____

_____

Division or Branch _____

Plant _____

Requested by _____

_____

Scope _____

_____

_____

_____

_____

_____

_____

Date authorized _____   Approved by _____

Date Closed _____   Approved by _____

Date Final Report _____   Reference _____

Annual Saving _____

Engineering Dept. Expense _____

Total Engineering Costs _____

Figure 9-5

Engineering Department
MONTHLY PROGRESS REPORT – SUMMARY

Report No. ——————— Month ——————— Year ———————

Title ———————————————————————————————————

Project No. ———————————— Date AR Approved ————————————

Engineer in Charge ————————————

	At the Beginning of the Work	Now
Objectives	————————	————————
	————————	————————
	————————	————————
	————————	————————
	————————	————————
	————————	————————
	————————	————————
	————————	————————
Costs		
Complete Job	————————	————————
Spent Plus Committed, to Date	xxxxxxxx	————————
Uncommitted, Contingency	————————	————————
Uncommitted, Escalation	————————	————————
Schedule		
Physical Completion Date	————————	————————
Project Sign–off	————————	————————
Remarks	————————————————————	

Figure 9-6

To: Distribution   **Unit:**

From: Erick Kasner   **Unit:**

Subject: REPORT FORMAT

Project No.:   **Date:**

                            TITLE:

Summary -- A brief, to-the-point abstract of report content;
           why, what, when, where, or how. The reader should be
           able to determine from the summary what is to be
           expected in the report.

Conclusions -- Should be concise and thorough, numbered with the
           most important points first--that is, benefits (savings,
           sales increase, etc.), then cost (what it will cost
           to carry out the project and the anticipated ROI
           or DCF or payback time).

Recommendations -- As with conclusions, should be concise and
           thorough, numbered with the most important points
           first. Conclusions and recommendations are to
           be handled separately. Recommendations of hedging
           or indecision should be avoided.

Discussion -- The discussion of the items listed in Conclusions
           and Recommendations should be in the same order.
           Each topic should be logically developed to the
           level given in Conclusions and Recommendations.
           It should contain all pertinent engineering data
           and all the information supporting the conclusions.

           Small tables and graphs are to be included (if
           available) in the body of the Discussion.

Appendix -- Full page tables, graphs, and other supporting
           information should be put into an appendix,
           sequentially numbered and referred to in the
           Discussion.

Figure 9-7

5. *Proofreading of the final report.* The completely corrected report should be read and retyped for the last time, proofread very carefully for typographical errors, consistency of data, grammatical errors, spelling errors, and similar obvious mistakes, then distributed to the individuals concerned.

9.4   Presentation of the Results

How results are presented or how the report looks does not necessarily reflect its quality; it does, however, have a psychological effect on the reader. Neat reports are easier to follow and understand. A professional-looking report nearly always implies a professional job. If possible, it is suggested that the report have an attractive cover since this adds prestige as well as protecting the report in handling.

Accuracy and logic throughout any report are very essential. Facts must be presented accurately, and the reader must not be misled with incorrect or dubious statements. There is nothing wrong with making approximations or assumptions as long as their accuracy is reflected in the results.

Everything possible must be done to assure that the report is readable and free from annoyances. If reports are lengthy, they should have a table of contents. Extremely long reports should have an index.

SUBHEADINGS AND PARAGRAPHS

Effective, well-placed subheadings can improve the readability of a report. If they follow the logical sequence of the report outline, they help orient the reader and prepare him or her for the upcoming subject.

Paragraphs, on the other hand, are used to cover one general thought. Long paragraphs are a strain on the reader. Paragraphs longer than 10 to 12 typed lines will usually fail to hold the reader's attention.

TABLES

An effective use of tables can save many words, especially if quantitative results are involved. Only tables essential to the understanding of the report are to be included in the body of the report. Any tabulated data not directly related to the discussion should be located in the appendix.

Tables should have clear headings with clear abbreviations. Often it is a good idea to number the columns and lines. A table should never be presented on two pages. With modern copying machines it is possible to reduce large tables into 8 × 11-inch pages and still retain the quality (see the appendix to this chapter).

GRAPHS

In comparison with tables, which present numerical values, graphs serve to show trends or comparisons. The interpretation of results can often be simplified for the reader if the tabulated results are presented graphically as well.

Points on the graph, being calculated or based on experimental results, can be represented by large dots, small circles, squares, triangles, or some other identifying symbol. The best curve is usually drawn on the basis of the plotted points, or connecting each point with a broken line may perhaps be more appropriate. In any case, the fitted curve should not extend through the open symbols representing the data points. If extrapolation or interpolation from the available data points is called for, the uncertain region should be designated by a dotted or dashed line. Here are additional suggestions for preparation of graphs:

1. The independent or controlled variable should be plotted as the abscissa (x-axis) and the variable that is being determined or the dependent variable should be plotted as the ordinate (y-axis).
2. To prevent a cluttered appearance, sufficient space between grid elements is recommended, if graph paper is used. Ordinarily, two to four grid lines per inch are adequate.
3. The values assigned to the grids should permit easy and convenient interpolation.
4. Unless families of curves are involved, it is advisable to limit the number of curves per plot to three or less.
5. The curve should be drawn as the heaviest line on the plot, and the coordinate axes (y and x) should be heavier than the grid lines, that is, if graph paper is used.

ILLUSTRATIONS

Flow diagrams, photographs, and line drawings of equipment can be inserted in the body of the text or included in the appendix. These can be photographed and reproduced economically by a photo-offset process; pasted insertions should be avoided.

REFERENCES TO LITERATURE

The source of any published literature or unpublished reports referred to in the report should be listed at the end of the body of the report. The references are usually tabulated and numbered in alphabetical order by author's last name, although the listing is occasionally by order of appearance in the report.

ACKNOWLEDGMENT

Only significant contributions should be acknowledged at the end of the discussion section of the report. Comments and input that improved the cohesiveness of the report or contributions of data and results should be acknowledged; routine cooperation, however, should not be.

9.5　Writing Style

Clarity of writing style is an obvious requirement for any report. Many engineers and technologists submit unimpressive reports because they do not concern themselves with style, clarity, and complexity—often yielding complex reports about the simplest subject. The aim of this section is to present some hints on formal writing as well as to point out some common errors which should be avoided when reporting results of an engineering or feasibility study.[1]

The use of personal pronouns such as I, we, you, etc., should be avoided unless absolutely necessary. "It is recommended that the new product be introduced because . . ." is more effective than "We recommend that the new product be introduced because . . ."

Humorous, witty, or personal statements are out of place in engineering or technical reports, even though the writer may feel justified in making them in order to hold interest. Such tactics usually irritate and often bore the reader. A good report is made interesting through clarity of expression, skillful organization, and the significance of its contents.

Hyphens should be employed to connect words that are compounded into adjectives. Examples are "a high-pressure split," "raw-materials inventory," and "in-process cost." No hyphen appears, however, in a "a highly sensitive cost system."

Split infinitives should be avoided in engineering or technical reports. They bother and irritate many readers by misplacing the emphasis. Instead of "The engineer intended to carefully check the new system," the sentence should say, "The engineer intended to check the new system carefully."

Finally, before sitting down to write a report, one should bear in mind the following essential principles of good writing:

1. Write to express, not to impress.
2. Write the way you speak.
3. Be concise.
4. Use familiar words.
5. Put action in the verbs.
6. Gear your writing to the reader's experience.

To tie in the sections of this chapter, several engineering feasibility reports have been provided in Appendixes 9.1 through 9.3. These deal with a make-versus-buy analysis, a new products feasibility study, and an experimental run with an improved process.

---

[1] For more details see: Ryan, C. W., "Writing: A Practical Guide for Business and Industry," John Wiley & Sons, Inc., New York, 1974.

Summary

Students who have prepared many reports in their chemistry, physics, or engineering laboratories often have the wrong impression of the true purpose of a report. They feel that it is a chore that must be completed and is used as a measure of the student's accomplishments in the laboratory. In industry an engineering or technical report has a far more vital function. It is a basis for management decision. Should a venture be undertaken? Study feasibility reports. Should a company manufacture a given product? Study the process reports. An engineering or technical report is not a mere exercise in accomplishment but an important factor in the daily routine of doing business.

Problems

1. Prepare a skeleton outline for a report on one of the following:
    a. A study to determine whether maintenance should be done by company employees (in-house) or by outside contractors
    b. A study made to determine the feasibility of a new product recently developed by a research group
    c. An analysis made to determine the best location for a railroad crossing
    d. A site survey to select the location for a new oil refinery
2. Write a report on a problem you have worked on.
3. Write a report on the last experiment conducted in your chemistry laboratory.
4. Write a report covering the purchase of your latest car. Include decisions and alternatives considered.
5. Correct the following sentences:
    a. Cast iron is just as good as stainless steel because no temperatures will be used at above 70°F.
    b. This property makes the steel stronger than any steel.
    c. The conclusions and recommendations are the following from the process development study.
    d. Agitation and batch temperature during the raw materials addition step was found to be most significant of the variables in question.
    e. Fans are installed in tunnels that circulate cold air.
    f. While his task was difficult, he did it well.

Appendix 9.1
Make-Versus-Buy Analysis Report

INTERNAL
MEMORANDUM   Date: May 22, 1979

To: Unit:

From: E. Roberts   Unit:

Subject: Manufacturing of product XYZ in Building 66

Make-Versus-Buy Analysis

SUMMARY
An investigation has been made into the feasibility of manufacturing XYZ in Building 66 rather than purchasing the product.

INTRODUCTION
At present, all the XYZ provided for our customers (approximately 250,000 lb/yr, on dry basis) is purchased from an outside source.

CONCLUSIONS
1. Product XYZ can be manufactured in Building 66 at an anticipated savings of $0.36/lb over the purchase price, or a realized savings of $90,720, $94,680 and $98,640 for the first, second, and third year, respectively.
2. The capital expenditure necessary for the above would amount to $41,000. However, return on assets realized would be 104.7, 102.4 and 107.2% for the first, second, and third year, respectively, or an average of 104.7% for the three years. Furthermore, the payout time would be 0.80 years.

DISCUSSION
Production of XYZ in Building 66 via one step in solvent (isopropyl alcohol) appears to be an attractive venture. The reaction step has been run on a full production scale[a] (two batches) earlier this month in Building 66, and the isopropyl alcohol recovered by distillation in Building 69.

Building 66 would be the most logical location to manufacture the

---

[a] See report of May 16th, "Experimental XYZ."

product. The 750-gallon CPB reactor which has a light CPB and ARA schedule could be used for production after minor piping changes. The stripped 950-gallon stainless steel reactor would serve as the receiver for the solvent.

The 1000-gallon precipitator presently in operation would continue to be used for the other ONE STEP products.

The theoretical production schedule for the 1000-gallon precipitator, the 750-gallon reactor, sales forecasts and productivity of the One Step products are summarized in the Tables A-1 through A-4.

TABLE A-1 Sales Forecast for "One Step" Products, Dry Basis (in 1000 lb)

Product	1979	1980	1981	1982	1983
E	16	16	16	16	16
M	60	60	60	60	60
M UO	268	279	290	302	314
E 50U	354	369	383	396	411
M 50U	180	200	219	227	236
XYZ*	252	263	274	286	300

Based on material to be purchased from an outside source.

TABLE A-2 Cycle Time, Batch Size, and Productivity per Day
Basis: 1000-Gallon precipitator

Product	Cycle Time	Batch Size (lb)	Productivity per Day (lb)
E	20	2450	2940
M	20	2627	3150
M UO	20	2600	3120
E 50U	20	3454	4150
M 50U	20	3380	4060
XYZ	20	3000	3600

TABLE A-3 Cycle Time, Batch Size, and Productivity per Day
Basis: 750-Gallon Reactor

Product	Cycle Time	Batch Size (lb)	Productivity per Day
XYZ	19	2300	2900

Note: For the 50U products and XYZ, the cycle time taken is reaction time only, since grinding is internal to the cycle.

TABLE A-4   Production Days for Precipitator Required to Meet the Sales
             Forecast

Product	1979	1980	1981	1982	1983
E	6	6	6	6	6
M	19	19	19	19	19
M UO	86	90	93	97	101
E 50U	85	89	92	96	99
M 50U	44	49	54	59	62
XYZ	70	73	76	80	84
Subtotal	310	326	340	357	371
Plus 15% due to washing & repairs	4	5	5	5	6
Total days required per year	314	331	345	362	377

As can be seen, the forecast would not be met with the precipitator
alone, and as such, the 750-gallon reactor would have to be utilized to
make XYZ. The list below shows the theoretical production days required
for the 750-gallon reactor to meet the XYZ forecast.

· Product	1979	1980	1981	1982	1983
· XYZ	87	91	95	99	104

It should be mentioned that in the event that a large amount of any
one particular product is to be made at short notice, both reactors, that
is, the 1000-gallon precipitator and the 750-gallon reactor, could be used
simultaneously to meet the requirement.

The existing finishing system, consisting of the attritor and two aux-
iliary tanks, is adequate for grinding the 50U products and XYZ. The
average grinding time per 3200 lb[b] batch is 14 hours (including clean-up
time between types) or 5480 lb/day. Table A-5 shows grinding days required to meet the forecast.

It should also be mentioned that presently on the average only one
batch (average 3400 lb) is ground per day since the bottleneck is the
existing 1000-gallon precipitator. With the 750-gallon reactor in operation,
the use of the attritor can be maximized with the aid of dynamic programming.

[b] This figure includes XYZ, i.e. $\dfrac{(3454 + 3380 + 3000)}{3} \cong 3200$ lb

TABLE A-5   Grinding Days Required to Meet the Forecast

Product	1979	1980	1981	1982	1983
E 50U	65	67	70	72	75
M 50U	33	37	40	42	43
XYZ	46	48	50	52	55
Total days required per year	144	152	160	166	173

Equipment Requirement (with installation)   *Cost*

1. Raw material—A-scale tank $ 6,460
2. Raw materials B- and C-scale tank   5,660
3. Raw material B Feed Pump   2,000
4. Converting existing second raw material D hold tank to hold tank for raw material C (includes pump and piping)[c]   3,430
5. Shell and tube condensor stainless steel (100 ft^2 surface area)   3,400
6. Vacuum pump   4,040
7. Raw material A balance feed line   6,310
8. Water heating system   4,870
9. Modify old 1000-gallon reactor   1,100

Subtotal	$32,270
10% contingency	3,730
Grand total	$41,000

Based on the two plant runs, the cost can be estimated as follows:

Raw materials	lb/lb	$/lb of raw materials	$/lb of product	Total
C	0.592	0.270	0.160	
ZnO	0.186	0.185	0.034	
A	0.349	0.055	0.019	
B[d]	0.065	0.075	0.005	

[c] At present, raw material C is received in drums at a standard cost of $0.300/lb. Purchasing the raw material in tank cars will reduce the standard cost to $0.270/lb. Furthermore, last year 148,800 lb of the above were used in 88 Building, purchased in drums, to make LAIC, the intermediate for XYZ. Since 148,800 lb will be used again this year and next, the savings realized will be:

$$148,800(0.03) = \$4,460/\text{yr}$$

This savings is not included in the financial statement.

[d] Although B would be recovered and reused, it is assumed that approximately 150 lb of it would be lost.

Raw materials	lb/lb	$/lb of raw materials	$/lb of product	Total
Aeresol OT	0.027	0.350	0.009	
K	0.002	1.573	0.002	
				0.229

Production[e]			
Variable		0.015	
Package		0.027	0.042
Total manufacturing cost			$0.271
Purchase price			$0.630
Savings			$0.359

The financial statement appears in Table A-6 and, as can be seen, the venture would be worthwhile.

An appropriation request is presently being written up.

TABLE A-6   Financial Information XYZ in Building 66

	First Year	Second Year	Third Year
Pounds processed on this equipment (dry basis)	252,000	263,000	274,000
Estimated gross savings			
Manufacturing over purchase price, @ $0.36/lb	$ 90,720	$ 94,680	$ 92,640
Less expenses			
Depreciation @ 7.75% on expenditure	3,180	3,180	3,180
Taxes & insurance @ 2% on expenditure	820	820	820
Maintenance @ 5% on expenditure	2,050	2,050	2,050
Interest @ 7% on expenditures	2,870	2,870	2,870
Total estimated expense	8,920	8,920	8,920
Net savings before taxes	81,800	85,760	89,720
Provisions for taxes @ 51%	41,720	43,740	45,760
Subtotal	40,080	42,020	43,960
Investment credit @ 7% on expenditure	2,870	—	—
Net savings after taxes	42,950	42,020	43,960
Total expenditure required	41,000	41,000	41,000
% ROA gross	104.7	102.4	107.2
3-yr average gross			
Payout time 0.80 Years			

[e] The fixed cost is included on the financial statement as depreciation, taxes and insurance, maintenance and interest.

Appendix 9.2
New Products Feasibility Study Report

	INTERNAL	
	MEMORANDUM	**Date:** December 24,1975
To:	**Unit:**	
From: E. Roberts	**Unit**	

Subject: Synthetic products

SUMMARY
An investigation has been made into the process, feasibility, and manufacturing site to produce 200 tons per year and up of Rite and Nite products. The Chester and Rose plants were visited and evaluated with regard to capability, process economics, and capital expenditure required to meet these demands. The investigation yielded the following conclusions and recommendations:

CONCLUSIONS
1. The Rite process though technologically sound is not ready for scale-up at this time. Additional engineering development work is still needed at the pilot plant level.
2. The Nite process is not ready for process development. Considerable research work is still needed. At this time, the product can not be reproduced to meet G's specifications. This report does, however, provide process economics around the limited information available.
3. The Rose plant appears to be the better choice for a semiworks site for the following reasons:
   a. More square footage of free space is available for expansions in the event the demand for these products increases beyond 200 tons per year.
   b. The plant is completely shut down. This will secure efficient scale-up, and actual semiworks production will follow smoothly without potential breaks in continuity.
   c. The working capital required to get the contaminants out of the system is estimated to be $20,000-$25,000, or 2 to 2.5 times less than required for Chester.
4. Based on the information available to date, the capital expenditure required for Rose to realize 200 tons and 4200 tons per year is $187,200 and $1,822,200, respectively.
5. Based on the information available to date, the manufacturing cost for Rite at the 200- and 4200-ton level is $1.458 and $0.8732 per

pound, respectively; and for the Nite $1,3255 and $0.7408 per pound, respectively.

6. Again, based on the information available and developed, this appears to be an attractive venture. Given a GTM (gross trading margin) of 50%, distribution costs at $0.05 per pound, and sales and administrative cost at 5.1%[f] of sales, the ROI at 200 and 4200 ton-per-year levels for Rite are 148% and 177%, respectively, and for Nite 127% and 147%, respectively.

RECOMMENDATIONS
1. Synthetic Rite should be transferred from the MSG Group to the development department allowing MSG to concentrate fully on developing reproducible synthetic Nite. The 100- and 900-gallon reactors available at the pilot plant should be utilized for piloting along with our knowledge of computer analysis of processing conditions.
2. No piloting is to be done at the Rose or Chester plants. Production-size equipment is not for piloting. The learning costs are too great and variables too many. When and only when all process parameters are fully defined and systematized, can the process be scaled up for production.
3. The green light should be given to begin the necessary pilot work.

DISCUSSION
The first week in December, ..., ..., ..., and Eric Roberts visited the Chester and Rose plants to evaluate equipment and facilities available at both locations and the capital expenditure required to realize 200 tons of product per year. In addition, feasibility and manufacturing cost were to be evaluated at this and other levels of production.

Both the Chester and Rose plants can readily adapt to produce 200 tons per year, although the working capital required to get the contaminants out of the system at Chester will be approximately 2 to 2.5 times that of Rose, or $40,000 to $50,000. There is more square footage of free space available for expansion at Rose in the event demand for these products exceeds 200 tons per year. Since production at Rose is completely shut down, scale-up for production and actual semiworks production can proceed more smoothly without possible breaks in continuity. Given the above information, the choice is clearly Rose.

The process itself (in the case of Rite only) although feasible, requires one month of hard-core engineering development work to provide a process statistically producible to within 99% confidence and ready for introduction into the semiworks production. This will require development of data and models which must be transformed into systematized quantitative information that will predict performance of large-scale processes from small-scale experimental models. Much of this data needed is already available from work done by the MSG Group. It is just a matter

[f] divisional average

of developing the missing data, linking it all together, then building such models with the aid of a computer, dimensional analysis, and simulation. As stated, it is recommended that the project (only the Rite process at this time) be transferred to the development department and that use be made of equipment available at the pilot plant and the development department's experience in computer analysis.

Based on the information available about the processes, Figures A, B, and C have been developed followed by Tables A-7, A-8, A-9, A-10, A-11 and Figures D, E, and F. For all calculations, the following constants were used:

1. Production efficiency = 73% (illness, equipment breakdown, off-grade, set-up batches, grievances, etc.). Hence, to produce 200 tons per year of either product, the manufacturing cost (or cost of goods sold) is equated to the cost of

$$\frac{200}{0.73} = 274 \text{ tons.}$$

2. Labor costs = hourly cost ($6.00) + fringe benefits ($2.50) = $8.50/hr
3. 47 weeks of operation per year.

It should be pointed out that the output levels shown in Table A-8 (expanded equipment estimate) indicate the level and distribution of required capital expenditure. It should be recognized, however, that these costs pertain to the Rose plant only; that is, adding equipment to an existing facility. If a new plant is to be built (new facility and equipment), the expenditure that will be required to realize 4000-4200 tons per year will be approximately between $5,000,000 and $7,000,000.

As an added attraction, Table A-10 provides financial information at the 200- and 4200-ton levels based on the following assumptions:

1. GTM = 50%
2. Distribution costs = $0.05 per pound
3. Sales and administration cost = 5.1% of sales

Figure A

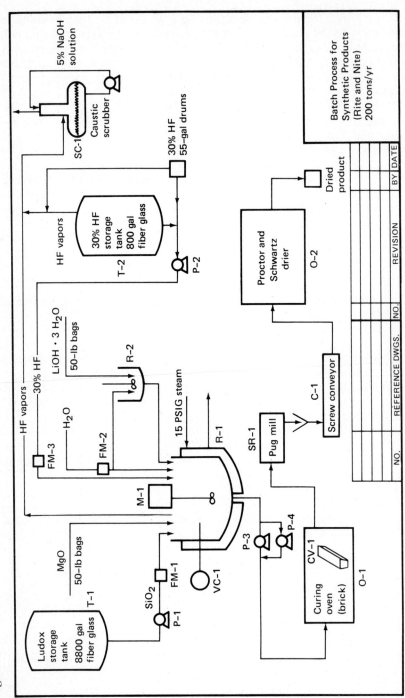

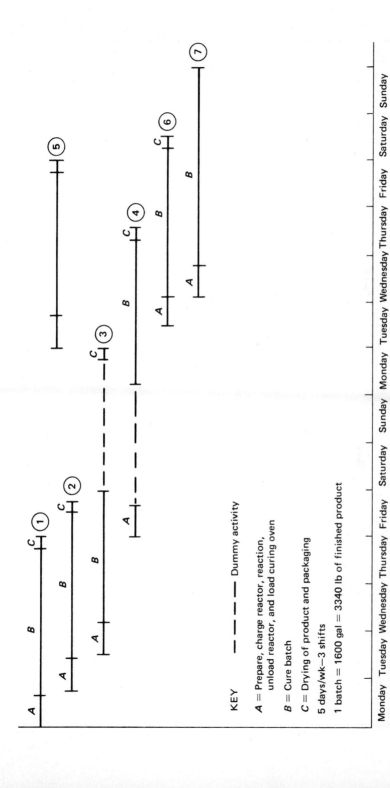

Figure B Time logic network.

KEY ▬ ▬ ▬ Dummy activity

A = Prepare, charge reactor, reaction,
    unload reactor, and load curing oven

B = Cure batch

C = Drying of product and packaging

5 days/wk–3 shifts

1 batch = 1600 gal = 3340 lb of finished product

Rite/Nite – 200 tons/yr

Monday Tuesday Wednesday Thursday Friday Saturday Sunday Monday Tuesday Wednesday Thursday Friday Saturday Sunday

Figure C Time logic network.

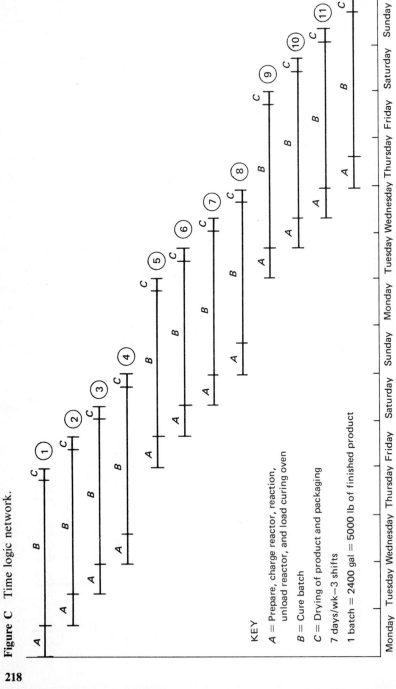

KEY

A = Prepare, charge reactor, reaction,
    unload reactor, and load curing oven

B = Cure batch

C = Drying of product and packaging

7 days/wk—3 shifts

1 batch = 2400 gal = 5000 lb of finished product

Rite/Nite — 4000 tons/yr

TABLE A-7 **Rose Plant Synthetic Products: Equipment Available and an Estimate of Needed Equipment, 200 tons/yr Production**

	Drawing no.	Cost
Equipment available		
1 - Ludox storage tank	T-1	—
1 - 300-gal. reactor	R-1	—
1 - 100-gal. LiOH solution make-up tank	R-2	—
1 - 800-gal. 30% HF storage tank	T-2	—
1 - 80-ft P&S belt drier	O-2	—
Equipment needed		
1 - Jacket for 3000-gallon reactor	R-1	$8,000
3 - Magnetic meters & recorders	FM-1,2,3	$12,000
1 - Variable speed Reeves agitator drive for 300-gal. reactor	M-1	$5,000
1 - Viscosity recorder, controller and alarm system	VC-1	$10,000
32 - ⅛"—10 Gauge 304 S.S.—200-gal. capacity curing vessels with lids @ $1500 each	CV-1	$48,000
1 - 18-ft × 18-ft × 8 ft curing oven—brick	O-1	$15,000
1 - HF scrubbing system	SC-1	$3,000
1 - Ludox feed pump—S.S.—50 GPM	P-1	$8,000
1 - Acid transfer pump—plastic; 5-10 GPM	P-2	$1,000
2 - Product transfer pumps—Moyns—S.S.—50 GPM	P-3,4	$16,000
1 - Pug mill & conveyor system	SR-1 & C-1	$25,000
100 - feet 2-in Sch. 10 S.S. piping		$5,000
4 - 2-in S.S. ball valves		
Subtotal		$156,000
20% contingency		31,200
Total fixed investment		$187,200

TABLE A-8 Expanded Equipment Estimate, Synthetic Products Rose Plant

	200	600	700	1,200	1,400	1,800	2,100
Yearly production—tons	200	600	700	1,200	1,400	1,800	2,100
Jacket for 3000-gal. reactor	8,000	—	8,000	—	—	—	—
Magnetic meters	12,000	—	—	—	—	—	—
Variable speed Reeves agitator drive for 3000-gal. reactor	5,000	—	5,000	—	5,000	—	5,000
Viscosity recorder, controller and alarm system	10,000	—	10,000	—	10,000	—	10,000
Curing vessels with lids @ $1500 each	48,000	—	72,000	—	72,000	—	72,000
Curing oven—brick	15,000	—	25,000	—	25,000	—	25,000
HF scrubbing system	3,000	—	—	—	—	—	—
Ludox feed pump	8,000	8,000	—	8,000	—	8,000	—
Acid transfer pump—plastic	1,000	1,000	—	1,000	—	1,000	—
Product transfer pumps—Moyns	16,000	—	—	—	—	—	16,000
Pug mill and conveyor system	25,000	—	25,000	—	25,000	—	25,000
Piping & valves	5,000	—	2,000	—	2,000	—	2,000
Additional reactor	—	—	—	—	60,000	—	60,000
Additional Ludox storage tank	—	10,000	—	10,000	—	10,000	—
Additional HF storage tank	—	5,000	—	5,000	—	5,000	—
Subtotal	$156,000	180,000	327,000	351,000	550,000	574,000	789,000
20% Contingency	31,200	36,000	65,400	70,200	110,000	114,800	157,800
Total expenditure	$187,200	216,000	392,400	421,200	660,000	688,800	946,800

TABLE A-8 Expanded Equipment Estimate, Synthetic Products Rose Plant (*Continued*)

Yearly production—tons	2,400	2,800	3,000	3,500	3,600	4,200
Jacket for 3000-gal. reactor	—	—	—	—	—	5,000
Magnetic meters	—	—	—	—	—	—
Variable speed Reeves agitator drive for 3000-gal. reactor	—	5,000	—	5,000	—	5,000
Viscosity recorder, controller and alarm system	—	10,000	—	10,000	—	10,000
Curing vessels with lids @ $1500 each	—	72,000	—	72,000	—	72,000
Curing oven—brick	—	25,000	—	25,000	—	25,000
HF scrubbing system	—	—	—	—	—	—
Ludox feed pump	8,000	—	8,000	—	8,000	8,000
Acid transfer pump—plastic	1,000	—	1,000	—	1,000	1,000
Product transfer pumps—Moyns	—	—	—	—	—	16,000
Pug mill and conveyor system	—	25,000	—	25,000	—	25,000
Piping & valves	—	2,000	—	2,000	—	2,000
Additional reactor	—	60,000	—	60,000	—	60,000
Additional Ludox storage tank	10,000	—	10,000	—	10,000	10,000
Additional HF storage tank	5,000	—	5,000	—	5,000	5,000
Subtotal	813,000	1,028,000	1,053,000	1,268,000	1,293,000	1,518,500
20% Contingency	162,600	205,600	210,600	253,600	258,600	303,700
Total expenditure	975,600	1,233,600	1,263,600	1,521,600	1,551,600	1,822,200

TABLE A-9 Process Economics—Rite/Nite—Basis: 200 Tons/yr—Rose Plant*—
Variable and Semivariable Costs†

		Raw Material Costs		
Raw material	Quantity Rite/Nite	Raw material per lb of product Rite/Nite	Unit cost ($)	Cost per lb Rite/Nite ($)
MgO	3,330/4,385	0.2846/0.3751	0.1100	0.0313/0.0413
30% HF	2,085/1,820	0.1784/0.1557	0.3800	0.0677/0.0592
$LiOH \cdot 3H_2O$	780/0	0.0667/0.0000	1.2200	0.0813/0.0000
$Na_2Al_2O_3$	0/1,070	0.0000/0.0915	0.1800	0.0000/0.0165
Ludox	22,315/18,930	1.9089/1.6193	0.2408	0.4596/0.3900
H_2O	25,400/29,700	2.1762/2.5406	0.0010	0.0021/0.0025

Yield = 11,690 lb @ 100%

Bulk cost per lb (Rite/Nite) =	$0.6420/0.5095

Packaging
Raw material cost—Rite $0.0300
Raw material cost—Nite $0.5395

Labor

(6 workers) (8 hr/worker-day) (5 days/wk) (52 wk/yr) ($8.50)‡
= $106,080/yr. $106,080/400,000 = $0.2652/lb

Utilities (Basis 3.5 Batches = 5-Day Week)

1. *Steam*
   a. *Reaction*
      Heat up   6,391,270 BTU
      Hold at temperature   5,414,080 BTU
                                 ‾‾‾‾‾‾‾‾‾‾‾‾‾‾
                                 11,805,350 BTU

   b. *Curing oven*
      Hold at temperature   48,726,720 BTU
   c. *Dryer*   57,213,550 BTU
                                 ‾‾‾‾‾‾‾‾‾‾‾‾‾‾
      Total   117,745,620 BTU

(117,745,620 BTU) (1 lb steam/1190 BTU) ($2.50/1000 lb steam) = $247.36/wk
$247.36/11,960 lb = $0.0211/lb of product

TABLE A-9   Process Economics—Rite/Nite—Basis: 200 Tons/yr—Rose Plant*—Variable and Semivariable Costs† *(Continued)*

2.   *Electricity*

a.	Lights	432 kwh @	$0.023/kwh
b.	Equipment	430 kwh @	$0.023/kwh
	Total		$0.0130/lb of product

Total utilities	
Steam	$0.0211/lb
Electricity	0.0130/lb
	$0.0341/lb of product

Supervision

$28,000/400,000 lb/yr = $0.0700

Overhead and general expense

50% of total expense for labor and supervision
$(106,080 + 28,000) (0.50)/400,000 = 0.1676$

Variable and Semivariable Cost Summary

	Hectorite	Saponite
Raw materials	0.6720	0.5395
Labor	0.2652	0.2652
Utilities	0.0341	0.0341
Supervision	0.0700	0.0700
Overhead & general expense	0.1676	0.1676
Total	1.2089	1.0764

*From quantitative flow diagram, Figure C.
†Fixed costs appear in Table A-10.
‡Includes fringe benefits = 40% of cost of labor.

TABLE A-10 Expanded Process Economics, Rite Production at Rose Plant

Yearly production, tons	200	600	700	1,200	1,400	1,800	2,100
Variable & semivariable costs							
Raw materials	268,800	806,400	940,800	1,612,800	1,881,600	2,419,200	2,822,400
Labor	106,080	106,080	141,440	141,440	194,480	194,480	247,520
Utilities	13,640	40,920	47,740	81,840	95,480	122,760	143,220
Supervision	28,000	28,000	28,000	28,000	48,000	48,000	48,000
Overhead & general expense	67,040	67,040	84,720	84,720	121,240	121,240	147,760
Total variable & semivariable cost	482,560	1,048,440	1,242,700	1,948,800	2,340,800	2,905,680	3,408,900
Total variable & semivariable cost per lb	1.2089	0.8737	0.8876	0.8120	0.8360	0.8071	0.8116
Fixed costs							
Depreciation @ 10% on expenditure plus undepreciated existing equipment utilized	33,720	36,600	54,250	57,120	81,000	83,900	109,680
Taxes and insurance @ 4% on expenditure plus existing equipment utilized	13,490	14,640	21,700	22,850	32,400	33,550	43,870
Maintenance @ 10% as above	33,720	36,600	54,240	57,120	81,000	83,900	109,680
Interest @ 10% on expenditure	18,720	21,600	39,240	42,120	66,000	68,800	94,680
Total fixed cost	99,650	109,440	169,420	179,210	260,040	270,150	357,910
Total fixed cost per lb	0.2491	0.0912	0.1210	0.0746	0.0930	0.0750	0.0852
Cost of goods sold per pound	1.4580	0.9649	1.0086	0.8866	0.9290	0.8821	0.8968
Capital expenditure*	187,200	216,000	392,400	421,200	660,000	688,800	946,800

*Includes 20% for contingency

TABLE A-10 Expanded Process Economics, Rite Production at Rose Plant *(Continued)*

	2,400	2,800	3,000	3,500	3,600	4,200
Yearly production, tons						
Variable & semivariable costs						
Raw materials	3,225,600	3,763,200	4,032,000	4,704,000	4,838,400	5,644,800
Labor	247,520	300,560	300,560	353,600	353,600	424,320
Utilities	163,680	190,960	204,600	238,700	245,520	286,440
Supervision	48,000	75,000	75,000	75,000	75,000	75,000
Overhead & general expense	147,760	187,780	187,780	214,300	214,300	249,660
Total variable & semivariable cost	3,832,560	4,517,500	4,799,940	5,585,600	5,726,820	6,680,220
Total variable & semivariable cost per lb	0.7985	0.8067	0.8009	0.7979	0.7953	0.7952
Fixed costs						
Depreciation @ 10% on expenditure plus undepreciated existing equipment utilized	112,560	138,360	141,360	167,160	170,160	197,220
Taxes and insurance @ 4% on expenditure plus existing equipment utilized	45,020	55,340	56,540	66,860	68,060	78,890
Maintenance @ 10% as above	112,560	138,360	141,360	167,160	170,160	197,220
Interest @ 10% on expenditure	97,560	123,360	126,360	152,160	155,160	182,220
Total fixed cost	367,700	455,420	465,620	553,340	563,540	655,550
Total fixed cost per lb	0.0766	0.0813	0.0776	0.0790	0.0782	0.0780
Cost of goods sold per pound	0.8751	0.8880	0.8776	0.8769	0.8735	0.8732
Capital expenditure*	975,600	1,233,600	1,263,600	1,521,600	1,551,600	1,822,200

*Includes 20% for contingency

TABLE A-11 Expanded Process Economics, Nite Production at Rose Plant

	200	600	700	1,200	1,400	1,800	2,100
Yearly production, tons							
Variable & semivariable costs							
Raw materials	215,800	647,400	755,300	1,294,800	1,510,600	1,942,200	2,265,900
Labor	106,080	106,080	141,440	141,440	194,480	194,480	247,520
Utilities	13,640	40,920	47,740	81,840	95,480	122,760	143,220
Supervision	28,000	28,000	28,000	28,000	48,000	48,000	48,000
Overhead & general expense	67,040	67,040	84,720	84,720	121,240	121,240	147,760
Total variable and semivariable cost	430,560	889,440	1,057,200	1,630,800	1,969,800	2,428,680	2,852,400
Total variable and semivariable cost/lb	1.0764	0.7412	0.7551	0.6795	0.7035	0.6746	0.6791
Fixed costs							
Total fixed cost	99,650	109,440	169,420	179,210	260,040	270,150	357,910
Total fixed cost/lb	0.2491	0.0912	0.1210	0.0746	0.0930	0.0750	0.0852
Cost of goods sold per pound	1.3255	0.8324	0.8761	0.7541	0.7965	0.7496	0.7643
Capital expenditure*	187,200	216,000	392,400	412,200	660,000	688,800	946,800

*Includes 20% for contingency

TABLE A-11 Expanded Process Economics, Nite Production at Rose Plant (*Continued*)

	2,400	2,800	3,000	3,500	3,600	4,200
Yearly production, tons						
Variable & semivariable costs						
Raw materials	2,589,600	3,021,200	3,237,000	3,776,500	3,884,400	4,531,800
Labor	247,520	300,560	300,560	353,600	353,600	424,320
Utilities	163,680	190,960	204,600	238,700	245,520	286,440
Supervision	48,000	75,000	75,000	75,000	75,000	75,000
Overhead & general expense	147,760	187,780	187,780	214,300	214,300	249,660
Total variable and semivariable cost	3,196,560	3,775,500	4,004,940	4,658,100	4,772,820	5,567,220
Total variable and semivariable cost/lb	0.6660	0.6742	0.6675	0.6654	0.6630	0.6628
Fixed costs						
Total fixed cost	367,700	455,420	465,620	553,340	563,540	655,550
Total fixed cost/lb	0.0766	0.0813	0.0776	0.0790	0.0782	0.0780
Cost of goods sold per pound	0.7426	0.7555	0.7451	0.7444	0.7412	0.7408
Capital expenditure*	975,600	1,233,600	1,263,600	1,521,600	1,551,600	1,822,200

*Includes 20% for contingency

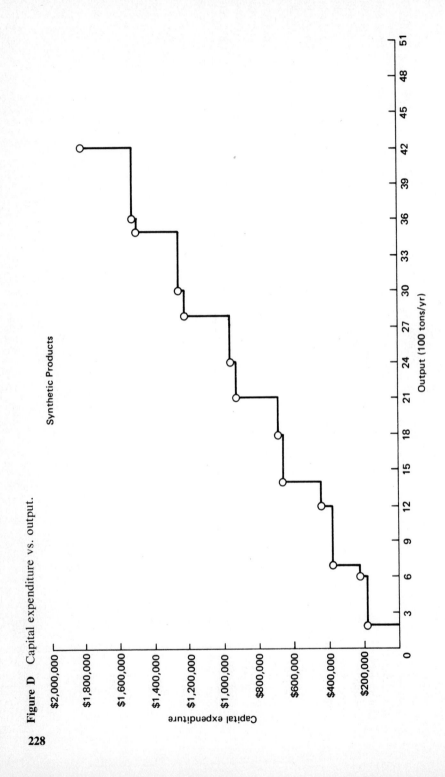

Figure D Capital expenditure vs. output.

Synthetic Products

Figure E Cost of goods sold vs. output.

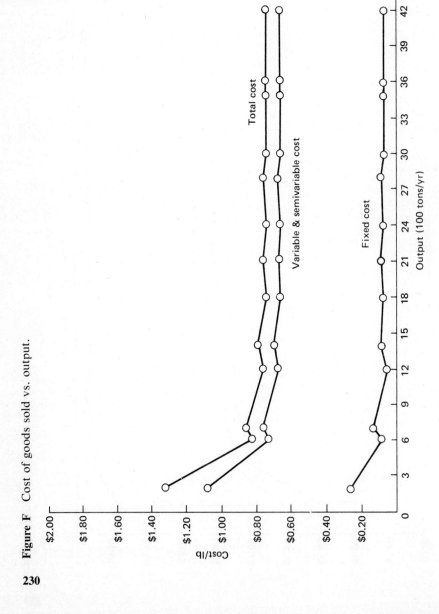

Figure F Cost of goods sold vs. output.

230

TABLE A-12   Financial Information—Synthetic Products

	Rite		Nite	
Tons produced				
Net sales	200	4,200	200	4,200
Less cost of	$1,200,000	14,700,000	$1,060,400	12,445,400
goods sold	583,200	7,334,880	530,200	6,222,720
Gross margin	616,800	7,365,120	530,200	6,222,680
Less distribution				
cost	20,000	420,000	20,000	420,000
Net trading				
margin	596,800	6,945,120	510,200	5,802,680
Less sales and				
administrative				
cost	61,200	749,700	54,080	635,000
Gross profit	535,600	6,195,420	456,120	5,167,680
Income tax @				
48%	257,100	2,973,800	218,940	2,480,490
Net income after				
taxes	$ 278,500	3,221,620	$ 237,180	2,687,190
Capital				
expenditure	$ 187,200	1,822,200	$ 187,200	1,822,200
ROI	148%	177%	127%	147%

Appendix 9.3
Experimental Run with an Improved Process Report

INTERNAL
MEMORANDUM   Date: June 1, 1976

To: **Unit:**

From: E. Roberts/J. Doe   **Unit:**

Subject: Product XYZ: Process improvement/cost reduction

35,000 pounds of XYZ have been prepared on an experimental basis via the zinc oxide route May 11 through 21 without any processing problems. 20,000 pounds of the above quantity has been spray-dried and evaluated already as well as placed in inventory. All of it meets specifications. The remaining 15,000 pounds is being stored to be spray-dried the week of June 7th.

This modified process is easily adaptable to existing equipment at Building #9 of the .... Plant. A capital expenditure of $4000-$5000 will be necessary, however, to secure a homogenizer for the zinc oxide. The homogenizer that had been rented for the above trial must now be returned.

In comparison to the old double decomposition process, the following benefits are realized:

1. The cost of making this product has decreased by $0.84/lb. hence, the 35,000 pounds just produced will contribute $29,400 before taxes to the division's earnings. If the yearly demand of 90,000 pounds remains as forecasted, an additional $46,200 will be contributed, or a grand total of $75,600 per year. As one can see, two days of production will pay back the above recommended homogenizer.
2. Productivity has been increased from 1800 to 8000 dry pounds per 16-hour day, amounting to an increase of 400%.
3. Utilization of existing equipment for production of XYZ has decreased by 76%. This will allow other water-insoluble soaps as well as other profitable products to be produced there.
4. Since water is the only by-product of this reaction, no longer is sodium sulfate being sent to the sewer (0.32 lb/lb of product) with the wash water. Based on the above demand for XYZ this amounts to 28,000 lbs. of sodium sulfate per year that will *not* have to be waste-treated in the future.

It is recommended with this note that the zinc oxide process be transferred to manufacturing, making the old double decomposition process obsolete. A final manufacturing procedure is being prepared which will be turned over to manufacturing during the transfer meeting. Although we do not foresee any problems during succeeding runs, the development department should be present during the next run.

Last, but not least, the writers wish to extend sincere thanks to ...., ..., and the plant manager, for all their help. Their support has made the idea a reality.

Glossary

amortization Repayment of debt by a sequence of payments.

analysis An examination of a complex, its elements, and their interrelation.

annuity A sequence of equal payments made at equal time intervals.

assets The things which a firm owns.

average cost Total cost divided by the quantity of output at that level of cost.

book value The accounting value of an asset.

break-even analysis An arithmetic or graphic technique utilized to determine the level of sales (dollars or units) necessary to recover all costs.

break-even point The level (amount of sales or number of units) at which sales and costs are equal.

budget A statement of plans and expected results expressed quantitatively.

capital Assets needed to operate a business.

capital gains Profit made from the sale of a property.

capital investment The amount of money needed to establish the assets (equipment and facilities) required to do a business.

capital losses Losses on the sale of a property.

carry back, carry forward For income tax purposes, losses that can be carried backward or forward to reduce federal income taxes.

compound interest An interest rate that is applicable when interest in succeeding periods is earned not only on the initial principal but also on the accumulated interest of prior periods.

compounding The mathematical process of determining the final value of a payment or series of payments when compound interest is applied.

consumption   Spending for goods and services by consumers or industry.

continuous compounding   The process of adding interest continuously rather than at discrete points of time (hourly versus quarterly).

control   The process of making events conform according to plan.

corporation   A form of business formed under state law in which ownership is vested in shares of stock and owner liability limited to the investment.

correlation   The degree to which two or more variables within a system are mutually related.

correlation coefficient   A measure of the degree of relationship between two variables.

cost   The value that must be given up in order to produce a good or a service.

cost index   A figure which represents the relative change in costs between a particular period of time and a base year.

cost of distribution   The cost of moving goods from the manufacturer to the consumer.

decision making   The process of choosing between alternatives.

demand   The willingness and ability to purchase goods or services.

depreciation   The loss in value of a property, such as a machine, over a period of time.

direct labor   Labor that is directly related to the production of a good or service.

discounting   The process of finding the present value of a series of future cash flows.

economics   The study of the efforts of human beings to satisfy their unlimited wants by utilizing their limited resources.

expenditure   That which is paid out.

feedback   Information concerning any type of planned operation relayed to the responsible person for evaluation.

fixed costs   Costs that remain constant at different levels of business activity.

flow diagram   A diagram depicting the sequence of operations involved in achieving a final goal.

gross profit   Sales price minus the cost of the good sold.

incremental analysis   A comparative examination of an existing situation and a proposal.

incremental cash flow   Net cash flow attributable to an investment project.

incremental costs   The difference in costs between an existing situation and a proposal.

index   An indicator.

inflation   An economic situation in which the supply of money increases at a faster rate than the supply of goods and services, resulting in a decrease in buying power.

innovation   A change made by bringing in something new which can lead to a profit for a firm.

interest   The cost of using borrowed money.

investment   The putting of money into a business or securities to obtain an income.

management   The process of coordination of labor, capital goods, and natural resources to produce a good or service.

manufacturing   The conversion of raw materials into a finished product by means of a chemical or a mechanical process.

manufacturing overhead   All costs associated with the manufacturing process other than direct labor and direct material.

objective   The goal of a business.

payback time   The length of time required for the net revenues of an investment to return the cost of the investment.

planning   Management's function which deals with developing a course of action or pattern of directives. It determines what should be done, by whom, when, and how.

present worth   The value today of a future payment, or stream of payments, discounted at the appropriate discount rate.

price   The amount of money that a good demands.

production   The creation of value.

production capacity   A quantity that can be produced within a specified unit of time (such as kilograms per hour, week, or year).

productivity   The amount of output per fixed unit of input.

relation   A connection between ordered pairs of real numbers.

rent   An amount paid for the use of another's property.

resources   Human beings and nonhuman items (e.g. land or machinery) that can be used for production of goods or services.

responsibility   The obligation to accomplish expected results.

salvage value   The value of an asset at the end of its useful life.

savings   The part of income which is not spent on consumption or investment. The part of cost which is not incurred because of technological improvements.

scheduling   A timetable showing when an activity should be started in order to achieve a goal.

sinking fund   A fund formed in order to pay an obligation due at a future date.

supply   The amount of goods available for sale.

supply curve   A graphical indication of the quantity of goods a producer would be willing to offer for sale at various prices.

surtax   A tax levied in addition to the normal tax.

value   The relative worth or importance of anything such as an idea, product, or process.

variable costs   Costs which vary directly with the level of production.

variance   The degree to which numerical data tend to spread about an average value.

wages   The price of labor.

working capital   Those assets that will be converted to cash within a year (inventory, accounts receivable).

x-axis   The horizontal line in the rectangular coordinate system.

y-axis   The vertical line in the rectangular coordinate system.

Time Value
of Money

Appendix A

A.1   Interest Rates and Their Determination

Interest rates vary according to the type of loan. Furthermore, interest rates overall are a function of monetary supply and demand. When demand for money is heavy but the supply is short, short-term interest rates will rise. To illustrate, consider a typical supply-demand relationship as shown in Figure A-1. The supply line represents the relationship between the quantity of money that lenders will make available for loans and the interest they receive. The demand line, on the other hand, represents the relationship between the quantity of money that borrowers will borrow and the interest they will pay. At the point where the lines intersect (point E), equilibrium, or stability, exists. As the supply of money decreases, as represented by the S' line, and the demand remains constant, the equilibrium point must shift to E' and the annual interest rate rises from 9.0 to 9.5%. As the supply of money increases (S'' line) the equilibrium point shifts to E'', yielding a lower interest rate (8.0%).

As short-term (prime) rates go up, long-term (mortgage) rates unavoidaly get affected; for long-term rates, too, must take into account the supply-demand relationship. To illustrate, consider individuals or firms reducing their savings accounts by shifting their income to high-yield treasury bills or short-term securities. The supply of money to banks decreases, forcing them to look to other sources of supply and pay a premium (interest) for these funds. These premiums are then passed on to borrowers in the form of higher interest rates. Hence, when such situations exist (typically during inflationary periods) and a firm is in the need of capital to build or expand a facility, it has to bear these higher rates.

Interestingly enough, however, during such inflationary periods, borrowers are willing to pay high interest rates to obtain money, since they anticipate being able to increase their prices and cover these higher costs. As will be shown later, such practice is very risky.

The government can exert a strong influence on interest rates because of its ability to manipulate the money market. It can increase or decrease the amount of money available, and it can also lower or raise the price banks must pay in order to get money with which to make loans. This latter method of affecting the banks' costs is called changing the discount rate. The Federal Reserve is the agency which decides upon and implements these policies. It can also specify the maximum amount of interest that banks are allowed to pay on savings accounts.

Often these rates are hard to control, as was seen during 1974. The money market gets out of hand, and sometimes wage and price controls are instituted, or at least threatened, in an attempt to restore order.

A.2   Effects of Interest Rates

As seen above, interest rates are directly related to the supply of money. A tight money supply gets reflected in the nation's economy in several ways:

1. High interest rates make new capital investments more expensive. Public utilities and municipalities are especially strongly affected, because their funds are raised through bond issues. These bonds, because of their low fixed yield and long term, are unattractive to an investor who sees a better return from short-term securities.

2. High rates make major capital projects less desirable, because such rates reduce the effective return on a firm's investment. If the difference between expected return on investment and minimum rate is small, a firm will not consider the project because of the high risk, especially for a small firm.

3. High interest rates have a major effect on the construction industry, especially home building, since doubling the rate of interest on a mortgage more than doubles the amount of interest paid. For example, a 50% increase in interest rate on a 20-year mortgage increases interest payments by approximately 65%. Consequently, the demand for new homes drops, followed by a drop in supply as illustrated in Figure A-1.

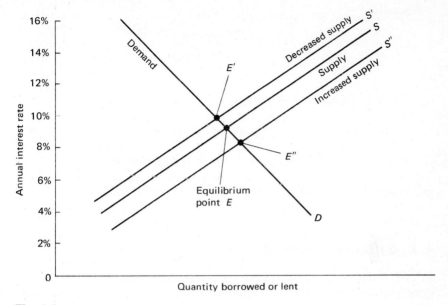

Fig. A-1.

A.3   Frequency of Compounding

In common industrial practice, the length of the discrete interest period is assumed to be one year and the fixed interest rate i is based on one year as well. Often however, other time units are employed. If compounding occurs m times per year and the interest rate is expressed on an annual basis, then Equation (5-3) can be expressed as

$$S = PW(1 + i/m)^{n \cdot m} \qquad \text{(A-1)}$$

where $n \cdot m$ is the number of periods and i/m is the interest rate per period while i always refers to annual interest rate.

The above equation can also be written in terms of present worth:

$$PW = S/(1 + i/m)^{n \cdot m} \qquad \text{(A-2)}$$

Example A-1

A firm wishes to borrow $11,000 to meet financial obligations. The monthly interest rate is 2%. What is the total amount due after two years if no intermediate payments are made?

Solution:

$$i/m = 2\% = 0.02$$
$$m = 12 \text{ months}$$
$$n = 2 \text{ years}$$

Then by Equation A-1

$$S = \text{PW}(1 + i/m)^{n \cdot m} = 11{,}000(1 + 0.02)^{(2)(12)} = 11{,}000(1 + 0.02)^{24}$$

From Appendix B the present-worth factor $= 1.6084$. Then

$$S = 11{,}000(1.6084) = \$17{,}692.40$$

A.4   Effective Interest Rate

Often it is desirable to express the exact interest rate based on the original principal and the convenient time unit of 1 year. This type of rate is known as the *effective interest rate* and can be expressed as

$$i_{\text{eff}} = (1 + i/m)^m - 1 \tag{A-3}$$

The next example will illustrate the importance of Equation A-3 and the meaning of the effective interest rate.

Example A-2
   What is the annual rate on an unpaid department store balance if the carrying charge per month is 1%?

Solution:
   By Equation A-3

$$i_{\text{eff}} = (1 + i/m)^m - 1 = (1 + 0.01)^{12} - 1 = (1.01)^{12} - 1$$
$$= 1.1268 - 1 = 0.1268 \text{ or } 12.68\%$$

As can be seen, the frequency of compounding has a significant effect on the true interest rate, and one pays 0.68% more per year than is assumed.

A.5   Continuous Interest

As the frequency of compounding increases, that is, as the number of interest periods m in Equation A-1 becomes very large or approaches infinity, Equation A-1 is transformed to[1]

$$S = PW \lim_{m \to \infty} (1 + i/m)^{n \cdot m} = PW \lim_{m \to \infty} (1 + i/m)^{(m/i)(i \cdot n)}$$

$$= PW(e^{i \cdot n})$$

where $\lim_{m \to \infty} (1 + i/m)^{(m/i)} = e = 2.71828 \ldots$

which is the fundamental definition for the base of the natural system of logarithims.

Similarly Equation 5-4 becomes

$$PW = \frac{S}{e^{in}} \tag{A-5}$$

Equation A-4 and A-5 express the process of adding interest continuously rather than at a discrete point in time (hourly versus quarterly or semi-annually, etc.).

Example A-3

If a firm borrows \$1000 at an annual rate of 10%, what is the total amount after 1 year with continuous compounding?

Solution:

By Equation A-5

$$S = PW(e^{i \cdot n}) = 1000[e^{(0.10)(1)}] = 1000(1.1052) = \$1105.20$$

It is interesting to note that if compounding were done annually rather than continuously, the final amount would be \$1100 (by Equation 5-3).

The concept of continuous interest is not widely used because industrial and financial practices are based on methods which executives, engineers, and the public are used to and can understand. This concept however should not be totally ignored since the frequency with which interest is compounded has an important influence on the total interest charges associated with an investment.

A.6   Average Interest Rate Estimation

Since a loan, for instance a car loan, is usually repaid in a series of equal installments, the interest rate decreases over the life of the loan. That is,

[1] For more details on derivation, see any book on advanced calculus.

the interest rate at the beginning of the loan is greater than the interest rate at the end of the loan. Accordingly, the average interest rate over the life of the loan is approximately one-half the prescribed annual interest rate. Mathematically, the relationship can be expressed as follows:

$$\bar{i} = \frac{i}{2}\left(\frac{n + 1}{n}\right) \qquad \text{(A-6)}$$

where
    $\bar{i}$ = average interest rate
    i = prescribed annual interest rate
    n = number of years or life of the loan

The above relatonship is only a rough approximation and should be used with discretion. It does, however, provide sufficient information for quick and crude analysis.

Example A-4
    If a car loan is taken for 3 years at 12% annual interest rate, what is the average interest rate?

Solution:
    By Equation A-6

$$\bar{i} = \frac{12}{2}\left(\frac{3 + 1}{3}\right) = (6)\left(\frac{4}{3}\right) = 8.0$$

Example A-5
    What is the average interest rate on a home improvement loan to be repaid in 7 years at an annual interest rate of 10.75%?

Solution:

$$\bar{i} = \frac{10.25}{2}\left(\frac{7 + 1}{7}\right) = 5.86\%$$

Interest Tables

Appendix B

These tables are reproduced by permission from *Interest Tables: 0 to 25 Percent,* published by the Edison Electric Institute (EEI Pub. No. 67-21).

The following notations are used:

$$I = \text{interest rate per period}$$
$$N = \text{number of interest periods}$$
$$P = \text{present worth of money}$$
$$S = \text{future worth of money}$$
$$R = \text{uniform end-of-period payment}$$
$$(1 + I)^{**}N = (1 + I)^{N}$$

1.00 PERCENT COMPOUND INTEREST FACTORS

	SINGLE PAYMENT		UNIFORM ANNUAL SERIES				
N PERIODS	COMPOUND AMOUNT FACTOR GIVEN P TO FIND S $(1+I)^N$	PRESENT WORTH FACTOR GIVEN S TO FIND P $\dfrac{1}{(1+I)^N}$	SINKING FUND FACTOR GIVEN S TO FIND R $\dfrac{I}{(1+I)^N-1}$	CAPITAL RECOVERY FACTOR GIVEN P TO FIND R $\dfrac{I(1+I)^N}{(1+I)^N-1}$	COMPOUND AMOUNT FACTOR GIVEN R TO FIND S $\dfrac{(1+I)^N-1}{I}$	PRESENT WORTH FACTOR GIVEN R TO FIND P $\dfrac{(1+I)^N-1}{I(1+I)^N}$	N PERIODS
1	1.0100000	.9900990	1.0000000	1.0100000	1.0000000	.9900990	1
2	1.0201000	.9802960	.4975124	.5075124	2.0100000	1.9703951	2
3	1.0303010	.9705901	.3300221	.3400221	3.0301000	2.9409852	3
4	1.0406040	.9609803	.2462811	.2562811	4.0604010	3.9019656	4
5	1.0510101	.9514657	.1960398	.2060398	5.1010050	4.8534312	5
6	1.0615202	.9420452	.1625484	.1725484	6.1520151	5.7954765	6
7	1.0721354	.9327181	.1386283	.1486283	7.2135352	6.7281945	7
8	1.0828567	.9234832	.1206903	.1306903	8.2856706	7.6516778	8
9	1.0936853	.9143398	.1067404	.1167404	9.3685273	8.5660176	9
10	1.1046221	.9052870	.0955821	.1055821	10.4622125	9.4713045	10
11	1.1156683	.8963237	.0864541	.0964541	11.5668347	10.3676282	11
12	1.1268250	.8874492	.0788488	.0888488	12.6825030	11.2550775	12
13	1.1380933	.8786626	.0724148	.0824148	13.8093280	12.1337401	13
14	1.1494742	.8699630	.0669012	.0769012	14.9474213	13.0037030	14
15	1.1609690	.8613495	.0621238	.0721238	16.0948955	13.8650525	15
16	1.1725786	.8528213	.0579446	.0679446	17.2578645	14.7178738	16
17	1.1843044	.8443775	.0542581	.0642581	18.4304431	15.5622513	17
18	1.1961475	.8360173	.0509820	.0609820	19.6147476	16.3982686	18
19	1.2081090	.8277399	.0480518	.0580518	20.8108950	17.2260085	19
20	1.2201900	.8195445	.0454153	.0554153	22.0190040	18.0455530	20
21	1.2323919	.8114302	.0430308	.0530308	23.2391940	18.8569831	21
22	1.2447159	.8033962	.0408637	.0508637	24.4715860	19.6603793	22
23	1.2571630	.7954418	.0388858	.0488858	25.7163018	20.4558211	23
24	1.2697346	.7875661	.0370735	.0470735	26.9734649	21.2433873	24
25	1.2824320	.7797684	.0354068	.0454068	28.2431995	22.0231557	25
26	1.2952563	.7720480	.0338689	.0438689	29.5256315	22.7952037	26
27	1.3082089	.7644039	.0324455	.0424455	30.8208878	23.5596076	27
28	1.3212910	.7568356	.0311244	.0411244	32.1290967	24.3164432	28
29	1.3345039	.7493421	.0298950	.0398950	33.4503877	25.0657853	29
30	1.3478489	.7419229	.0287481	.0387481	34.7848915	25.8077082	30
31	1.3613274	.7345771	.0276757	.0376757	36.1327404	26.5422854	31
32	1.3749407	.7273041	.0266709	.0366709	37.4940679	27.2695895	32
33	1.3886901	.7201031	.0257274	.0357274	38.8690085	27.9896925	33
34	1.4025770	.7129733	.0248400	.0348400	40.2576986	28.7026659	34
35	1.4166028	.7059142	.0240037	.0340037	41.6602756	29.4085801	35
36	1.4307688	.6989249	.0232143	.0332143	43.0768784	30.1075050	36
37	1.4450765	.6920049	.0224680	.0324680	44.5076471	30.7995099	37
38	1.4595272	.6851534	.0217615	.0317615	45.9527236	31.4846633	38
39	1.4741225	.6783697	.0210916	.0310916	47.4122509	32.1630330	39
40	1.4888637	.6716531	.0204556	.0304556	48.8863734	32.8346861	40

NOTE— **N IS EXPONENT N

2.00 PERCENT COMPOUND INTEREST FACTORS

N PERIODS	SINGLE PAYMENT — COMPOUND AMOUNT FACTOR GIVEN P TO FIND S $(1 + I)^{**N}$	PRESENT WORTH FACTOR GIVEN S TO FIND P $\dfrac{1}{(1 + I)^{**N}}$	SINKING FUND FACTOR GIVEN S TO FIND R $\dfrac{I}{(1 + I)^{**N} - 1}$	UNIFORM ANNUAL SERIES — CAPITAL RECOVERY FACTOR GIVEN P TO FIND R $\dfrac{I(1 + I)^{**N}}{(1 + I)^{**N} - 1}$	COMPOUND AMOUNT FACTOR GIVEN R TO FIND S $\dfrac{(1 + I)^{**N} - 1}{I}$	PRESENT WORTH FACTOR GIVEN R TO FIND P $\dfrac{(1 + I)^{**N} - 1}{I(1 + I)^{**N}}$	N PERIODS
1	1.0200000	.9803922	1.0000000	1.0200000	1.0000000	.9803922	1
2	1.0404000	.9611688	.4950495	.5150495	2.0200000	1.9415609	2
3	1.0612080	.9423223	.3267547	.3467547	3.0604000	2.8838833	3
4	1.0824322	.9238454	.2426238	.2626238	4.1216080	3.8077287	4
5	1.1040808	.9057308	.1921584	.2121584	5.2040402	4.7134595	5
6	1.1261624	.8879714	.1585258	.1785258	6.3081210	5.6014309	6
7	1.1486857	.8705602	.1345120	.1545120	7.4342834	6.4719911	7
8	1.1716594	.8534904	.1165098	.1365098	8.5829691	7.3254814	8
9	1.1950926	.8367553	.1025154	.1225154	9.7546284	8.1622367	9
10	1.2189944	.8203483	.0913265	.1113265	10.9497210	8.9825850	10
11	1.2433743	.8042630	.0821779	.1021779	12.1687154	9.7868480	11
12	1.2682418	.7884932	.0745596	.0945596	13.4120897	10.5753412	12
13	1.2936066	.7730325	.0681184	.0881184	14.6803315	11.3483737	13
14	1.3194788	.7578750	.0626020	.0826020	15.9739382	12.1062486	14
15	1.3458683	.7430147	.0578255	.0778255	17.2934169	12.8492635	15
16	1.3727857	.7284458	.0536501	.0736501	18.6392853	13.5777093	16
17	1.4002414	.7141626	.0499698	.0699698	20.0120710	14.2918719	17
18	1.4282462	.7001594	.0467021	.0667021	21.4123124	14.9920313	18
19	1.4568112	.6864308	.0437818	.0637818	22.8405586	15.6784620	19
20	1.4859474	.6729713	.0411567	.0611567	24.2973698	16.3514333	20
21	1.5156663	.6597758	.0387848	.0587848	25.7833172	17.0112092	21
22	1.5459797	.6468390	.0366314	.0566314	27.2989835	17.6580482	22
23	1.5768993	.6341559	.0346681	.0546681	28.8449632	18.2922041	23
24	1.6084372	.6217215	.0328711	.0528711	30.4218625	18.9139256	24
25	1.6406060	.6095309	.0312204	.0512204	32.0302997	19.5234565	25
26	1.6734181	.5975793	.0296992	.0496992	33.6709057	20.1210358	26
27	1.7068865	.5858620	.0282931	.0482931	35.3443236	20.7068978	27
28	1.7410242	.5743746	.0269897	.0469897	37.0512103	21.2812724	28
29	1.7758447	.5631123	.0257784	.0457784	38.7922345	21.8443847	29
30	1.8113616	.5520709	.0246499	.0446499	40.5680792	22.3964556	30
31	1.8475888	.5412460	.0235963	.0435963	42.3794408	22.9377015	31
32	1.8845406	.5306333	.0226106	.0426106	44.2270296	23.4683348	32
33	1.9222314	.5202287	.0216865	.0416865	46.1115702	23.9885636	33
34	1.9606760	.5100282	.0208187	.0408187	48.0338016	24.4985917	34
35	1.9998896	.5000276	.0200022	.0400022	49.9944776	24.9986193	35
36	2.0398873	.4902232	.0192329	.0392329	51.9943672	25.4888425	36
37	2.0806851	.4806109	.0185068	.0385068	54.0342545	25.9694534	37
38	2.1222988	.4711872	.0178206	.0378206	56.1149396	26.4406406	38
39	2.1647448	.4619482	.0171711	.0371711	58.2372384	26.9025888	39
40	2.2080397	.4528904	.0165557	.0365557	60.4019832	27.3554792	40

NOTE— **N IS EXPONENT N

5.00 PERCENT COMPOUND INTEREST FACTORS

	SINGLE PAYMENT		UNIFORM ANNUAL SERIES				
N PERIODS	COMPOUND AMOUNT FACTOR GIVEN P TO FIND S $(1+I)^{**N}$	PRESENT WORTH FACTOR GIVEN S TO FIND P $\frac{1}{(1+I)^{**N}}$	SINKING FUND FACTOR GIVEN S TO FIND R $\frac{I}{(1+I)^{**N}-1}$	CAPITAL RECOVERY FACTOR GIVEN P TO FIND R $\frac{I(1+I)^{**N}}{(1+I)^{**N}-1}$	COMPOUND AMOUNT FACTOR GIVEN R TO FIND S $\frac{(1+I)^{**N}-1}{I}$	PRESENT WORTH FACTOR GIVEN R TO FIND P $\frac{(1+I)^{**N}-1}{I(1+I)^{**N}}$	N PERIODS
1	1.0500000	.9523810	1.0000000	1.0500000	1.0000000	.9523810	1
2	1.1025000	.9070295	.4878049	.5378049	2.0500000	1.8594104	2
3	1.1576250	.8638376	.3172086	.3672086	3.1525000	2.7232480	3
4	1.2155063	.8227025	.2320118	.2820118	4.3101250	3.5459505	4
5	1.2762816	.7835262	.1809748	.2309748	5.5256313	4.3294767	5
6	1.3400956	.7462154	.1470175	.1970175	6.8019128	5.0756921	6
7	1.4071004	.7106813	.1228198	.1728198	8.1420085	5.7863734	7
8	1.4774554	.6768394	.1047218	.1547218	9.5491089	6.4632128	8
9	1.5513282	.6446089	.0906901	.1406901	11.0265643	7.1078217	9
10	1.6288946	.6139133	.0795046	.1295046	12.5778925	7.7217349	10
11	1.7103394	.5846793	.0703889	.1203889	14.2067872	8.3064142	11
12	1.7958563	.5568374	.0628254	.1128254	15.9171265	8.8632516	12
13	1.8856491	.5303214	.0564558	.1064558	17.7129828	9.3935730	13
14	1.9799316	.5050680	.0510240	.1010240	19.5986320	9.8986409	14
15	2.0789282	.4810171	.0463423	.0963423	21.5785636	10.3796580	15
16	2.1828746	.4581115	.0422699	.0922699	23.6574918	10.8377696	16
17	2.2920183	.4362967	.0386991	.0886991	25.8403664	11.2740662	17
18	2.4066192	.4155207	.0355462	.0855462	28.1323847	11.6895869	18
19	2.5269502	.3957340	.0327450	.0827450	30.5390039	12.0853209	19
20	2.6532977	.3768895	.0302426	.0802426	33.0659541	12.4622103	20
21	2.7859626	.3589424	.0279961	.0779961	35.7192518	12.8211527	21
22	2.9252607	.3418499	.0259705	.0759705	38.5052144	13.1630026	22
23	3.0715238	.3255713	.0241368	.0741368	41.4304751	13.4885739	23
24	3.2250999	.3100679	.0224709	.0724709	44.5019989	13.7986418	24
25	3.3863549	.2953028	.0209525	.0709525	47.7270988	14.0939446	25
26	3.5556727	.2812407	.0195643	.0695643	51.1134538	14.3751853	26
27	3.7334563	.2678483	.0182919	.0682919	54.6691264	14.6430336	27
28	3.9201291	.2550936	.0171225	.0671225	58.4025828	14.8981273	28
29	4.1161356	.2429463	.0160455	.0660455	62.3227119	15.1410736	29
30	4.3219424	.2313774	.0150514	.0650514	66.4388475	15.3724510	30
31	4.5380395	.2203595	.0141321	.0641321	70.7607899	15.5928105	31
32	4.7649415	.2098662	.0132804	.0632804	75.2988294	15.8026767	32
33	5.0031885	.1998725	.0124900	.0624900	80.0637708	16.0025492	33
34	5.2533480	.1903548	.0117554	.0617554	85.0669594	16.1929040	34
35	5.5160154	.1812903	.0110717	.0610717	90.3203074	16.3741943	35
36	5.7918161	.1726574	.0104345	.0604345	95.8363227	16.5468517	36
37	6.0814069	.1644356	.0098398	.0598398	101.6281389	16.7112873	37
38	6.3854773	.1566054	.0092842	.0592842	107.7095458	16.8678927	38
39	6.7047512	.1491480	.0087646	.0587646	114.0950231	17.0170407	39
40	7.0399887	.1420457	.0082782	.0582782	120.7997742	17.1590864	40

NOTE— **N IS EXPONENT N

6.00 PERCENT COMPOUND INTEREST FACTORS

N PERIODS	SINGLE PAYMENT COMPOUND AMOUNT FACTOR GIVEN P TO FIND S $(1 + I)^{**N}$	SINGLE PAYMENT PRESENT WORTH FACTOR GIVEN S TO FIND P $\dfrac{1}{(1 + I)^{**N}}$	SINKING FUND FACTOR GIVEN S TO FIND R $\dfrac{I}{(1+I)^{**N} - 1}$	UNIFORM ANNUAL SERIES CAPITAL RECOVERY FACTOR GIVEN P TO FIND R $\dfrac{I(1 + I)^{**N}}{(1 + I)^{**N} - 1}$	UNIFORM ANNUAL SERIES COMPOUND AMOUNT FACTOR GIVEN R TO FIND S $\dfrac{(1 + I)^{**N} - 1}{I}$	PRESENT WORTH FACTOR GIVEN R TO FIND P $\dfrac{(1 + I)^{**N} - 1}{I(1 + I)^{**N}}$	N PERIODS
1	1.0600000	.9433962	1.0000000	1.0600000	1.0000000	.9433962	1
2	1.1236000	.8899964	.4854369	.5454369	2.0600000	1.8333927	2
3	1.1910160	.8396193	.3141098	.3741098	3.1836000	2.6730119	3
4	1.2624770	.7920937	.2285915	.2885915	4.3746160	3.4651056	4
5	1.3382256	.7472582	.1773964	.2373964	5.6370930	4.2123638	5
6	1.4185191	.7049605	.1433626	.2033626	6.9753185	4.9173243	6
7	1.5036303	.6650571	.1191350	.1791350	8.3938376	5.5823814	7
8	1.5938481	.6274124	.1010359	.1610359	9.8974679	6.2097938	8
9	1.6894790	.5918985	.0870222	.1470222	11.4913160	6.8016923	9
10	1.7908477	.5583948	.0758680	.1358680	13.1807949	7.3600871	10
11	1.8982986	.5267875	.0667929	.1267929	14.9716426	7.8868746	11
12	2.0121965	.4969694	.0592770	.1192770	16.8699412	8.3838439	12
13	2.1329283	.4688390	.0529601	.1129601	18.8821377	8.8526830	13
14	2.2609040	.4423010	.0475849	.1075849	21.0150659	9.2949839	14
15	2.3965582	.4172651	.0429628	.1029628	23.2759699	9.7122490	15
16	2.5403517	.3936463	.0389521	.0989521	25.6725281	10.1058953	16
17	2.6927728	.3713644	.0354448	.0954448	28.2128798	10.4772597	17
18	2.8543392	.3503438	.0323565	.0923565	30.9056525	10.8276035	18
19	3.0255995	.3305130	.0296209	.0896209	33.7599917	11.1581165	19
20	3.2071355	.3118047	.0271846	.0871846	36.7855912	11.4699212	20
21	3.3995636	.2941554	.0250045	.0850045	39.9927267	11.7640766	21
22	3.6035374	.2775051	.0230456	.0830456	43.3922903	12.0415817	22
23	3.8197497	.2617973	.0212785	.0812785	46.9958277	12.3033790	23
24	4.0489346	.2469785	.0196790	.0796790	50.8155774	12.5503575	24
25	4.2918707	.2329986	.0182267	.0782267	54.8645120	12.7833562	25
26	4.5493830	.2198100	.0169043	.0769043	59.1563827	13.0031662	26
27	4.8223459	.2073680	.0156972	.0756972	63.7057657	13.2105341	27
28	5.1116867	.1956301	.0145926	.0745926	68.5281116	13.4061643	28
29	5.4183879	.1845567	.0135796	.0735796	73.6397983	13.5907210	29
30	5.7434912	.1741101	.0126489	.0726489	79.0581862	13.7648312	30
31	6.0881006	.1642548	.0117922	.0717922	84.8016774	13.9290860	31
32	6.4533867	.1549574	.0110023	.0710023	90.8897780	14.0840434	32
33	6.8405899	.1461862	.0102729	.0702729	97.3431647	14.2302296	33
34	7.2510253	.1379115	.0095984	.0695984	104.1837546	14.3681411	34
35	7.6860868	.1301052	.0089739	.0689739	111.4347799	14.4982464	35
36	8.1472520	.1227408	.0083948	.0683948	119.1208667	14.6209871	36
37	8.6360871	.1157932	.0078574	.0678574	127.2681187	14.7367803	37
38	9.1542523	.1092389	.0073581	.0673581	135.9042058	14.8460192	38
39	9.7035075	.1030555	.0068938	.0668938	145.0584581	14.9490747	39
40	10.2857179	.0972222	.0064615	.0664615	154.7619656	15.0462969	40

NOTE- **N IS EXPONENT N

7.00 PERCENT COMPOUND INTEREST FACTORS

| | SINGLE PAYMENT | | UNIFORM ANNUAL SERIES | | | | |
N PERIODS	COMPOUND AMOUNT FACTOR GIVEN P TO FIND S $(1+I)^{**N}$	PRESENT WORTH FACTOR GIVEN S TO FIND P $\frac{1}{(1+I)^{**N}}$	SINKING FUND FACTOR GIVEN S TO FIND R $\frac{I}{(1+I)^{**N}-1}$	CAPITAL RECOVERY FACTOR GIVEN P TO FIND R $\frac{I(1+I)^{**N}}{(1+I)^{**N}-1}$	COMPOUND AMOUNT FACTOR GIVEN R TO FIND S $\frac{(1+I)^{**N}-1}{I}$	PRESENT WORTH FACTOR GIVEN R TO FIND P $\frac{(1+I)^{**N}-1}{I(1+I)^{**N}}$	N PERIODS
1	1.0700000	.9345794	1.0000000	1.0700000	1.0000000	.9345794	1
2	1.1449000	.8734387	.4830918	.5530918	2.0700000	1.8080182	2
3	1.2250430	.8162979	.3110517	.3810517	3.2149000	2.6243160	3
4	1.3107960	.7628952	.2252281	.2952281	4.4399430	3.3872113	4
5	1.4025517	.7129862	.1738907	.2438907	5.7507390	4.1001974	5
6	1.5007304	.6663422	.1397958	.2097958	7.1532907	4.7665397	6
7	1.6057815	.6227497	.1155532	.1855532	8.6540211	5.3892894	7
8	1.7181862	.5820091	.0974678	.1674678	10.2598026	5.9712985	8
9	1.8384592	.5439337	.0834865	.1534865	11.9779887	6.5152322	9
10	1.9671514	.5083493	.0723775	.1423775	13.8164480	7.0235815	10
11	2.1048520	.4750928	.0633569	.1333569	15.7835993	7.4986743	11
12	2.2521916	.4440120	.0559020	.1259020	17.8884513	7.9426863	12
13	2.4098450	.4149644	.0496508	.1196508	20.1406429	8.3576507	13
14	2.5785342	.3878172	.0443449	.1143449	22.5504879	8.7454680	14
15	2.7590315	.3624460	.0397946	.1097946	25.1290220	9.1079140	15
16	2.9521637	.3387346	.0358576	.1058576	27.8880536	9.4466486	16
17	3.1588152	.3165744	.0324252	.1024252	30.8402173	9.7632230	17
18	3.3799323	.2958639	.0294126	.0994126	33.9990325	10.0590869	18
19	3.6165275	.2765083	.0267530	.0967530	37.3789648	10.3355952	19
20	3.8696845	.2584190	.0243929	.0943929	40.9954923	10.5940142	20
21	4.1405624	.2415131	.0222890	.0922890	44.8651768	10.8355273	21
22	4.4304017	.2257132	.0204058	.0904058	49.0057392	11.0612405	22
23	4.7405299	.2109466	.0187139	.0887139	53.4361409	11.2721874	23
24	5.0723670	.1971466	.0171890	.0871890	58.1766708	11.4693340	24
25	5.4274326	.1842492	.0158105	.0858105	63.2490377	11.6535832	25
26	5.8073529	.1721955	.0145610	.0845610	68.6764704	11.8257787	26
27	6.2138676	.1609304	.0134257	.0834257	74.4838233	11.9867090	27
28	6.6488384	.1504022	.0123919	.0823919	80.6976909	12.1371113	28
29	7.1142570	.1405628	.0114487	.0814487	87.3465293	12.2776741	29
30	7.6122550	.1313671	.0105864	.0805864	94.4607863	12.4090412	30
31	8.1451129	.1227730	.0097969	.0797969	102.0730414	12.5318142	31
32	8.7152708	.1147411	.0090729	.0790729	110.2181543	12.6465553	32
33	9.3253398	.1072347	.0084081	.0784081	118.9334251	12.7537900	33
34	9.9781135	.1002193	.0077967	.0777967	128.2587648	12.8540094	34
35	10.6765815	.0936629	.0072340	.0772340	138.2368784	12.9476723	35
36	11.4239422	.0875355	.0067153	.0767153	148.9134598	13.0352078	36
37	12.2236181	.0818088	.0062368	.0762368	160.3374020	13.1170166	37
38	13.0792714	.0764569	.0057951	.0757951	172.6610202	13.1934735	38
39	13.9948204	.0714550	.0053868	.0753868	185.6602916	13.2649285	39
40	14.9744578	.0667804	.0050091	.0750091	199.6351120	13.3317088	40

NOTE- **N IS EXPONENT N

8.00 PERCENT COMPOUND INTEREST FACTORS

	SINGLE PAYMENT		UNIFORM ANNUAL SERIES				
N PERIODS	COMPOUND AMOUNT FACTOR GIVEN P TO FIND S $(1+I)^{**}N$	PRESENT WORTH FACTOR GIVEN S TO FIND P $\frac{1}{(1+I)^{**}N}$	SINKING FUND FACTOR GIVEN S TO FIND R $\frac{I}{(1+I)^{**}N-1}$	CAPITAL RECOVERY FACTOR GIVEN P TO FIND R $\frac{I(1+I)^{**}N}{(1+I)^{**}N-1}$	COMPOUND AMOUNT FACTOR GIVEN R TO FIND S $\frac{(1+I)^{**}N-1}{I}$	PRESENT WORTH FACTOR GIVEN R TO FIND P $\frac{(1+I)^{**}N-1}{I(1+I)^{**}N}$	N PERIODS
1	1.0800000	.9259259	1.0000000	1.0800000	1.0000000	.9259259	1
2	1.1664000	.8573388	.4807692	.5607692	2.0800000	1.7832647	2
3	1.2597120	.7938322	.3080335	.3880335	3.2464000	2.5770970	3
4	1.3604890	.7350299	.2219208	.3019208	4.5061120	3.3121268	4
5	1.4693281	.6805832	.1704565	.2504565	5.8666010	3.9927100	5
6	1.5868743	.6301696	.1363154	.2163154	7.3359290	4.6228797	6
7	1.7138243	.5834904	.1120724	.1920724	8.9228034	5.2063701	7
8	1.8509302	.5402689	.0940148	.1740148	10.6366276	5.7466389	8
9	1.9990046	.5002490	.0800797	.1600797	12.4875578	6.2468879	9
10	2.1589250	.4631935	.0690295	.1490295	14.4865625	6.7100814	10
11	2.3316390	.4288829	.0600763	.1400763	16.6454875	7.1389643	11
12	2.5181701	.3971138	.0526950	.1326950	18.9771265	7.5360780	12
13	2.7196237	.3676979	.0465218	.1265218	21.4952966	7.9037759	13
14	2.9371936	.3404610	.0412969	.1212969	24.2149203	8.2442370	14
15	3.1721691	.3152417	.0368295	.1168295	27.1521139	8.5594787	15
16	3.4259426	.2918905	.0329769	.1129769	30.3242830	8.8513692	16
17	3.7000181	.2702690	.0296294	.1096294	33.7502257	9.1216381	17
18	3.9960195	.2502490	.0267021	.1067021	37.4502437	9.3718871	18
19	4.3157011	.2317121	.0241276	.1041276	41.4462632	9.6035992	19
20	4.6609571	.2145482	.0218522	.1018522	45.7619643	9.8181474	20
21	5.0338337	.1986557	.0198323	.0998323	50.4229214	10.0168032	21
22	5.4365404	.1839405	.0180321	.0980321	55.4567552	10.2007437	22
23	5.8714636	.1703153	.0164222	.0964222	60.8932966	10.3710589	23
24	6.3411807	.1576993	.0149780	.0949780	66.7647592	10.5287583	24
25	6.8484752	.1460179	.0136788	.0936788	73.1059400	10.6747762	25
26	7.3963532	.1352018	.0125071	.0925071	79.9544151	10.8099780	26
27	7.9880615	.1251868	.0114481	.0914481	87.3507684	10.9351648	27
28	8.6271064	.1159137	.0104889	.0904889	95.3388298	11.0510785	28
29	9.3172749	.1073275	.0096185	.0896185	103.9659362	11.1584060	29
30	10.0626569	.0993773	.0088274	.0888274	113.2832111	11.2577883	30
31	10.8676694	.0920160	.0081073	.0881073	123.3458680	11.3497994	31
32	11.7370830	.0852000	.0074508	.0874508	134.2135374	11.4349994	32
33	12.6760496	.0788889	.0068516	.0868516	145.9506204	11.5138884	33
34	13.6901336	.0730453	.0063041	.0863041	158.6266701	11.5869337	34
35	14.7853443	.0676345	.0058033	.0858033	172.3168037	11.6545682	35
36	15.9681718	.0626246	.0053447	.0853447	187.1021480	11.7171928	36
37	17.2456256	.0579857	.0049244	.0849244	203.0703198	11.7751785	37
38	18.6252756	.0536905	.0045389	.0845389	220.3159454	11.8288690	38
39	20.1152977	.0497134	.0041851	.0841851	238.9412210	11.8785824	39
40	21.7245215	.0460309	.0038602	.0838602	259.0565187	11.9246133	40

NOTE— $**N$ IS EXPONENT N

9.00 PERCENT COMPOUND INTEREST FACTORS

	SINGLE PAYMENT		SINKING FUND FACTOR	UNIFORM ANNUAL SERIES			
N PERIODS	COMPOUND AMOUNT FACTOR GIVEN P TO FIND S	PRESENT WORTH FACTOR GIVEN S TO FIND P	GIVEN S TO FIND R	CAPITAL RECOVERY FACTOR GIVEN P TO FIND R	COMPOUND AMOUNT FACTOR GIVEN R TO FIND S	PRESENT WORTH FACTOR GIVEN R TO FIND P	N PERIODS
	$(1 + I)^{**N}$	$\dfrac{1}{(1 + I)^{**N}}$	$\dfrac{I}{(1 + I)^{**N} - 1}$	$\dfrac{I(1 + I)^{**N}}{(1 + I)^{**N} - 1}$	$\dfrac{(1 + I)^{**N} - 1}{I}$	$\dfrac{(1 + I)^{**N} - 1}{I(1 + I)^{**N}}$	
1	1.0900000	.9174312	1.0000000	1.0900000	1.0000000	.9174312	1
2	1.1881000	.8416800	.4784689	.5684689	2.0900000	1.7591112	2
3	1.2950290	.7721835	.3050548	.3950548	3.2781000	2.5312947	3
4	1.4115816	.7084252	.2186687	.3086687	4.5731290	3.2397199	4
5	1.5386240	.6499314	.1670925	.2570925	5.9847106	3.8896513	5
6	1.6771001	.5962673	.1329198	.2229198	7.5233346	4.4859186	6
7	1.8280391	.5470342	.1086905	.1986905	9.2004347	5.0329528	7
8	1.9925626	.5018663	.0906744	.1806744	11.0284738	5.5348191	8
9	2.1718933	.4604278	.0767988	.1667988	13.0210364	5.9952469	9
10	2.3673637	.4224108	.0658201	.1558201	15.1929297	6.4176577	10
11	2.5804264	.3875329	.0569467	.1469467	17.5602934	6.8051906	11
12	2.8126648	.3555347	.0496507	.1396507	20.1407198	7.1607253	12
13	3.0658046	.3261786	.0435666	.1335666	22.9533846	7.4869039	13
14	3.3417270	.2992465	.0384332	.1284332	26.0191892	7.7861504	14
15	3.6424825	.2745380	.0340589	.1240589	29.3609162	8.0606884	15
16	3.9703059	.2518698	.0302999	.1202999	33.0033987	8.3125582	16
17	4.3276334	.2310732	.0270462	.1170462	36.9737046	8.5436314	17
18	4.7171204	.2119997	.0242123	.1142123	41.3013380	8.7556251	18
19	5.1416613	.1944897	.0217304	.1117304	46.0184584	8.9501148	19
20	5.6044108	.1784309	.0195465	.1095465	51.1601196	9.1285457	20
21	6.1088077	.1636981	.0176166	.1076166	56.7645304	9.2922237	21
22	6.6586004	.1501817	.0159050	.1059050	62.8733381	9.4424264	22
23	7.2578745	.1377814	.0143819	.1043819	69.5319386	9.5802068	23
24	7.9110832	.1264049	.0130226	.1030226	76.7898131	9.7066118	24
25	8.6230807	.1159678	.0118063	.1018063	84.7008962	9.8225796	25
26	9.3991579	.1063925	.0107154	.1007154	93.3239769	9.9289721	26
27	10.2450821	.0976078	.0097349	.0997349	102.7231348	10.0265799	27
28	11.1671395	.0895484	.0088520	.0988520	112.9682169	10.1161284	28
29	12.1721821	.0821545	.0080557	.0980557	124.1355565	10.1982829	29
30	13.2676785	.0753711	.0073364	.0973364	136.3075385	10.2736540	30
31	14.4617695	.0691478	.0066856	.0966856	149.5752170	10.3428019	31
32	15.7633288	.0634384	.0060962	.0960962	164.0369865	10.4062403	32
33	17.1820284	.0582003	.0055617	.0955617	179.8003153	10.4644406	33
34	18.7284109	.0533948	.0050766	.0950766	196.9823437	10.5178354	34
35	20.4139679	.0489861	.0046358	.0946358	215.7107547	10.5668215	35
36	22.2512250	.0449413	.0042350	.0942350	236.1247226	10.6117628	36
37	24.2538353	.0412306	.0038703	.0938703	258.3759476	10.6529934	37
38	26.4366805	.0378262	.0035382	.0935382	282.6297829	10.6908196	38
39	28.8159817	.0347030	.0032356	.0932356	309.0664633	10.7255226	39
40	31.4094201	.0318376	.0029596	.0929596	337.8824450	10.7573602	40

NOTE- **N IS EXPONENT N

10.00 PERCENT COMPOUND INTEREST FACTORS

N PERIODS	SINGLE PAYMENT		SINKING FUND FACTOR GIVEN S TO FIND R	UNIFORM ANNUAL SERIES			N PERIODS
	COMPOUND AMOUNT FACTOR GIVEN P TO FIND S	PRESENT WORTH FACTOR GIVEN S TO FIND P		CAPITAL RECOVERY FACTOR GIVEN P TO FIND R	COMPOUND AMOUNT FACTOR GIVEN R TO FIND S	PRESENT WORTH FACTOR GIVEN R TO FIND P	
	$(1+I)^{**N}$	$\dfrac{1}{(1+I)^{**N}}$	$\dfrac{I}{(1+I)^{**N}-1}$	$\dfrac{I(1+I)^{**N}}{(1+I)^{**N}-1}$	$\dfrac{(1+I)^{**N}-1}{I}$	$\dfrac{(1+I)^{**N}-1}{I(1+I)^{**N}}$	
1	1.1000000	.9090909	1.0000000	1.1000000	1.0000000	.9090909	1
2	1.2100000	.8264463	.4761905	.5761905	2.1000000	1.7355372	2
3	1.3310000	.7513148	.3021148	.4021148	3.3100000	2.4868520	3
4	1.4641000	.6830135	.2154708	.3154708	4.6410000	3.1698654	4
5	1.6105100	.6209213	.1637975	.2637975	6.1051000	3.7907868	5
6	1.7715610	.5644739	.1296074	.2296074	7.7156100	4.3552607	6
7	1.9487171	.5131581	.1054055	.2054055	9.4871710	4.8684188	7
8	2.1435888	.4665074	.0874440	.1874440	11.4358881	5.3349262	8
9	2.3579477	.4240976	.0736405	.1736405	13.5794769	5.7590238	9
10	2.5937425	.3855433	.0627454	.1627454	15.9374246	6.1445671	10
11	2.8531167	.3504939	.0539631	.1539631	18.5311671	6.4950610	11
12	3.1384284	.3186308	.0467633	.1467633	21.3842838	6.8136918	12
13	3.4522712	.2896644	.0407785	.1407785	24.5227121	7.1033562	13
14	3.7974983	.2633313	.0357462	.1357462	27.9749834	7.3666875	14
15	4.1772482	.2393920	.0314738	.1314738	31.7724817	7.6060795	15
16	4.5949730	.2176291	.0278166	.1278166	35.9497299	7.8237086	16
17	5.0544703	.1978447	.0246641	.1246641	40.5447028	8.0215533	17
18	5.5599173	.1798588	.0219302	.1219302	45.5991731	8.2014121	18
19	6.1159090	.1635080	.0195469	.1195469	51.1590904	8.3649201	19
20	6.7274999	.1486436	.0174596	.1174596	57.2749995	8.5135637	20
21	7.4002499	.1351306	.0156244	.1156244	64.0024995	8.6486943	21
22	8.1402749	.1228460	.0140051	.1140051	71.4027494	8.7715403	22
23	8.9543024	.1116782	.0125718	.1125718	79.5430243	8.8832184	23
24	9.8497327	.1015256	.0112998	.1112998	88.4973268	8.9847440	24
25	10.8347059	.0922960	.0101681	.1101681	98.3470594	9.0770400	25
26	11.9181765	.0839055	.0091590	.1091590	109.1817654	9.1609455	26
27	13.1099942	.0762777	.0082576	.1082576	121.0999419	9.2372232	27
28	14.4209936	.0693433	.0074510	.1074510	134.2099361	9.3065665	28
29	15.8630930	.0630394	.0067281	.1067281	148.6309297	9.3696059	29
30	17.4494023	.0573086	.0060792	.1060792	164.4940227	9.4269145	30
31	19.1943425	.0520987	.0054962	.1054962	181.9434250	9.4790132	31
32	21.1137767	.0473624	.0049717	.1049717	201.1377675	9.5263756	32
33	23.2251544	.0430568	.0044994	.1044994	222.2515442	9.5694324	33
34	25.5476699	.0391425	.0040737	.1040737	245.4766986	9.6085749	34
35	28.1024368	.0355841	.0036897	.1036897	271.0243685	9.6441590	35
36	30.9126805	.0323492	.0033431	.1033431	299.1268053	9.6765082	36
37	34.0039486	.0294083	.0030299	.1030299	330.0394859	9.7059165	37
38	37.4043434	.0267349	.0027469	.1027469	364.0434344	9.7326514	38
39	41.1447778	.0243044	.0024910	.1024910	401.4477779	9.7569558	39
40	45.2592556	.0220949	.0022594	.1022594	442.5925557	9.7790507	40

NOTE- **N IS EXPONENT N

11.00 PERCENT COMPOUND INTEREST FACTORS

	SINGLE PAYMENT		UNIFORM ANNUAL SERIES				
N PERIODS	COMPOUND AMOUNT FACTOR GIVEN P TO FIND S $(1 + I)^{N}$	PRESENT WORTH FACTOR GIVEN S TO FIND P $\dfrac{1}{(1 + I)^{N}}$	SINKING FUND FACTOR GIVEN S TO FIND R $\dfrac{I}{(1 + I)^{N} - 1}$	CAPITAL RECOVERY FACTOR GIVEN P TO FIND R $\dfrac{I(1 + I)^{N}}{(1 + I)^{N} - 1}$	COMPOUND AMOUNT FACTOR GIVEN R TO FIND S $\dfrac{(1 + I)^{N} - 1}{I}$	PRESENT WORTH FACTOR GIVEN R TO FIND P $\dfrac{(1 + I)^{N} - 1}{I(1 + I)^{N}}$	N PERIODS
1	1.1100000	.9009009	1.0000000	1.1100000	1.0000000	.9009009	1
2	1.2321000	.8116224	.4739336	.5839336	2.1100000	1.7125233	2
3	1.3676310	.7311914	.2992131	.4092131	3.3421000	2.4437147	3
4	1.5180704	.6587310	.2123264	.3223264	4.7097310	3.1024457	4
5	1.6850582	.5934513	.1605703	.2705703	6.2278014	3.6958970	5
6	1.8704146	.5346408	.1263766	.2363766	7.9128596	4.2305379	6
7	2.0761602	.4816584	.1022153	.2122153	9.7832741	4.7121963	7
8	2.3045378	.4339265	.0843211	.1943211	11.8594343	5.1461228	8
9	2.5580369	.3909248	.0706017	.1806017	14.1639720	5.5370475	9
10	2.8394210	.3521845	.0598014	.1698014	16.7220090	5.8892320	10
11	3.1517573	.3172833	.0511210	.1611210	19.5614300	6.2065153	11
12	3.4984506	.2858408	.0440273	.1540273	22.7131872	6.4923561	12
13	3.8832802	.2575143	.0381510	.1481510	26.2116378	6.7498704	13
14	4.3104410	.2319948	.0332282	.1432282	30.0949180	6.9818652	14
15	4.7845895	.2090043	.0290652	.1390652	34.4055590	7.1908696	15
16	5.3108943	.1882922	.0255167	.1355167	39.1899485	7.3791618	16
17	5.8950927	.1696326	.0224715	.1324715	44.5008428	7.5487944	17
18	6.5435529	.1528222	.0198429	.1298429	50.3995355	7.7016166	18
19	7.2633437	.1376776	.0175625	.1275625	56.9394884	7.8392942	19
20	8.0623115	.1240339	.0155756	.1255756	64.2028321	7.9633281	20
21	8.9491658	.1117423	.0138379	.1238379	72.2651437	8.0750704	21
22	9.9335740	.1006687	.0123131	.1223131	81.2143095	8.1757391	22
23	11.0262672	.0906925	.0109712	.1209712	91.1478835	8.2664316	23
24	12.2391566	.0817050	.0097872	.1197872	102.1741507	8.3481366	24
25	13.5854638	.0736081	.0087402	.1187402	114.4133073	8.4217447	25
26	15.0798648	.0663136	.0078126	.1178126	127.9987711	8.4880583	26
27	16.7386500	.0597420	.0069892	.1169892	143.0786359	8.5478002	27
28	18.5799014	.0538216	.0062571	.1162571	159.8172859	8.6016218	28
29	20.6236906	.0484879	.0056055	.1156055	178.3971873	8.6501098	29
30	22.8922966	.0436828	.0050246	.1150246	199.0208779	8.6937926	30
31	25.4104492	.0393539	.0045063	.1145063	221.9131745	8.7331465	31
32	28.2055986	.0354540	.0040433	.1140433	247.3236237	8.7686004	32
33	31.3082145	.0319405	.0036294	.1136294	275.5292223	8.8005409	33
34	34.7521180	.0287752	.0032591	.1132591	306.6374368	8.8293161	34
35	38.5748510	.0259236	.0029275	.1129275	341.5895548	8.8552398	35
36	42.8180846	.0233545	.0026304	.1126304	380.1644058	8.8785944	36
37	47.5280740	.0210402	.0023642	.1123642	422.9824905	8.8996346	37
38	52.7561621	.0189551	.0021254	.1121254	470.5105644	8.9185897	38
39	58.5599399	.0170767	.0019111	.1119111	523.2667265	8.9356664	39
40	65.0008673	.0153844	.0017187	.1117187	581.8260664	8.9510508	40

NOTE— $**N$ IS EXPONENT N

12.00 PERCENT COMPOUND INTEREST FACTORS

N PERIODS	SINGLE PAYMENT		UNIFORM ANNUAL SERIES				N PERIODS
	COMPOUND AMOUNT FACTOR GIVEN P TO FIND S	PRESENT WORTH FACTOR GIVEN S TO FIND P	SINKING FUND FACTOR GIVEN S TO FIND R	CAPITAL RECOVERY FACTOR GIVEN P TO FIND R	COMPOUND AMOUNT FACTOR GIVEN R TO FIND S	PRESENT WORTH FACTOR GIVEN R TO FIND P	
	$(1 + I)$**N	$\dfrac{1}{(1 + I)$**$N}$	$\dfrac{I}{(1 + I)$**$N - 1}$	$\dfrac{I(1 + I)$**$N}{(1 + I)$**$N - 1}$	$\dfrac{(1 + I)$**$N - 1}{I}$	$\dfrac{(1 + I)$**$N - 1}{I(1 + I)$**$N}$	
1	1.1200000	.8928571	1.0000000	1.1200000	1.0000000	.8928571	1
2	1.2544000	.7971939	.4716981	.5916981	2.1200000	1.6900510	2
3	1.4049280	.7117802	.2963490	.4163490	3.3744000	2.4018313	3
4	1.5735194	.6355181	.2092344	.3292344	4.7793280	3.0373493	4
5	1.7623417	.5674269	.1574097	.2774097	6.3528474	3.6047762	5
6	1.9738227	.5066311	.1232257	.2432257	8.1151890	4.1114073	6
7	2.2106814	.4523492	.0991177	.2191177	10.0890117	4.5637565	7
8	2.4759632	.4038832	.0813028	.2013028	12.2996931	4.9676398	8
9	2.7730788	.3606100	.0676789	.1876789	14.7756563	5.3282498	9
10	3.1058482	.3219732	.0569842	.1769842	17.5487351	5.6502230	10
11	3.4785500	.2874761	.0484154	.1684154	20.6546833	5.9376991	11
12	3.8959760	.2566751	.0414368	.1614368	24.1331333	6.1943742	12
13	4.3634931	.2291742	.0356772	.1556772	28.0291093	6.4235484	13
14	4.8871123	.2046198	.0308772	.1508772	32.3926024	6.6281682	14
15	5.4735658	.1826963	.0268242	.1468242	37.2797147	6.8108645	15
16	6.1303937	.1631217	.0233900	.1433900	42.7532804	6.9739862	16
17	6.8660409	.1456443	.0204567	.1404567	48.8836741	7.1196305	17
18	7.6899658	.1300336	.0179373	.1379373	55.7497150	7.2496701	18
19	8.6127617	.1161068	.0157630	.1357630	63.4396808	7.3657769	19
20	9.6462931	.1036668	.0138788	.1338788	72.0524424	7.4694436	20
21	10.8038483	.0925596	.0122401	.1322401	81.6987355	7.5620032	21
22	12.1003101	.0826425	.0108105	.1308105	92.5025838	7.6446457	22
23	13.5523473	.0737880	.0095600	.1295600	104.6028939	7.7184337	23
24	15.1786289	.0658821	.0084634	.1284634	118.1552411	7.7843158	24
25	17.0000644	.0588233	.0075000	.1275000	133.3338701	7.8431391	25
26	19.0400721	.0525208	.0066519	.1266519	150.3339345	7.8956599	26
27	21.3248808	.0468936	.0059041	.1259041	169.3740066	7.9425535	27
28	23.8836665	.0418693	.0052439	.1252439	190.6988874	7.9844228	28
29	26.7497305	.0373833	.0046602	.1246602	214.5827539	8.0218060	29
30	29.9599221	.0333779	.0041437	.1241437	241.3326843	8.0551840	30
31	33.5551128	.0298017	.0036861	.1236861	271.2920065	8.0849857	31
32	37.5817263	.0266087	.0032803	.1232803	304.8477192	8.1115944	32
33	42.0915335	.0237577	.0029203	.1229203	342.4294455	8.1353521	33
34	47.1425175	.0212123	.0026006	.1226006	384.5207790	8.1565644	34
35	52.7996196	.0189355	.0023166	.1223166	431.6634965	8.1755039	35
36	59.1355739	.0169103	.0020641	.1220641	484.4631161	8.1924142	36
37	66.2318428	.0150985	.0018396	.1218396	543.5986900	8.2075127	37
38	74.1796639	.0134808	.0016398	.1216398	609.8305328	8.2209935	38
39	83.0812236	.0120364	.0014620	.1214620	684.1019167	8.2330299	39
40	93.0509704	.0107468	.0013036	.1213036	767.0914203	8.2437767	40

NOTE- **N IS EXPONENT N

253

15.00%

15.00 PERCENT COMPOUND INTEREST FACTORS

	------SINGLE PAYMENT------			------UNIFORM ANNUAL SERIES------			
	COMPOUND AMOUNT FACTOR GIVEN P TO FIND S	PRESENT WORTH FACTOR GIVEN S TO FIND P	SINKING FUND FACTOR GIVEN S TO FIND R	CAPITAL RECOVERY FACTOR GIVEN P TO FIND R	COMPOUND AMOUNT FACTOR GIVEN R TO FIND S	PRESENT WORTH FACTOR GIVEN R TO FIND P	
N PERIODS	$(1 + I)**N$	$\dfrac{1}{(1 + I)**N}$	$\dfrac{I}{(1 + I)**N - 1}$	$\dfrac{I(1 + I)**N}{(1 + I)**N - 1}$	$\dfrac{(1 + I)**N - 1}{I}$	$\dfrac{(1 + I)**N - 1}{I(1 + I)**N}$	N PERIODS
1	1.1500000	.8695652	1.0000000	1.1500000	1.0000000	.8695652	1
2	1.3225000	.7561437	.4651163	.6151163	2.1500000	1.6257089	2
3	1.5208750	.6575162	.2879770	.4379770	3.4725000	2.2832251	3
4	1.7490063	.5717532	.2002654	.3502654	4.9933750	2.8549784	4
5	2.0113572	.4971767	.1483156	.2983156	6.7423813	3.3521551	5
6	2.3130608	.4323276	.1142369	.2642369	8.7537384	3.7844827	6
7	2.6600199	.3759370	.0903604	.2403604	11.0667992	4.1604197	7
8	3.0590229	.3269018	.0728501	.2228501	13.7268191	4.4873215	8
9	3.5178763	.2842624	.0597740	.2095740	16.7858419	4.7715839	9
10	4.0455577	.2471847	.0492521	.1992521	20.3037182	5.0187686	10
11	4.6523914	.2149432	.0410690	.1910690	24.3492760	5.2337118	11
12	5.3502501	.1869072	.0344808	.1844808	29.0016674	5.4206190	12
13	6.1527876	.1625280	.0291105	.1791105	34.3519175	5.5831470	13
14	7.0757058	.1413287	.0246885	.1746885	40.5047051	5.7244756	14
15	8.1370616	.1228945	.0210171	.1710171	47.5804109	5.8473701	15
16	9.3576209	.1068648	.0179477	.1679477	55.7174725	5.9542349	16
17	10.7612640	.0929259	.0153669	.1653669	65.0750934	6.0471608	17
18	12.3754536	.0808051	.0131863	.1631863	75.8363574	6.1279659	18
19	14.2317716	.0702653	.0113364	.1613364	88.2118110	6.1982312	19
20	16.3665374	.0611003	.0097615	.1597615	102.4435826	6.2593315	20
21	18.8215180	.0531307	.0084168	.1584168	118.8101200	6.3126422	21
22	21.6447457	.0462006	.0072658	.1572658	137.6316380	6.3586627	22
23	24.8914576	.0401744	.0062784	.1562784	159.2763837	6.3988372	23
24	28.6251762	.0349343	.0054298	.1554298	184.1678413	6.4337714	24
25	32.9189526	.0303776	.0046994	.1546994	212.7930175	6.4641491	25
26	37.8567955	.0264153	.0040698	.1540698	245.7119701	6.4905644	26
27	43.5353148	.0229699	.0035265	.1535265	283.5687656	6.5135343	27
28	50.0656121	.0199738	.0030571	.1530571	327.1040804	6.5335081	28
29	57.5754539	.0173685	.0026513	.1526513	377.1696925	6.5508766	29
30	66.2117720	.0151031	.0023002	.1523002	434.7451464	6.5659796	30
31	76.1435378	.0131331	.0019962	.1519962	500.9569183	6.5791127	31
32	87.5650684	.0114201	.0017328	.1517328	577.1004561	6.5905328	32
33	100.6998287	.0099305	.0015045	.1515045	664.6655245	6.6004633	33
34	115.8048030	.0086352	.0013066	.1513066	765.3653532	6.6090985	34
35	133.1755234	.0075089	.0011349	.1511349	881.1701561	6.6166074	35
36	153.1518519	.0065295	.0009859	.1509859	1014.3456796	6.6231369	36
37	176.1246297	.0056778	.0008565	.1508565	1167.4975315	6.6288147	37
38	202.5433242	.0049372	.0007443	.1507443	1343.6221612	6.6337519	38
39	232.9248228	.0042932	.0006468	.1506468	1546.1654854	6.6380451	39
40	267.8635462	.0037332	.0005621	.1505621	1779.0903082	6.6417784	40

NOTE- **N IS EXPONENT N

254

20.00 PERCENT COMPOUND INTEREST FACTORS

	SINGLE PAYMENT		SINKING	UNIFORM ANNUAL SERIES			
N PERIODS	COMPOUND AMOUNT FACTOR GIVEN P TO FIND S	PRESENT WORTH FACTOR GIVEN S TO FIND P	SINKING FUND FACTOR GIVEN S TO FIND R	CAPITAL RECOVERY FACTOR GIVEN P TO FIND R	COMPOUND AMOUNT FACTOR GIVEN R TO FIND S	PRESENT WORTH FACTOR GIVEN R TO FIND P	N PERIODS
	$(1+I)^{**N}$	$\frac{1}{(1+I)^{**N}}$	$\frac{I}{(1+I)^{**N}-1}$	$\frac{I(1+I)^{**N}}{(1+I)^{**N}-1}$	$\frac{(1+I)^{**N}-1}{I}$	$\frac{(1+I)^{**N}-1}{I(1+I)^{**N}}$	
1	1.2000000	.8333333	1.0000000	1.2000000	1.0000000	.8333333	1
2	1.4400000	.6944444	.4545455	.6545455	2.2000000	1.5277778	2
3	1.7280000	.5787037	.2747253	.4747253	3.6400000	2.1064815	3
4	2.0736000	.4822531	.1862891	.3862891	5.3680000	2.5887346	4
5	2.4883200	.4018776	.1343797	.3343797	7.4415000	2.9906121	5
6	2.9859840	.3348980	.1007057	.3007057	9.9292000	3.3255101	6
7	3.5831808	.2790816	.0774239	.2774239	12.9159040	3.6045918	7
8	4.2998170	.2325680	.0606094	.2606094	16.4990848	3.8371598	8
9	5.1597804	.1938067	.0480795	.2480795	20.7989018	4.0309665	9
10	6.1917364	.1615056	.0385228	.2385228	25.9586821	4.1924721	10
11	7.4300837	.1345880	.0311038	.2311038	32.1504185	4.3270601	11
12	8.9161004	.1121567	.0252650	.2252650	39.5805022	4.4392167	12
13	10.6993205	.0934639	.0206200	.2206200	48.4966027	4.5326806	13
14	12.8391846	.0778866	.0168931	.2168931	59.1959232	4.6105672	14
15	15.4070216	.0649055	.0138821	.2138821	72.0351079	4.6754726	15
16	18.4884259	.0540879	.0114361	.2114361	87.4421294	4.7295605	16
17	22.1861111	.0450732	.0094401	.2094401	105.9305553	4.7746338	17
18	26.6233333	.0375610	.0078054	.2078054	128.1166664	4.8121948	18
19	31.9479999	.0313009	.0064625	.2064625	154.7399997	4.8434957	19
20	38.3375999	.0260841	.0053565	.2053565	186.6879996	4.8695797	20
21	46.0051199	.0217367	.0044439	.2044439	225.0255995	4.8913164	21
22	55.2061439	.0181139	.0036896	.2036896	271.0307195	4.9094304	22
23	66.2473727	.0150949	.0030653	.2030653	326.2368633	4.9245253	23
24	79.4968472	.0125791	.0025479	.2025479	392.4842360	4.9371044	24
25	95.3962166	.0104826	.0021187	.2021187	471.9810832	4.9475870	25
26	114.4754600	.0087355	.0017625	.2017625	567.3772999	4.9563225	26
27	137.3705520	.0072796	.0014666	.2014666	681.8577598	4.9636021	27
28	164.8446624	.0060663	.0012207	.2012207	819.2233118	4.9696684	28
29	197.8135948	.0050553	.0010162	.2010162	984.0679742	4.9747237	29
30	237.3763138	.0042127	.0008461	.2008461	1181.8815690	4.9789364	30
31	284.8515766	.0035106	.0007046	.2007046	1419.2578828	4.9824470	31
32	341.8218919	.0029255	.0005868	.2005868	1704.1094594	4.9853725	32
33	410.1862702	.0024379	.0004888	.2004888	2045.5313512	4.9878104	33
34	492.2235243	.0020316	.0004071	.2004071	2456.5176215	4.9898420	34
35	590.6682292	.0016930	.0003392	.2003392	2948.3411458	4.9915350	35
36	708.8018750	.0014108	.0002826	.2002826	3538.0093749	4.9929458	36
37	850.5622500	.0011757	.0002354	.2002354	4247.8112499	4.9941215	37
38	1020.6747000	.0009797	.0001961	.2001961	5098.3734999	4.9951013	38
39	1224.8096400	.0008165	.0001634	.2001634	6119.0481999	4.9959177	39
40	1469.7715680	.0006804	.0001362	.2001362	7343.8578398	4.9965981	40

NOTE- **N IS EXPONENT N

25.00 PERCENT COMPOUND INTEREST FACTORS

	SINGLE PAYMENT		SINKING FUND FACTOR GIVEN S TO FIND R	UNIFORM ANNUAL SERIES			
N PERIODS	COMPOUND AMOUNT FACTOR GIVEN P TO FIND S $(1+i)^n$	PRESENT WORTH FACTOR GIVEN S TO FIND P $\frac{1}{(1+i)^n}$	$\frac{i}{(1+i)^n-1}$	CAPITAL RECOVERY FACTOR GIVEN P TO FIND R $\frac{i(1+i)^n}{(1+i)^n-1}$	COMPOUND AMOUNT FACTOR GIVEN R TO FIND S $\frac{(1+i)^n-1}{i}$	PRESENT WORTH FACTOR GIVEN R TO FIND P $\frac{(1+i)^n-1}{i(1+i)^n}$	N PERIODS
1	1.2500000	.8000000	1.0000000	1.2500000	1.0000000	.8000000	1
2	1.5625000	.6400000	.4444444	.6944444	2.2500000	1.4400000	2
3	1.9531250	.5120000	.2622951	.5122951	3.8125000	1.9520000	3
4	2.4414063	.4096000	.1734417	.4234417	5.7656250	2.3616000	4
5	3.0517578	.3276800	.1218467	.3718467	8.2070313	2.6892800	5
6	3.8146973	.2621440	.0888195	.3388195	11.2587891	2.9514240	6
7	4.7683716	.2097152	.0663417	.3163417	15.0734863	3.1611392	7
8	5.9604645	.1677722	.0503985	.3003985	19.8418579	3.3289114	8
9	7.4505806	.1342177	.0387562	.2887562	25.8023224	3.4631291	9
10	9.3132257	.1073742	.0300726	.2800726	33.2529030	3.5705033	10
11	11.6415322	.0858993	.0234929	.2734929	42.5661287	3.6564026	11
12	14.5519152	.0687195	.0184476	.2684476	54.2076609	3.7251221	12
13	18.1898940	.0549756	.0145434	.2645434	68.7595761	3.7800977	13
14	22.7373675	.0439805	.0115009	.2615009	86.9494702	3.8240781	14
15	28.4217094	.0351844	.0091169	.2591169	109.6568377	3.8592625	15
16	35.5271368	.0281475	.0072407	.2572407	138.1085472	3.8874100	16
17	44.4089210	.0225180	.0057592	.2557592	173.6356839	3.9099280	17
18	55.5111512	.0180144	.0045862	.2545862	218.0446049	3.9279424	18
19	69.3889390	.0144115	.0036556	.2536556	273.5557562	3.9423539	19
20	86.7361738	.0115292	.0029159	.2529159	342.9446952	3.9538831	20
21	108.4202172	.0092234	.0023273	.2523273	429.6808690	3.9631065	21
22	135.5252716	.0073787	.0018584	.2518584	538.1010862	3.9704882	22
23	169.4065895	.0059030	.0014845	.2514845	673.6263578	3.9763882	23
24	211.7582368	.0047224	.0011862	.2511862	843.0329473	3.9811105	24
25	264.6977960	.0037779	.0009481	.2509481	1054.7911841	3.9848884	25
26	330.8722450	.0030223	.0007579	.2507579	1319.4899801	3.9879107	26
27	413.5903063	.0024179	.0006059	.2506059	1650.3612251	3.9903286	27
28	516.9878828	.0019343	.0004845	.2504845	2063.9515314	3.9922629	28
29	646.2348536	.0015474	.0003875	.2503875	2580.9394142	3.9938103	29
30	807.7935669	.0012379	.0003099	.2503099	3227.1742678	3.9950482	30
31	1009.7419567	.0009904	.0002478	.2502478	4034.9678347	3.9960386	31
32	1262.1774484	.0007923	.0001982	.2501982	5044.7097934	3.9968309	32
33	1577.7218104	.0006338	.0001586	.2501586	6306.8872418	3.9974647	33
34	1972.1522631	.0005071	.0001268	.2501268	7884.6090522	3.9979718	34
35	2465.1903288	.0004056	.0001015	.2501015	9856.7613153	3.9983774	35
36	3081.4879110	.0003245	.0000812	.2500812	12321.9516441	3.9987019	36
37	3851.8598888	.0002596	.0000649	.2500649	15403.4395551	3.9989615	37
38	4814.8248610	.0002077	.0000519	.2500519	19255.2994439	3.9991692	38
39	6018.5310762	.0001662	.0000415	.2500415	24070.1243048	3.9993354	39
40	7523.1638453	.0001329	.0000332	.2500332	30088.6553811	3.9994683	40

NOTE- **N IS EXPONENT N

Logarithms

Appendix C

C.1 Use of Common Logarithms

As we saw in Chapter 5 (Example 5-5), logarithms are used to simplify calculation involving multiplication, division, and exponential functions among others.

A typical logarithmic function has the form $y = \log x$ which is equivalent to the exponential form $x = 10y$. In common logarithms y is always the exponent of the base 10. Accordingly, our objective, as we learn how to employ common logarithms, is to think of a logarithm as an exponent.

The common logarithm of a number is the power of 10 which equals that number. The list below illustrates.

Exponent	*Logarithm*
$1 = 10^0$	$\log 1 = 0$
$10 = 10^1$	$\log 10 = 1$
$100 = 10^2$	$\log 100 = 2$
$1000 = 10^3$	$\log 1000 = 3$
$10,000 = 10^4$	$\log 10,000 = 4$
$0.1 = 10^{-1}$	$\log 0.1 = -1$
$0.01 = 10^{-2}$	$\log 0.01 = -2$
$0.001 = 10^{-3}$	$\log 0.001 = -3$
$0.0001 = 10^{-4}$	$\log 0.0001 = -4$

Before proceeding any further it is necessary to understand the rules for using logarithms: To multiply numbers add their logarithms; thus

$$\log (x \cdot y) = \log x + \log y$$

To divide one number by another, subtract the logarithm of the denominator from the logarithm of the numerator; thus

$$\log \frac{x}{y} = \log x - \log y$$

We can now expand our list.

Exponent	*Logarithm*
$150 = 1.50 \times 10^2$	$\log 150 = \log 1.50 + \log 10^2 = \log 1.50 + 2$
$15 = 1.5 \times 10^1$	$\log 15 = \log 1.50 + \log 10^1 = \log 1.50 + 1$
$1.5 = 1.5 \times 10^0$	$\log 1.5 = \log 1.50 + \log 10^0 = \log 1.50 + 0$
$0.15 = 1.5 \times 10^{-2}$	$\log 0.15 = \log 1.50 + \log 10^{-2} = \log 1.50 - 2$
$0.015 = 1.5 \times 10^{-3}$	$\log 0.015 = \log 1.50 + \log 10^{-3} = \log 1.50 - 3$
$348 = 3.48 \times 10^2$	$\log 348 = \log 3.48 + \log 10^2 = \log 3.48 + 2$
$12.583.75 = 1.258375 \times 10^4$	$\log 12583.75 = \log 1.258375 + \log 1.258375 + 4$

The whole-number part of a logarithm, 1., 2., etc. is called the *characteristic,* and the fractional part, .1, .01, .2873, etc., is called the *mantissa.* Table C-1 shows four-place mantissas; it is accurate enough for most economic analysis data. Decimals have been omitted for printing convenience.

To find log 158 look for the first two digits on the vertical column N and over across the table to column 8 locating .1987 which is the mantissa of the logarithm, then from above two tables:

$$\log 158 = \log 1.58 + \log 10^2 = \log 1.58 + 2 = 0.1987 + 2 = 2.1987$$

The characteristic for a number between 0 and 1 is always negative. It is customary to indicate the logarithm of that number by a minus sign written above the characteristic or a positive number followed by -10.

$$\log 0.158 = \log 1.58 + \log 10^{-1} = \log 1.58 + (-1)$$
$$= 0.1987 + (-1)$$
$$= \bar{1}.1987 \text{ or } 9.1987 - 10$$
$$\log 0.0158 = \log 1.58 + (-2) = 0.1987 + (-2)$$
$$= \bar{2}.1987 \text{ or } 8.1987 - 10$$

C.1   Antilogarithms

To find the antilogarithm or natural number corresponding to a logarithm, the process above reverses. Hence, to find the antilogarithm of 4.2380, we locate .2380 in the table and read across to N and up to column number 173. Then from the rules on characteristics $1.73 \times 10^4 = 17,300$. To get the antilog of $\overline{1}.2920$ $(9.2920 - 10)$, we find the nearest mantissa in the table .2923 and read the number 196 which then equals $0.196(1.96 \times 10^{-1})$.

Example C-1
If a $9972 loan has a maturity of $14,600 after 5 years, what was the annual interest rate?

Solution:
By Equation 5-4

$$PW = S \ \frac{1}{(1 + i)^n} = 9,972 = 14,600 \ \frac{1}{(1 + i)^5}$$

Multiplying both sides of the equation by $(1 + i)^5$ yields

$9972 \ (1 + i)^5 = 14,600$

$(1 + i)^5 = \dfrac{14,600}{9972} = 1.4640$

$5 \log (1 + i) = \log 1.4640$
$4 \log (1 + i) = 0.1644$

$\log (1 + i) = \dfrac{0.1644}{5} = 0.0329$

Taking the antilogarithm by reading from the table, the number is 108. Then, from the rules on characteristics, $1.08 \times 10^0 = 1.08$. Hence

$$(1 + i) = 1.08$$
$$\text{and } i = 1.08 - 1 = 0.08, \text{ or } 8\%$$

Before concluding it should be pointed out that the $(1 + i)$ in the above example is in reality less than 1.08. If one seeks to be more precise, it is possible to do so by interpolation. Thus, to find the antilogarithm of .0329, and using high school algebra,

$$\begin{array}{cc} 107 & .0294 \\ x & .0329 \\ 108 & .0334 \end{array}$$

$$\frac{(108 - 107)}{(x - 107)} = \frac{(.0334 - .0294)}{(.0329 - .0294)}$$

$$\frac{1}{x - 107} = \frac{.0040}{.0035} = 1.1429$$

$$1.1429\,x - 122.2903 = 1$$

$$x = 107.88$$

Hence

$$(1 + i) = 1.0788 \text{ and } i = 0.0788, \text{ or } 7.88\%$$

PROBLEMS

1. Find the logarithm of each number
   a. 3.85
   b. 0.423
   c. 597
   d. 2/6
   e. 1.88×10^{-4}
   f. 1 8/9
   g. 8800
   h. 11,600
   i. 0.0131
   j. 17
   k. 1/300
   l. 683

2. Find the antilogarithms of the following logarithms. Interpolate where necessary.
   a. 0.4997
   b. 3.720
   c. 6.8 − 10
   d. 0.0066
   e. 1.0586
   f. 0.1620
   g. 6.3746
   h. $\overline{1}.8465 - 10$
   i. $\overline{1}.3139$
   j. $\overline{2}.4915$
   k. 2.0608
   l. 0.5011

3. Compute the following using logarithms
   a. (8.61)(42)
   b. 70/50
   c. 70(1 + 0.05)
   d. $(1.01)^3 - 17$
   e. $\sqrt{131}$
   f. $8^{0.67}$
   g. $50(1 + 0.4)^{1.7}$
   h. $\sqrt{923}$
   i. (1.01)(67)
   j. $65(1 + 0.06)^{10}$
   k. (108)(730)
   l. $(8.68)^{8.1}$

TABLE C-1 Common Logarithms of Numbers*

N	0	1	2	3	4	5	6	7	8	9
10	0000	0043	0086	0128	0170	0212	0253	0294	0334	0374
11	0414	0453	0492	0531	0569	0607	0645	0682	0719	0755
12	0792	0823	0864	0899	0934	0969	1004	1038	1072	1106
13	1139	1173	1206	1239	1271	1303	1335	1367	1399	1430
14	1461	1492	1523	1553	1584	1614	1644	1673	1703	1732
15	1761	1790	1818	1847	1875	1903	1931	1959	1987	2014
16	2041	2068	2095	2122	2148	2175	2201	2227	2253	2279
17	2304	2330	2355	2380	2405	2430	2455	2480	2504	2529
18	2553	2577	2601	2625	2648	2672	2695	2718	2742	2765
19	2788	2810	2833	2856	2878	2900	2923	2945	2967	2989
20	3010	3032	3054	3075	3096	3118	3139	3160	3181	3201
21	3222	3243	3263	3284	3304	3324	3345	3365	3385	3404
22	3424	3444	3464	3483	3502	3522	3541	3560	3579	3598
23	3617	3636	3655	3674	3692	3711	3729	3747	3766	3784
24	3802	3820	3838	3856	3874	3892	3909	3927	3945	3962
25	3979	3997	4014	4031	4048	4065	4082	4099	4116	4133
26	4150	4166	4183	4200	4216	4232	4249	4265	4281	4298
27	4314	4330	4346	4362	4378	4393	4409	4425	4440	4456
28	4472	4487	4502	4518	4533	4548	4564	4579	4594	4609
29	4624	4639	4654	4669	4683	4698	4713	4728	4742	4757
30	4771	4789	4800	4814	4829	4843	4857	4871	4886	4900
31	4914	4928	4942	4955	4969	4983	4997	5011	5024	5038
32	5051	5065	5079	5092	5105	5119	5132	5145	5159	5172
33	5185	5198	5211	5224	5237	5250	5263	5276	5289	5302
34	5315	5328	5340	5353	5366	5378	5391	5403	5416	5428
35	5441	5453	5465	5478	5490	5502	5514	5527	5539	5551
36	5563	5575	5587	5599	5611	5623	5635	5647	5658	5670
37	5682	5694	5705	5717	5729	5740	5752	5763	5775	5786
38	5798	5809	5821	5832	5843	5855	5866	5877	5888	5899
39	5911	5922	5933	5944	5955	5966	5977	5988	5999	6010
40	6021	6031	6042	6053	6064	6075	6085	6096	6107	6117
41	6128	6138	6149	6160	6170	6180	6191	6201	6212	6222
42	6232	6243	6253	6263	6274	6284	6294	6304	6314	6325
43	6335	6345	6355	6365	6375	6385	6395	6405	6415	6425
44	6435	6444	6454	6464	6474	6484	6493	6503	6513	6522
45	6532	6542	6551	6561	6571	6580	6590	6599	6609	6618
46	6628	6637	6646	6656	6665	6675	6684	6693	6702	6712
47	6721	6760	6739	6749	6758	6767	6776	6785	6794	6803
48	6812	6821	6830	6839	6848	6857	6866	6875	6884	6893
49	6902	6911	6920	6928	6937	6946	6955	6964	6972	6971

TABLE C-1   Common Logarithms of Numbers*

N	0	1	2	3	4	5	6	7	8	9
50	6990	6998	7007	7016	7024	7033	7042	7050	7059	7067
51	7076	7084	7093	7101	7110	7118	7126	7135	7143	7152
52	7160	7168	7177	7185	7193	7202	7210	7218	7226	7235
53	7243	7251	7259	7267	7275	7284	7292	7300	7308	7316
54	7324	7332	7340	7348	7356	7364	7372	7380	7388	7396
55	7404	7412	7419	7427	7435	7443	7451	7459	7466	7474
56	7482	7490	7497	7505	7513	7520	7528	7536	7543	7551
57	7559	7566	7574	7582	7589	7597	7604	7612	7619	7627
58	7634	7642	7649	7657	7664	7672	7679	7686	7694	7701
59	7709	7716	7723	7731	7738	7745	7752	7760	7767	7774
60	7782	7789	7796	7803	7810	7818	7825	7832	7839	7849
61	7853	7860	7868	7875	7882	7889	7896	7903	7910	7917
62	7924	7931	7938	7945	7652	7959	7966	7973	7980	7987
63	7993	8000	8007	8014	8021	8028	8035	8041	8048	8055
64	8062	8069	8075	8082	8089	8096	8102	8109	8116	8122
65	8129	8136	8142	8149	8156	8162	8169	8176	8182	8189
66	8195	8202	8209	8215	8222	8228	8235	8241	8248	8254
67	8261	8267	8274	8280	8287	8293	8299	8306	8312	8319
68	8325	8331	8338	8344	8351	8357	8363	8370	8376	8382
69	8388	8395	8401	8407	8414	8420	8426	8432	8439	8445
70	8451	8457	8463	8470	8476	8482	8488	8494	8500	8506
71	8513	8519	8525	8531	8537	8543	8549	8555	8561	8567
72	8573	8579	8585	8591	8597	8603	8609	8615	8621	8627
73	8633	8639	8645	8651	8657	8663	8669	8675	8681	8686
74	8692	8698	8704	8710	8716	8722	8727	8733	8739	8745
75	8751	8756	8762	8768	8774	8779	8785	8791	8797	8802
76	8808	8814	8820	8825	8831	8837	8842	8848	8854	8859
77	8865	8871	8876	8882	8887	8893	8899	8904	8910	8915
78	8921	8927	8932	8938	8943	8949	8954	8960	8965	8971
79	8976	8982	8987	8993	8998	9004	9009	9015	9020	9025
80	9031	9036	9042	9047	9053	9058	9063	9069	9074	9079
81	9085	9090	9096	9101	9106	9112	9117	9122	9128	9133
82	9138	9143	9149	9154	9159	9165	9170	9175	9180	9186
83	9191	9196	9201	9206	9212	9217	9222	9227	9232	9238
84	9243	9248	9253	9258	9263	9269	9274	9279	9284	9289
85	9294	9299	9304	9309	9315	9320	9325	9330	9335	9340
86	9345	9350	9355	9360	9365	9370	9375	9380	9385	9390
87	9395	9400	9405	9410	9415	9420	9425	9430	9435	9440
88	9445	9450	9455	9460	9465	9469	9474	9479	9484	9489
89	9494	9499	9504	9509	9513	9518	9523	9528	9533	9538

TABLE C-1   Common Logarithms of Numbers*

N	0	1	2	3	4	5	6	7	8	9
90	9542	9547	9552	9557	9562	9566	9571	9576	9581	9586
91	9590	9595	9600	9605	9609	9615	9619	9624	9628	9633
92	9638	9643	9647	9652	9657	9661	9666	9671	9675	9680
93	9685	9689	9694	9699	9703	9708	9713	9717	9722	9727
94	9731	9736	9741	9745	9750	9754	9759	9763	9768	9773
95	9777	9782	9786	9791	9795	9800	9805	9809	9814	9818
96	9823	9827	9832	9836	9841	9845	9850	9854	9859	9863
97	9868	9872	9877	9881	9886	9890	9894	9899	9903	9908
98	9912	9917	9921	9926	9930	9934	9939	9943	9948	9952
99	9956	9961	9965	9969	9974	9978	9983	9987	9991	9996

*Source: Lange, *Handbook of Chemistry,* 11th ed., McGraw-Hill, New York, 1973.

Suggested Readings

Appendix D

The following list of suggested readings is neither comprehensive nor exclusive. The books and articles suggested are, in the author's view, *among* the best published on the subjects presented in this book. These should give the engineer or technologist a good overall reference source on most important aspects of engineering economics.

Time Value of Money

Barish, N. H., *Economic Analysis for Engineering and Managerial Decision Making,* McGraw-Hill, New York, 1962.
DeGarmo, E. P., *Engineering Economy,* MacMillan, New York, 1967.
Smith, G. W., *Engineering Economy: Analysis of Capital Expenditures,* Iowa State University Press, Ames, Iowa, 1973.

Evaluation of Investment Alternatives

Grant, E. L. and W. G. Ireson, *Principles of Engineering Economy,* 5th ed., Ronald Press, New York, 1970.
Fleischer, G. A., *Capital Allocation Theory: The Study of Investment Decisions,* Appleton-Century-Crofts, New York, 1969.

Jeynes, P. H., *Profitability and Economic Choice,* Iowa State University Press, Ames, Iowa, 1968.

Schweyer, H. E., *Analytic Models for Managerial and Engineering Economics,* Van Nostrand Reinhold, New York, 1964.

Theusen, H. G., W. J. Fabrycky and G. J Thuesen, *Engineering Economy,* 5th ed., Prentice-Hall, Englewood Cliffs, N.J., 1977.

Winfrey, R., *Economic Analysis of Highways,* International Textbook Co., Scranton, Pa., 1969.

Cost Estimation and Analysis

Aries, R. S. and R. D. Newton, *Chemical Engineering Cost Estimation,* Mc-Graw-Hill, New York, 1955.

Jelen, F. C., (ed.), *Cost and Optimization Engineering,* McGraw-Hill, New York, 1955.

Popper, H., *Modern Cost Engineering Techniques,* McGraw-Hill, New York, 1970.

Ostwald, P. F., *Cost Estimating for Engineering and Management,* Prentice-Hall, Englewood Cliffs, N.J., 1974.

Vernon, I. R., (ed.), *Realistic Cost Estimating For Manufacturing,* Society of Manufacturing Engineers, Dearborn, Michigan, 1968.

Depreciation

Grant, E. L. and P. T. Norton, *Depreciation,* Ronald Press, New York, 1955.

Marston, A., R. Winfrey, and J. C. Hempstead, *Engineering Valuation and Depreciation,* Iowa State University Press, Ames, Iowa, 1953.

U.S. Treasury Department, Internal Revenue Service, *Depreciation Guidelines and Rules.*

Taxes

Thorne, H. C., R. O. Carlson, and L. D. Thomas, "How Taxes Affect Economic Evaluation," *Cost Engineers' Notebook,* D-7.8, 1965.

Tax Institute Inc., *Depreciation and Taxes: A Symposium,* Princeton, N.J., 1959.

Jelen, F. C., "Consider Income Tax in Cost Analysis," *Chemical Engineering,* September 1957, pp. 271-275.

Break-Even Analysis

Anthony, R. H., *Management Accounting,* 4th ed., Richard D. Irwin, Homewood, Ill., 1970.

Brigham, E. F. and J. L. Pappas 2d ed., *Managerial Economics,* The Dryden Press, Hinsdale, Ill., 1976.
Levin, R. I. and C. A. Kirkpatrick, *Quantitative Approaches to Management,* McGraw-Hill, New York, 1965.
Spurr, W. A. and C. P. Bonini, *Statistical Analysis for Business Decisions,* Irwin, Homewood, Ill., 1971.

Project Planning and Cost Control

Cleland, D. I. and W. R. King, *Systems Analysis and Project Management,* 2d ed., McGraw-Hill, New York, 1975.
Hoare, H. R., *Project Management Using Network Analysis,* McGraw-Hill, London, England, 1973.
Moder, J. J. and C. R. Phillips, *Project Management with CPM and PERT,* 2d ed., Van Nostrand Reinhold, New York, 1970.
O'Brien, J. J., *CPM In Construction Management,* McGraw-Hill, New York, 1965.

Results Reporting

Kierzek, J. M. and W. Gibson, *The MacMillan Handbook of English,* 5th ed., MacMillan, New York, 1966.
Lesikar, R. V., *How to Write a Report Your Boss Will Read and Remember,* Dow-Jones-Irwin, Homewood, Illinois, 1974.
Ryan, C. W., *Writing: A Practical Guide for Business and Industry,* Wiley, New York, 1974.

Solutions to Selected Problems

Appendix E

Chapter 1

1. *Capital investment*
   Purchase of lot
   Survey of lot
   Architect's fee
   Contruction costs
   Grading, seeding, sodding

   Working capital
   Legal fees, city permits
   Fire and liability insurance
   Advertising for tenants
   Interest costs
   Grass mowing and general
   preparations

2. Solar energy, electric cars, space shuttle.

4. **a.** $250,000
   b. $105,000
   c. 10.5%
   d. 9.52 yrs
   e. No

5. A $ROI_a = 65\%$
   B $ROI_b = 50\%$
   C $ROI_c = 40\%$

   Hence, alternative A.

6. **a.** ROI = 5%. The venture should not be undertaken.
   b. ROI = 8%. Still should not be undertaken.

Chapter 2

1. $938,351
2. $309,991
3. Fixed capital investment = $10,000,000
4. $4,066,209
5. $5,441,616
6. $2,251,404
7. $265,889
9. See Chapter 6
10. Total operating cost = $1,525,975
11. **b.** $428,629
12. **a.** Direct operating cost = $0.189/bar, $567,000/yr
    b. Total operating cost = $989,550
    c. $210,450
13. $431,454
14. Loss of $975
15. **a.** $132,000

Chapter 3

1. **a.** 10,000 calculators
    b. 11,000
    c. same
2. $150,000
3. **a.** $580,000
    b. $5,147,000
    c. $6,220,000
4. $403,225
5. $143,807
6. Price should be set at $10 since the highest gross profit will be realized.
7. **b.** 5 lots at $1.80 per lot
9. **a.** 51,217 kilograms per year.
10. 1000 units
11. **a.** $1.66 per ton   **b.** $9.00 per ton
12. $A - Bx^2 = C_F + Cx^3 + Dx^2$
13. 5000 units or 83.33% of capacity.
14. 11 units

15. At 35 cars the total cost in $3200; hence the profit is $3500 − $3200 = $300. Maximum profit of 500 per train will be realized if the train length is increased to 40 cars.

16. **a.** $Y_e = 1 + 2.5\,x$ **b.** 4885, 0.9090

c. For 10 employees, the average monthly operating cost should be $26,000. this cost is out of line. The store is operating at a lower cost than anticipated.

Chapter 4

1. **a.** 13.33 years
b. 6%
c. 10%

2. $PT_{MIN} = 2.56$ year ·

3. $PT_{MIN} = 12.56$ years

4. Second alternative

5. 1-inch insulation

6. On an individual basis, the batch system since it has a higher ROI (18% versus 15.6% for continuous). On an incremental basis however, continuous system is the choice since incremental ROI = 11%.

7. Make its own since ROI = 17.94% which is greater than interest rate.

8. No. ROI = 7.85%

9. Cone top

10. Gas turbine since the incremental interest cost exceeds the incremental saving in total costs.

11. Yes, since gross ROI = 44.44%

12. No. ROI on average net profit is 14.9%

13. None.

14. $A = 0.168$, $B = 0.778$, $C = 7.40$

15. **b.** At the end of the 23rd year after completion.

16. $A = 0.94$, $B = 0.804$, $C = 1.00$

18. alternative D.

19. At $ROI_m = 14\%$, E. At $ROI_m = 24\%$, C. At $ROI_m = 34\%$, A. At $ROI_m = 45\%$, none.

20. No, unless the $0.50 per gallon reduction in tolling charge brings in an additional 400,000 gallons of oil per year.

Chapter 5

1. 10.066 yrs
2. 25,900.58
3. $9982
4. 6.1%
5. $19,260.39
6. $11,040
7. 5.95 yrs
8. $1398/yr
9. $8951
10. 12.2%

11. $83,112
13. $A = 0.118$
    $B = 0.477$
    $C = 3.106$
14. $A = 0.102$
    $B = 0.395$
    $C = 2.358$
16. No since DCF is less than 1%
17. The total cost for B will be $234 less than A.

Chapter 6

2. a.   11 yrs.
    b. $f = 0.1675$
3. 8.33 yrs.
4. $n = 5$ yrs for alternative A
5. a. $12,800, $9320, $5760
    b. $8270, $5318, $3420
    c.   8192, $5244, $3356
6. $29,000
7. $2899
8. $45,000

9. $90,000
10. a. $2200
     b. $3453
     c. $3164
     d. $3385
     e. $500
11. $758,000, $38,000
12. a.   10 yr
     b.   20 yr
     c.   19 yr

Chapter 7

1. $220,500
2. $207,300
3. $3600 per year
4. First two years $3600, third year $4950
5. No. ROI = 9.36%
6. No again. ROI even lower.
7. a.   50.6%
    b.   49.4%

8.   Yes. DCF = 20.28%
9.   a. $137,800
     b. $18,200
10. a.   20%
     b.   22%
11. a. $32,700
     b. $12,000
12. 12.72%, yes.

13. $1,411,000

14. **a.** $200
 b. $962

15. Alternative *A* or *B*; Not none nor *C*.

16. BTROI$_{ave}$ = 8.41% ATROI$_{ave}$ = 4.37%

17. **a.** 7% **e.** 10.00%
 b. None **f.** 10.00%
 c. 6.67% **g.** 7.00%
 d. 3.33%

18. Alternative *B* via incremental analysis; ROI = 15%

19. 8.21%, 11.54%

Chapter 8

1. **c.** Critical path is 1–3–4 or *B*–*E*
 d. Project completion time is 13 weeks

2.

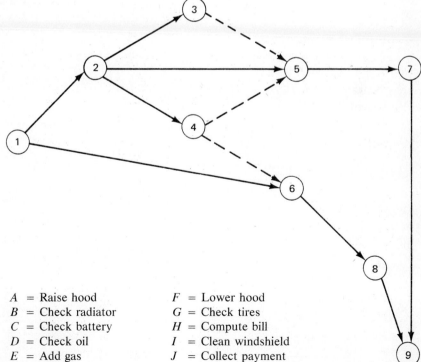

A = Raise hood   *F* = Lower hood
B = Check radiator *G* = Check tires
C = Check battery *H* = Compute bill
D = Check oil   *I* = Clean windshield
E = Add gas   *J* = Collect payment

Chapter 8 (Continued)

3.

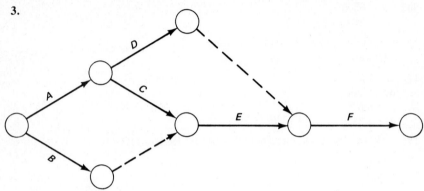

5. Critical path 1–2–4–5–6

6. Critical path 1–3–6–8–10

9. **b.** Critical path 1–2–4–6–7–10–11–12

Index